FREEDOM IN BROADCASTING

FREEDOM IN BROADCASTING

Edited by

Cento Veljanovski

Institute of Economic Affairs

1989

First published in March 1989

by

THE INSTITUTE OF ECONOMIC AFFAIRS
2 Lord North Street, Westminster, London SW1P 3LB

© The Institute of Economic Affairs 1989

Hobart Paperback 29

ISSN 0309-1783
ISBN 0-255 36218-8

Filmset by Goron Pro-Print Co. Ltd., Lancing, Sussex

Printed in Great Britain by Billing & Sons Limited, Worcester

Filmset in Times Roman 11 on 12 point

CONTENTS

PREFACE

Cento Veljanovski

Research & Editorial Director,
Institute of Economic Affairs

BRITISH BROADCASTING is undergoing one of its periodic convulsions. This time, however, the prospects of greater competition and choice will dwarf all past changes. It took nearly a quarter of a century for the number of television channels to expand from one to two, and another 20 years for this to double to the present four channels. In the next year or so the number of channels available to the British viewer will be measured in 10s. Already viewers in Europe can receive up to 17 satellite channels and this number will more than triple as we enter the next decade. Those who have access to the new generation of cable television networks in the UK can already receive 12 or more channels. The development of cable and satellite technologies has generated a momentum for more competition and more choice which no government, including the Eastern bloc, can stem or control. This has now been accepted by the British Government in its White Paper, *Broadcasting in the '90s.*[1]

Broadcasting has been the subject matter of several IEA monographs. Indeed, its publications were the only analyses of broadcasting policy by economists in the UK during the 1960s and 1970s. The main thrust of these works was to advocate greater choice and competition, and subscription television. These concepts are now the focal points of the current debate, if not yet actual policy.

In 1962, following the Pilkington Committee Report, the IEA published *TV – From Monopoly to Competition,* by Wilfred Altman, Denis Thomas

---

[1] Home Office, *Broadcasting in the '90s: Competition, Choice and Quality – The Government's Plans for Broadcasting Legislation,* Cm. 517, London: HMSO, 1988.

and David Sawers,[2] which put forward the case for more competition and subscription television. A quarter of a century later one of these authors, David Sawers, again examines Government broadcasting policy. In 1968 Sir Sidney Caine wrote *Paying for TV?*,[3] which put the case for subscription television.[4] This proposal formed the cornerstone of Professor Sir Alan Peacock's influential Report to the Government on broadcasting.[5]

Much later I (when at Oxford University), together with Bill Bishop (now Professor of Law at George Mason University), examined the prospects for cable television in *Choice by Cable*.[6] This developed a positive case for the complete deregulation of cable television in the UK, which up to then had been stifled by government protection of the BBC and ITV – the 'cosy duopoly' – from what was euphemistically called destructive competition. While cable television was deregulated under the Cable & Broadcasting Act 1984, it was hamstrung with restrictions which guaranteed that it would not grow rapidly. Many of these restrictions will be removed if the proposals in the broadcasting White Paper are accepted. *Choice by Cable* was influential in an indirect way. The Merriman Committee on the radio spectrum considered the argument that frequencies should be priced and allocated to uses and users by the market.[7] The Government has now investigated the idea further[8] and has accepted that radio frequencies should be auctioned.

Freedom in Broadcasting continues the IEA's efforts to present an economic view of British broadcasting untainted by the special pleading of interest groups. It gathers together a set of original contributions on the economics of broadcasting policy from economists who have been instrumental in bringing about change. These include two members of the Peacock Committee: Professor Sir Alan Peacock, Chairman of the Committee and a trustee of the IEA, and Samuel Brittan, a powerful advocate of the freedom-of-expression approach to broadcasting deregulation and one of the IEA's more prolific authors. The other contributors have also made important contributions to broadcasting policy and economic research. Indeed, *Freedom in Broadcasting* brings together a unique collection of experts.

---

2 W. Altman, D. Thomas, and D. Sawers, *TV: From Monopoly to Competition – and Back?*, Hobart Paper 15, London: Institute of Economic Affairs, 2nd edn., 1962.

3 S. Caine, *Paying for TV?*, Hobart Paper 43, London: IEA, 1968.

4 The IEA has also examined radio broadcasting: D. Thomas, *Competition in Radio*, Occasional Paper 5, London: IEA, 1965.

5 Home Office, *Report of the Committee on Financing the BBC*, London: HMSO, 1986.

6 *Choice by Cable – The Economics of a New Era in Television*, Hobart Paper 96, London: IEA, 1983.

7 Home Office, *The Report of the Independent Review of the Radio Spectrum (30-960 MHZ)*, Cmnd. 9000, London: HMSO, 1983.

8 This led to a further report, Department of Trade and Industry, *Deregulation of the Radio Spectrum in the UK*, London: HMSO, 1987.

All these contributors start from the principle that broadcasting is like any other economic activity. It should be provided competitively unless there are compelling reasons for not doing so. Not all of them agree on the best way to achieve a free market in broadcasting. But there is a consensus that the justification for the existing system and the rationale for the state's encroachment on the media are rapidly being undermined by techno-logical advances, and the growing demand that it is the viewers and not broadcasters and regulators who should decide what we see, hear and read.

The IEA is an educational charity and therefore does not have a corporate view. It publishes the work of academics and others who write in their own capacity as experts in their field of research. The contributors to *Freedom in Broadcasting* present their original analysis of the key policy issues from the standpoint of economic principles rather than practical politics. Their views will be of interest to everyone concerned with broadcasting and freedom of expression. Although the White Paper endorses the view that choice and competition should be the goals of broadcasting, it remains to be seen how this commitment will be translated into practical policy and regulation. The lessons from the past teach us that short-term expediency and political pressures often override economic principles to limit the chances of full deregulation which will permit the maximum level of competition and choice.

The IEA would like to thank Kelly Davies, Michael Solly and Ruth Croxford for providing the editorial and production assistance vital to producing this book.

January 1989   CENTO VELJANOVSKI
Research & Editorial Director

FOREWORD

THE ECONOMIST AND THE FUTURE OF BROADCASTING IN THE UK

Alan Peacock

Executive Director,
The David Hume Institute

THE CLEARLY SUCCESSFUL EFFORTS of the Institute of Economic Affairs, and those of many imitators, to improve public understanding of economic issues, are in marked contrast to an influential position taken by many academic economists who regard it as not really quite respectable to gauge professional reputation by success in marketing one's product. Instead, one should seek to maximise reputation with one's peer group as measured by the professional esteem attached to one's position in the academic hierarchy, the university in which that position is held and the accolade of membership of prestigious learned societies. It is given to only few to make both a popular and professional reputation of any consequence, and in such instances it is often said that the former must mar the latter. This position is one which prominent members of the broadcasting profession can fully appreciate. Several stated in evidence to the Committee on Financing the BBC[1] that the principal indicator of the value of a broadcasting company to the community was the relative number of trophies awarded to its programme-makers, actors and producers in any one year – but awarded by the broadcasting companies collectively!

A profession's estimate of the worth of its individual members may be defended as a guide to the benefits conferred on those who finance their activities. However, the comfortable position resulting from immunity from the pressures of the market can breed complacency so that it may

---

[1] Home Office, *Report of the Committee on Financing the BBC* (Peacock Report), Cmnd. 9824, London: HMSO, 1986.

come as a rude shock when taxpayers paying increasing amounts for higher education and research or for a licence to receive TV programmes begin to question whether they are obtaining value for money.

It is therefore not surprising that the intrusion of economic analysis of markets into the field of broadcasting has been accompanied by misunderstanding and, indeed, considerable hostility. As my introductory remarks imply, broadcasting interests often seem to assume that they have the monopoly of the truth when it comes to defining the objectives of the broadcasting system; furthermore, UK broadcasters have had few occasions when they have considered it necessary to employ professional economic analysis.

Nor have British economists displayed a continuing professional interest in broadcasting as an industry. Apart from some spasmodic concern with television and radio as examples of industries with 'public goods' characteristics when pricing of services may be technically difficult if not impossible and even undesirable on welfare grounds,[2] studies designed to command the attention of policy-makers have challenged prevailing broadcasting philosophy and associated government policies.[3] If we exclude attitude surveys, the use of quantitative economic analysis to throw light on the effects of different methods of financing television virtually began in the UK with the studies generated by the methodology adopted by the Committee on Financing the BBC.

The studies presented in this volume are designed to rectify this omission and it is no accident that they have been influenced by the present Government's decision to make the broadcasting system more responsive to the tastes and preferences of viewers. In the round, they offer an advertisement for the several ways in which economic analysis may be used to illuminate and sometimes to question aspects of this change in policy. They are directed to all those with a serious interest in and concern for the future of broadcasting in the UK and not merely towards fellow economists, though economists not working in this area should find much to interest them in their contents.

The unfamiliarity of economic analysis to the senior management of broadcasting in the UK means that there are more than the usual obstacles to be faced in persuading its members to take on board the fact that, whether they like it or not, the economist's perception of the problem of how broadcasting might be organised is highly relevant to present discussion.

The first misconception of the economist's position is that he is concerned solely with the promotion of material values. For instance, in

---

[2] P. Wiles, 'Pilkington and the Theory of Value', *Economic Journal*, Vol. LXXIII, 1963, pp. 185-200.

[3] For example, R. H. Coase, *British Broadcasting: A Study in Monopoly*, London: Longmans Green, 1950; Sir Sydney Caine, *Paying for TV?*, Hobart Paper 43, London: Institute of Economic Affairs, 1968; C. G. Veljanovski and W. G. Bishop, *Choice by Cable*, Hobart Paper 96, London: IEA, 1983.

an interview with the *Sunday Times* (13 November 1988), Mr Richard Dunn, Chief Executive of Thames Television and one of the leading figures in the present debate, described the White Paper on Broadcasting[4] as being 'about economic values, not social or cultural values'. If economic analysis has begun to penetrate government thinking on broadcasting, its concerns are completely independent of the question whose choices should determine what broadcasting programmes should be available and the content of those choices.

There is a further point to be made about the values which are to influence the structure of broadcasting. Whose aims are to be paramount? The question cannot be answered by saying that this is the prerogative of the broadcasting authorities. Aims must be based on value-judgements which cannot be ranked by economic or any other form of scientific inquiry. Neither broadcasters nor economists have any claim to dictate such aims. Unfortunately, much of the discussion about resource use in broadcasting is carried on as if objective valuations can be made which determine 'broadcasting needs', and that these valuations are best made by those who provide broadcasting services. Ask doctors to translate 'needs' for health care into resource costs and the optimum resource input is understandably illimitable; ask broadcasting engineers to translate broadcasting 'needs' into resource costs and the result is the same – there can never be a limit to improvements in the quality of the 'picture'. The resources to be used for broadcasting services can only be valued in terms of the alternatives foregone. This can be done only by those whom we identify as choosers and then only on the basis of their subjective valuations.

If the Committee on Financing the BBC and the White Paper take it as axiomatic that broadcasting services must reflect the interests of viewers and listeners, the justification must be found in arguments other than those which claim that there is some scientific way of ranking tastes and preferences. In fact, it is based on the widely accepted value-judgement that the function of any service is to benefit the consumer, and that in the case of broadcasting, as with other services, the viewer and listener are the best judges of their own interest.[5]

The second misconception of broadcasters is based on the failure (or refusal) to recognise that creating a market which gives viewers and listeners much more control over what they want to watch is not synonymous with the introduction of complete commercial *laissez-faire*. Viewers and listeners cannot give full expression to their preferences if channels are financed primarily by advertising revenue, although a marked increase in the number of radio or TV channels can make

---

4 Home Office, *Broadcasting in the '90s: Competition, Choice and Quality*, Cm. 517, London: HMSO, 1988.

5 See the Summary of Research commissioned by the Committee in Appendix G of the Peacock Report.

advertisers much more responsive to differences in consumer tastes.[6] This is the case for the introduction of subscription or 'pay-per-view' methods of financing. Nor can viewers and listeners develop their tastes and preferences unless these are challenged by a wide range of alternative forms of programme which can be supplied only if there is much greater freedom of entry into the programming business. The creation of such a market entails government intervention in order to prevent 'horizontal' integration (concentration of ownership in TV channels, for instance) and 'vertical' integration (concentration of ownership in programming, scheduling and transmission of programmes).

However, a major worry remains in the minds of those who fear that a consumer-driven market system in broadcasting would reduce 'programme quality' for programmes which could not pay their way and which would disappear or at least be reduced in number. Leaving aside the vexed question of the definition of quality, which can be derived only from value-judgements, the fact that the market might 'under-supply' such programmes does not mean that the viewing and listening public do not recognise the benefits of programmes of a cultural and educational nature and must regard the market as the sole means by which they can give expression to their preferences. The public may itself support further action to preserve quality, either through direct regulation of the composition of programmes and/or some form of financial inducement to companies to present them. This general line of argument is pursued in later contributions. It suffices to say here that the preservation of quality can be achieved without having to give up the very substantial increase in benefits which can be obtained by making the broadcasting system largely dependent on consumer choices expressed through payment for services rendered. Furthermore, if there are worries about reduced access to services by those who can ill afford to pay for them, either because of poverty or because they live in isolated and sparsely populated areas which could not guarantee a large enough market to TV companies, then government support may be justified, always provided that the amount of finance required is public knowledge.

While the following contributions explore the implications of a broadcasting system geared to acceptance of consumer sovereignty, there are pronounced differences of emphasis both in the interpretation of consumer welfare, in the precise characteristics of the broadcasting system that will best reflect consumer sovereignty, in the institutional changes that should characterise the broadcasting system, and in the pattern and timing of such changes. The limited experience in the UK of alternative broadcasting systems clearly requires that several contributions consider carefully the working of broadcasting in other countries, though this will

---

[6] For further discussion, Alan Peacock, *Making Sense of Broadcasting Finance*, Robbins Lecture, University of Stirling, 1986.

meet the sales resistance of those who assert in that imperious way typical of our more insular broadcasting pundits that we have the best broadcasting system in the world. At the same time, reasonable men can disagree about the relevance of experience in other countries and how far it could and should influence the British broadcasting scene.

In sum, to expect serious discussion of the economic aspects of broadcasting to result in a resolution of all disagreements would be patently naive, as it would be to expect broadcasting engineers to agree on which forecasts of technological progress in the use of the radio spectrum or in the quality of the TV picture will be the most accurate. Attention to the economic analysis of broadcasting may have entered rather late into British policy discussions, but it is now here to stay.

PART I

PRINCIPLES AND POLICY

ch! great change in in Live

White Pape 1988 — allaw great cherge in
(broadcasting)
ARGUMENT — who says those of "higher" tests
should have the say asto what is broadcost.

COMPETITION
IN BROADCASTING

Cento Veljanovski

Research & Editorial Director,
Institute of Economic Affairs

'There are no excuses now for pretending things will stay as they are. Choice is the objective; competition is the means to achieve it.'

ROGER LAUGHTON, BBC[1]

THE CHINESE HAVE A CURSE – may you live in a period of great change. The established broadcasting institutions are increasingly appreciating the wisdom of the Chinese. There has not been such a period of transition in British broadcasting since the invention of television. The central underpinnings of the British broadcasting system, that of public service broadcasting, are under attack and are looking less defensible. The *status quo* is no longer an option.

The Government's long-awaited White Paper, *Broadcasting in the '90s – Competition, Choice and Quality*,[2] sets out its proposals for the de-regulation of British broadcasting. In broad terms it advances the cause of freedom in the media.

Broadcasting has been treated as something that cannot be left to the market or to individual choice. Many reasonable and highly educated people believe that it must be controlled by the Government to protect the public. A patrician attitude (some would say arrogance) still pervades British broadcasting: that the average viewer must be given programmes

---

[1] 'Introduction', *Television After the White Paper*, London: Royal Television Society, 1988, p. 7.

[2] Home Office, *Broadcasting in the '90s: Competition, Choice and Quality – The Government's Plans for Broadcasting Legislation*, Cm. 517, HMSO, 1988 – hereinafter referred to simply as the White Paper.

which those with superior and more refined tastes regard as good, worthy and uplifting.

It is an extraordinary episode in history (paralleled by the experience of the printed word many centuries ago) that the state's control of broadcasting should have remained so entrenched and unchallenged for virtually 60 years in the UK. It would be hard to explain to the foreigner how the same department of state (the Home Office) controls both the police force and broadcasting without getting these functions confused. It was George Orwell in *1984*, drawing on his experiences in the BBC, who sketched the frightening portrait of state control of the citizen using the latest telecommunications technology. Orwell was wrong – technology, attracted by the beacon of profits and the call of consumer demand, has been the saviour of the citizen and has broken the state's stranglehold on broadcasting.

The last several years has witnessed an intense public debate over the future of British broadcasting. There is now a clear challenge to the British broadcasting industry to explain why it should be run as a public service in the public interest. The White Paper, if nothing else, uses the language of markets and freedom to express its policy. Like the influential Peacock Report[3] it accepts the case for choice and competition.[4] 'The Government', it proclaims, 'places the viewer and listener at the centre of broadcasting policy'.[5] Among the proposals of the White Paper are the authorisation of a fifth commercial channel by April 1993, the restructuring of the Independent Television system, the authorisation of two additional satellite channels which can broadcast directly to viewers, the further deregulation of cable and other local television systems, a major reform of the regulatory system including the abolition of the Cable Authority and the Independent Broadcasting Authority whose functions will be merged into a new Commercial Television Authority (CTA), and a greater role for independent producers through a system of programme quotas imposed on both the BBC and ITV.

Yet the White Paper still seeks to control television. British governments have a congenital inability to accept a completely free broadcasting system. The White Paper hedges by outlining a number of what it describes as 'consumer protection' and 'positive programme' requirements which in Samuel Brittan's view (see Chapter 2) amount to state censorship. These regulations will, however, be less restrictive than at present. But the Government does not explain why greater choice will necessarily threaten programme standards nor does it define what are acceptable programmes.

---

[3] Home Office, *Report of the Committee on Financing the BBC*, Cmnd. 9824, London: HMSO, 1986.

[4] A strong advocate of a deregulated broadcasting industry was the past Chairman of the Federal Communications Commission, Mark Fowler: M. Fowler and D. Brenner, 'A Market-Place Approach to Broadcast Regulation', *Texas Law Review*, Vol. 60, 1982, pp. 207-257.

[5] Cm. 517, para. 1.2.

THE STRUCTURE OF BRITISH BROADCASTING

The BBC/ITV Duopoly

The competitive commercial era of broadcasting began in Britain in 1954 with the creation of a second television channel financed by advertising revenue. Commercial television became known as Independent Television or the ITV system and is regulated by the Independent Broadcasting Authority (IBA). Prior to that the British Broadcasting Corporation (BBC), was the sole monopoly radio and television broadcaster in the UK. The BBC/ITV duopoly structure has persisted to the present day despite the expansion in television channels.

The overriding principle of Britain's broadcasting system is that it be run as a public service. Public service broadcasting is hard to define. At a bare minimum it involves the Reithian trinity – that the goal of broadcasting is to educate, inform and entertain – coupled with universality of service; both in the geographical sense of providing a television service to the whole country and in supplying a range of programming which caters to all tastes. These public service principles are imposed on the commercial broadcasters by statute (the various Broadcasting Acts) and the IBA.

The system of regulated competition, or rationed television, that has evolved out of public service broadcasting is uniquely British. The BBC provides two national television channels (BBC1 and BBC2) which compete for audiences with one regionalised television channel, ITV, composed of 15 regional contractors. Since February 1983 there has also been a separate breakfast TV contractor (TV-am). In addition there is a fourth channel (Channel 4) which began broadcasting a national service in 1982 and its Welsh-language cousin S4C. Channel 4 is owned by the IBA but financed by a 'subscription' imposed on the ITV contractors broadly in proportion to their advertising revenue. In return the ITV contractors have the right to sell advertising time on Channel 4 in their respective areas.

All the ITV contractors have a monopoly of advertising time in their respective franchise areas, except in the lucrative London area where Thames broadcasts during the weekdays and London Weekend Television on the weekends.

The ITV contractors are franchised in a competitive process held about every seven years, although the actual length of the franchise period has varied considerably. The Broadcasting Act 1987 extended the present franchises to 1992 in order to judge the impact that cable and satellite developments will have on the ITV system. The White Paper proposes fundamental changes to this method of franchising.

Competition between these channels is restrained. All channels have explicit controls on the type, nature and style of programmes. The second television channel of the BBC (BBC2) and the 'commercial' sector

5

(Channel 4) complement the programmes of BBC1 and ITV respectively. Furthermore, the programmes shown on the second channel are qualitatively different. Channel 4 is required by the Broadcasting Act 1980 to show programmes that ITV does not have time for and which cater for minority interests and are new and experimental. This is its so-called 'distinctive programming remit' which the White Paper states 'must be fully sustained'.[6] Channel 4 also differs from the three other channels in one other respect. It does not produce its own programmes – it is a commissioning house which has created a whole new independent programme production sector in the UK.

The New Media

The prospect of competition from the new media – principally cable and satellite – has been enhanced in the last several years.

The transmission of programmes through cables is older than over-the-air broadcasting. With the effective nationalisation of broadcasting in the 1920s, cable's role was greatly limited. Government regulation restricted the cable industry to the relay of broadcast television and radio programmes to areas where over-the-air reception was poor or unavailable.

The Cable & Broadcasting Act 1984 deregulated the cable industry. Cable systems would now be authorised to provide programmes in direct competition with the BBC/ITV duopoly. Their expansion was to be market-led and privately financed. The Act set up a new regulatory agency to award franchises and oversee the industry. The Cable Authority was, to use the oft-quoted words of the White Paper, to apply 'regulation with a light touch'.

At March 1988, 23 franchises had been awarded for new broadband cable systems. These are listed in Table 1. The great bulk of these systems have yet to begin construction and operation. Eleven of these systems are now operating (Swindon, Aberdeen, Coventry, Westminster, Windsor, Croydon, Glasgow, Ealing, Tower Hamlets, Camden and Bedfordshire). The total number of homes cabled (as at 1 April 1988) is 256,527, or 18.7 per cent of the number of homes passed by cable (Table 2). In addition, there are 11 new British 'national' channels which supply the cable systems with programme material (Sky Channel, Children's Channel, Screen Sport, Premiere, Music Box, Lifestyle, Arts Channel, Star, Home Video, Bravo).

The Cable & Broadcasting Act 1984 also empowered the IBA to award a franchise for a direct broadcast by satellite (DBS) television service consisting of three channels. This contract was awarded in 1986 to a consortium called British Satellite Broadcasting (BSB). The satellite is due to be launched in 1989 with three channels, although the White Paper

---

6 Cm. 517, para. 6.23.

TABLE 1

CABLE FRANCHISE AREAS

Area	Homes Passed
First Round 1983	
Belfast	136,000
Merseyside	125,000
Coventry	119,000
Windsor	99,000
Croydon	114,000
Glasgow	112,000
Ealing	100,000
Aberdeen	91,000
Westminster	73,000
Swindon	75,000
Guildford	22,000
Second Round 1985	
Tower Hamlets	127,000
West Surrey	115,000
Bolton	135,000
Wandsworth (London)	100,000
Cheltenham/Gloucester	90,000
Third Round 1985	
Cardiff & Penarth	103,000
Central Lancashire	114,000
Edinburgh	183,000
Camden (London)	70,000
Southampton & Eastleigh	97,000
Others	
Bedfordshire	97,000
Kensington and Chelsea	68,000
North Solihull	22,000
Andover	12,000
Blackburn, Accrington, Burnley, Nelson, Colne, Rossendale Valley	168,000
Birmingham and/or Solihull	466,000
Southend-on-Sea, Basildon, Brentwood, Chelmsford, etc.	221,000
Medway Towns, Gravesend, Maidstone & Sittingbourne	145,000
Hammersmith & Fulham, Brent and Barnet	280,000
Bristol, Bath, Weston-super-Mare, etc.	300,000
Redbridge, Bexley, Barking and Dagenham	229,000
Reading, Bracknell, Basingstoke, Newbury, etc.	215,000
Northampton	72,000
Total	4,495,000

Source: Cable Authority.

TABLE 2

BRITISH CABLE: KEY FACTS

	31 March 1988	31 March 1987
Number of broadband franchises awarded	23	22
Number of broadband franchises operating	10	8
Homes so far passed	307,453	168,436
Homes connected to franchises	44,565	21,873
Average connection rate	14·5%	13·0%
Average subscription paid per month	£17·86	£18·50
Homes passed by all UK cable	1,372,856	1,189,655
Homes connected to all UK cable	256,527	193,173
Average connection rate	18·7%	16·2%
Proportion of viewing of cable channels	39·0%	30·0%

Source: Cable Authority.

states that an additional two will be permitted (the UK having been allocated five DBS channels under international agreement).

In addition to DBS, a number of medium- and low-powered satellite television channels which are outside the control of the UK Government are or will be available to the British viewer. These will be broadcast via the Astra satellite successfully launched in 1988 which has the potential to broadcast 16 television channels. The major difference between DBS and medium-powered satellite television channels is the size of the reception dish (and hence expense). For DBS television small dishes (around 45 cm. or less in diameter) are required whereas Astra will require larger, more expensive dishes (approximately 65 cm.).

THE PROGRESS OF POLICY

The White Paper is the outcome of a vigorous and at times acrimonious debate over broadcasting policy. It would take a book, and I suspect a pretty racy one, to describe the machinations and absurdities, the exaggeration and prejudices, and the self-serving lobbying that has surrounded the debate over the future course of broadcasting policy.[7] To the Government's credit its approach has become progressively more radical as the claims of the producer groups have become more outrageous.

The White Paper follows on the heels of the Hunt Report,[8] which

---

[7] A. T. Peacock, 'The "Politics" of Investigating Broadcasting Finance', *Royal Bank of Scotland Review*, 153, 1987, pp. 3-16; S. Brittan, 'The Fight for Freedom in Broadcasting', *Political Quarterly*, Vol. 58, 1987, pp. 3-20.

[8] Home Office/Department of Trade & Industry, *Report of the Inquiry into Cable Expansion and Broadcasting Policy*, Cmnd. 8679, HMSO, 1982.

effectively deregulated cable television,[9] and the Peacock Report,[10] which was asked the narrow question: Should the BBC be funded by advertising?, but offered a coherent intellectual basis for the reform and deregulation of British broadcasting. In addition the Government has investigated a range of specific issues, many arising out of the Peacock Report and published reports on radio spectrum deregulation,[11] subscription television,[12] and microwave television (known in this country as Microwave Video Distribution System or MVDS).[13]

The Hunt Report

The Hunt Report marks a watershed in broadcasting policy. It recommended that cable television should be liberalised and permitted to compete outright with the BBC and ITV for audiences. This, or rather the *Principles* Cable & Broadcasting Act 1984, thus broke several of the tenets of public service broadcasting – those of universal service, the prohibition of direct viewer payment and the idea that no two broadcasting organisations should compete for the same source of revenue. It was also the case that cable television programmes would be less regulated.

The impetus for cable deregulation did not come from a concern with viewers but the Cabinet Office and Department of Trade & Industry's (DTI) desire to rejuvenate the British telecommunications manufacturing industry which had declined dramatically and as part of the overall scheme for telecommunications deregulation which accompanied the privatisation of British Telecommunications (BT) in 1984.[14] At the time the Government believed that broadband cable networks (that is, cable

---

9 Also see Home Office/Department of Trade & Industry, *The Development of Cable Systems and Services*, Cmnd. 8866, London: HMSO, 1985.

10 Cmnd. 9824, *op. cit.*

11 Home Office, *The Report of the Independent Review of the Radio Spectrum (30-960 MHZ)*, Cmnd. 9000, London: HMSO, 1983; Department of Trade & Industry, *Deregulation of the Radio Spectrum in the UK*, London: HMSO, 1987.

12 Home Office, *Subscription Television*, London: HMSO, 1987. Also see the earlier (unpublished) analysis by R. Bowles, M. Cave & P. Swann, *An Economic Appraisal of Subscription Television*, Home Office: Report for the Committee on Financing the BBC, 1986.

13 Department of Trade & Industry, *Report on the Potential for Microwave Video Distribution Systems in the UK*, London: HMSO, 1988.

14 For an extensive discussion of cable television policy throughout this period see the following articles and monographs by me: (with W. D. Bishop), *Choice by Cable – The Economics of a New Era in Television*, Hobart Paper 96, London: IEA, 1983; 'UK Cable Policy in the Eighties', *Fiscal Studies*, Vol. 4, 1983, pp. 29-45; 'Cable Television – Agency Franchising and Economics', in R. Baldwin & C. McCruddin (eds.), *Regulation and Public Law*, London: Weidenfeld & Nicolson, 1987; 'British Cable and Satellite Television Policies', *National Westminster Bank Quarterly Review*, November 1987, pp. 28-40. The reader interested in this area should also consult the consultants' reports and findings of the MacDonald Committee (an internal DTI review of UK communications infrastructure policy): DTI, *The Development of UK Communications Systems*, Discussion Document, April 1987, PA Consulting Group, *Evolution of the United Kingdom Communications Infrastructure Phase 1 – Discussion Paper*, London: DTI, September 1987; DTI, *Evolution of the United Kingdom Communications Infrastructure*, London: HMSO, 1988; DTI Communications Steering Group Report, *The Infrastructure for Tomorrow*, London: HMSO, 1988.

systems with in excess of 30 television channels and the capability to provide telephone and other services) would eventually provide effective competition with BT in the one area it had an unassailed monopoly – the provision of local telephone services. As part of this policy the Government imposed on cable systems a range of technical requirements and limited cable providers' ability to use other technology to bring programmes to viewers in their franchise areas. In addition cable operators were not permitted to 'cherry pick' – they were required to cable their whole franchise area to an agreed timetable.

This policy has been decisively rejected in the White Paper, largely because the expansion of the cable system has been slow. The Cable Authority will be abolished and merged into the proposed Commercial Television Authority (CTA) which will replace the IBA. Cable companies and others wishing to provide local television services will be free to use the mix of technologies and the level of technical sophistication which are dictated by commercial considerations. Moreover, they will not have to cable the whole franchise area. The White Paper also proposes that the ownership of delivery (the cable infrastructure) and the retailing of cable services should be separated. This was again decisively rejected in the Hunt Report but proposed by Peacock (Recommendation 15) as a way of fostering genuine competition in ideas and programmes in broadcasting.[15]

The Peacock Report

The Peacock Committee was given a narrow brief which it interpreted liberally (in both senses of the word). The Committee was set up to consider the vexed question of how to fund the BBC. The licence fee (essentially an annual tax on households which owned television sets) required periodic Parliamentary approval. Each time it came before the politicians a major debate on the BBC occurred, generating controversy and uncertainty. The Peacock Committee concluded that, because of the limited number of channels in the UK, financing the BBC by advertising would be undesirable since it would intensify competition for audiences which, in the Committee's opinion, would reduce the choice to the viewer. Like the White Paper, it rejected advertising on the BBC. The Peacock Committee recommended that the licence fee should continue for the foreseeable future but be pegged to the Retail Price Index. This was accepted by the Government.

The White Paper proposes that the licence fee should be pegged to the RPI for the next three years (1988-91) but thereafter rise by less than the increase in the RPI and that the BBC should seek funding from developing subscription television. This will clearly put a squeeze on the BBC's finances.

---

15 For a discussion of this question, C. G. Veljanovski, 'Regulatory Options for Cable TV in the UK', *Telecommunications Policy*, Vol. 7, 1984, pp. 290-306.

The Peacock Committee went on to outline its vision of the evolution of British broadcasting to a freer and more competitive industry. It rested on competition fostered by the development of multi-channel cable systems and payment for television directly by viewers through subscription.[16] This it argued would lead to the eventual withering away of the state's regulation of programmes and channels.

The Peacock Committee stated the goals that broadcasting should serve in clear and unequivocal terms:

> 'The fundamental aim of broadcasting should in our view be to enlarge both the freedom of choice of the consumer and the opportunities available to programme makers to offer alternative wares to the public.'[17]

It saw the consumer as the ultimate arbitrator of what should be shown on television, although it accepted that there was a role for public service broadcasting. The latter should be restricted to the areas of knowledge, culture, criticism and experiment, and 'should account for only a modest proportion of total broadcasting'.

What has not been fully understood is how the Peacock Report fundamentally altered the terms of the debate over the future of broadcasting from those based on subjective values, preferences and tastes to economic and factual propositions.

Prior to the Peacock Report the debate followed the pattern of many which had preceded it in the turbulent history of British broadcasting policy – long on clichés and unsupported claims but short on facts: namely, that any change to the present system would lead to the destruction of British culture and the ruination of the best television system in the world. Indeed, a considerable mythology has developed around the ethnocentric claim that British television is the best in, or more boastfully that it is the envy of, the world. This is a claim, one is bound to say, that issues mainly from the lips of British broadcasters or by those from public service broadcasting institutions in North America and the Commonwealth rather than from viewers. Notwithstanding this, any argument to the contrary was simply ridiculed. For 60 years the above claims had been effectively deployed to block or limit competition.

While it is undeniably true that British public service broadcasting has some enviable features, it is hardly true that this can be said of the whole system or that reform is thereby precluded because a programme of high artistic merit is occasionally produced. This is particulary true of ITV which has been vigorous in protecting its monopoly of television

---

16 For my analysis of the Peacock Report's views see: C. G. Veljanovski, 'Cable and Satellite: The Market for Programmes?', London: Centre for Economic Policy Research, Working Paper No. 176, 1987; 'Commercial Broadcasting in the UK – Over Regulation or Mis-Regulation?', London: Centre for Economic Policy Research, Working Paper No. 175, 1987.

17 Peacock Report, para. 547.

BOX 1

The Rehabilitation of a Much-Maligned Report

Raymond Snoddy

When the Peacock Report on the financing of British broadcasting was published two years ago this month, opponents queued up to kick it to death.

Broadcasters from the BBC and ITV bristled at being described as 'a comfortable duopoly'. There was horror at the radical recommendation that ITV franchises should be put out to competitive tender and contempt for the idea that, in future, public service programmes would have to be funded by an 'arts council of the air'. . . .

It has not been kicked into the long grass. Instead, with the powerful backing of senior members of Mrs Thatcher's government, bit by bit its main recommendations have won increasing favour in Downing Street. It is now clear that they will form the basic template for the most dramatic changes in British broadcasting since the introduction of commercial television more than 30 years ago.

Ideas once seen as outrageously radical have become almost common-place, through changes in the market-place, the passage of time and the imminence of many new channels of satellite television.

'I think we have had a very good run for our money,' says Professor – now Sir Alan – Peacock, who chaired the committee. 'We have stirred the pot a bit and given a point of reference and departure.'

Just how much a point of departure became clear on Thursday when a Cabinet Committee chaired by Mrs Thatcher backed a comprehensive package of changes to be included in a broadcasting white paper due in November. It includes awarding ITV franchises by competitive tender next time round – a recommendation supported by only four of the seven Peacock committee members.

With a strike rate of about two-thirds on recommendations that are either already accepted or are very likely to appear in next year's broadcasting bill, Sir Alan believes he has done better than he had a right to expect.

But the Government has ignored the report's final argument that the recommendations were designed to form a coherent strategy and that it was not possible 'to pick and choose at will among them without destroying the whole thrust'.

That, in fact, is what the Government has done. Most of the recommendations that would increase competition and consumer choice have been warmly embraced. But one that did not make it was the recommendation that broadcasters should be as free as publishers, subject only to laws relating to obscenity, defamation, blasphemy and sedition.

Far from accepting such a libertarian approach, the Government set up a Broadcasting Standards Council under Sir William Rees-Mogg to monitor how sex and violence is portrayed in broadcasting.

Four recommendations of the Peacock Committee have already either been accepted or implemented: that the BBC should not have to take advertising; its licence fee should be indexed to retail prices; the Corporation should have the responsibility for collecting the licence fee and – most important of all – that both ITV and BBC should take a significant proportion of their programmes from independent producers.

The Government also accepted the recommendation that regulation of commercial radio by the Independent Broadcasting Authority should be replaced by a looser régime. A new Radio Authority is being set up to do just that with a similar looser régime for commercial television from a new Commercial Television Authority. A linked proposal that BBC Radios 1 and 2 should be privatised and be financed by advertising was rejected.

A further five recommendations are likely to happen in some form. Apart from competitive tendering they are: the sale to other broadcasters of night-time hours; Channel 4 TV to have the option of selling its own airtime; removal of restrictions on non-EC ownership of cable franchises and ending restrictions on both pay-per-channel and pay-per-programme television. . . .

As well as a new freedom for broadcasters, three other Peacock recommendations were rejected: £10 car radio licences to help fund the BBC; a free licence for pensioners drawing supplementary pension and competitive tenders for direct broadcasting by satellite franchises.

Despite the successes, Mr Samuel Brittan, a member of the Peacock Committee and chief economic commentator of the *Financial Times*, says he does not support the emerging government broadcasting policy because on 'first amendment' rights to free speech it has actually gone backwards.

The central theme of Peacock – that there should be an orderly progress towards a full consumer market in broadcasting which would mean greater liberty for both citizen and broadcasters – has not been respected.

In a study to be published by the Institute of Economic Affairs [the present book], Brittan argues: 'To the extent that the Government endorsed some Peacock recommendations, it is the letter that was accepted, and the spirit rejected. As the proposed fifth channel is likely to be financed exclusively by advertising, even the letter, in its up-to-date form, has now been rejected' (below, pp. 39-40).

(Reprinted from the *Financial Times*, 31 July 1988.)

advertising revenue. As the Home Secretary, Douglas Hurd, countered after the publication of the White Paper:

> '... to suppose that when my constituents ... turn on ITV on a Saturday night they are entering some temple of high culture is something they would be very surprised to hear'.[18]

The Peacock Committee forced the protagonists to substantiate their claims. And since some of the Committee were economists, including the Chairman, the most persuasive assembly of facts and analysis would be those in an explicit economic framework. The Peacock Committee must be one of the few public inquiries in which the outcome rested, or appeared to rest, on the findings of several statistical studies of the elasticity of demand for television advertising.[19] But the framework developed by Peacock and the issues that it drew attention to – essentially fundamental questions about the nature and purpose of broadcasting in a free society – required all to reconsider the basis of broadcasting policy. This we can now see in retrospect led to a major transformation in a public debate over the future of broadcasting and a more radical broadcasting White Paper than would have been conceivable when the Government set up the Committee.

Post-Peacock Developments

Despite its subsequent success the Peacock Report was initially greeted with apparent disappointment by the Government (which wanted the BBC to take advertising) and with good cheer by the BBC and established broadcasters. It appeared a dead letter.

However, the Prime Minister and senior members of the Cabinet held the view that something had to be done about broadcasting, particulary the inefficiencies perceived to exist in the ITV system. ITV, for example, was seen by the Prime Minister as the last bastion of restrictive labour practices. A special Cabinet Committee chaired by the Prime Minister was set up and a number of reports commissioned to investigate some of Peacock's recommendations and other key matters.

One of the key recommendations of the Peacock Committee was that the best method of funding television was direct payment by the viewer, i.e. subscription television. In direct response to this recommendation the Home Office commissioned a study entitled *Subscription Television* on the technical and commercial feasibility of funding the existing television channels by subscription. This concluded, rather lamely, that subscription

---

[18] P. Fiddick, 'Hurd v. Grade in Big Match', *Guardian*, 21 November 1988, p. 25.

[19] For example, the consultants' reports commissioned by the Peacock Committee: M. Cave & P. Swann, *The Effects on Advertising Revenues of Allowing Advertising on BBC Television – A Report for the Committee on Financing the BBC*, London: Home Office, 1985; G. K. Yarrow, C. Veljanovski *et al.*, *The Effects on Other Media of the Introduction of Advertising on the BBC – A Report for the Committee on Financing the BBC*, London: Home Office, 1985.

television, while possible, would not generate sufficient revenue to fund the present four television channels. Its methodology and conclusions are critically examined in Sawers's chapter in this volume.

The high costs of television advertising time also attracted attention, particularly by the Department of Trade and Industry. During the Peacock Committee's deliberations the growth of advertising revenue had slowed. This added fuel to the claim that there was insufficient advertising to support four channels if the BBC were required to take advertisements. The econometric studies commissioned by Peacock concluded that the demand elasticity for advertising was unity, implying that an increase in its availability would drive down its price so that total advertising revenue would remain more or less constant but be shared between more channels. However, in 1987 the cost of television advertising skyrocketed largely as a result of the consumer boom in the UK economy. Increasingly, advertisers became agitated and began lobbying for increased competition in the broadcasting sector to bring rates down. This occurred just at the time when the Home Office had lost momentum and broadcasting policy appeared to be drifting from one indecision to another. In the first half of 1988 the Home Office was galvanised by the interest shown by Lord Young (the Secretary of State for Trade and Industry). Young's concern revolved around the need to introduce more competition in broadcasting to break ITV's monopoly and thereby make more time available to British industry to advertise its goods and services.

The Deregulation of Independent Radio

During these deliberations over television the Government moved on local independent radio, the commercial limb of Britain's radio system. The radio Green Paper[20] took a fundamental look at the future of commercial radio. It recommended the deregulation of radio, the authorisation of three new national commercial radio stations, and the creation of a new regulatory body, the Radio Authority, to take over from the IBA.[21]

The Green Paper contained a scathing attack on the IBA's approach to regulating radio. The industry was in chaos. The Independent Local Radio (ILR) is a system of local radio stations with substantial public service obligations which competed with four BBC national channels and BBC local radio. The radio Green Paper pointed to the unmet demand for radio broadcasting, the evidence of stagnation, the weak financial base of the industry with at the time (1987) only 26 of the 49 ILR stations in profit, and the burdensome regulation placed on each ILR station which increased their costs substantially.

---

[20] Home Office, *Radio: Choices and Opportunities – A Consultative Document*, Cm. 92, London: HMSO, 1987.

[21] See M. Oliver's chapter in this volume, below, Ch. 9, pp. 165-177.

In early January 1988 the Government announced that it intended to legislate along the lines of the Green Paper's recommendation. The broadcasting White Paper which followed stated that the 'case for substantial deregulation of independent local radio is compelling'.[22]

The White Paper

The White Paper is a complex document. It is in fact more in the nature of a Green Paper on some key issues and has unnecessarily prolonged the uncertainty concerning government policy, e.g. on the future of Channel 4.

There are at least two distinct approaches in the White Paper. The first concerns local television. The White Paper represents a radical reversal in cable and local television policy. The Cable Authority, less than four years old, is to be abolished and its functions taken over by the proposed CTA. The idea that cable systems should also be capable of providing telecommunications services has been rejected and a host of technical restrictions will be relaxed. It states that no longer will the Government attempt to pick and back winners or choose the mix of technologies. These will be left to the commercial decisions of the private sector.

The more cautious and conservative strand of the White Paper shows the interventionist hand of the Home Office with its continued attempt to control programmes and the activities of the UHF licensees, i.e. the BBC, ITV and Channel 4 and the proposed Channel 5. Here the Government is moving with an unsure foot and without the courage to deregulate fully. All these channels, including the proposed new Channel 5, are to have public service obligations and programme controls. Thus the nature of these channels, including their competitive character, will largely be determined by regulation. Broadcasting is being given the appearance of more competition by independent production quotas (which will require the BBC and ITV to buy or commission at least 25 per cent of programmes from independent producers) and the splitting of channels by time of day, that is, having separate companies broadcast on the same frequencies but for different parts of the day such as during the breakfast hours, during the day and the night hours. It is unclear to what extent this re-structuring of the industry is in any way dictated by commercial logic.

FAILURE TO DEFINE PUBLIC SERVICE BROADCASTING

A major gap in the White Paper is its refusal to define public service broadcasting. It side-steps the issue by outlining a set of positive programme regulations which will ensure the maintenance of standards and the preservation of the BBC and Channel 4. Yet nowhere does the White Paper state why competition and commercialism will lead to a fall in programme standards, or what are good programmes.

---

[22] Cm. 517, para. 8.1. ·

If, as the White Paper accepts, the object of broadcasting is to give viewers what they want and if it claims that competition and more choice will achieve this result – then the question can fairly be asked: What is public service broadcasting? Unless the Government provides a clear answer to this question, then it will be impossible to assess to what extent the White Paper is consistent with a free market in broadcasting.

It is often said that public service broadcasting is no more and no less than the Reithian trinity – to educate, entertain and inform – adapted to modern circumstances. While this definition may satisfy those broadcasters responsible for administering the system, it is at best a vague concept that has defied expression in terms which would permit one to assess whether its purported objectives have been achieved. It is undeniably paternalistic, which many find offensive; others reassuring. All those subscribing to the concept will say that public service broadcasting is a changing notion, while its enemies will say that it is whatever the BBC and IBA say it is.

The White Paper does nothing to resolve these concerns or to put public service broadcasting on a firm basis. Instead it attempts to embed into its proposals for the whole broadcasting sector a commitment to some ill-defined but different concept of public service. Thus Channel 3 (the present ITV system) will have public service obligations, Channel 4 will continue with its distinctive programme remit (which it says has been a 'striking success' and 'must be fully sustained'[23]), and the BBC will continue with its own approach to public service broadcasting.

Effectively this is an attempt to link PSB with the existing public service broadcasters. However, this serves only to preserve these broadcasting organisations rather than maximise the choice and quality of programmes in an increasingly competitive television market-place.

Indicative of confusion is the tentative and ambiguous way the plans for the future of Channel 4 are stated in the White Paper. Channel 4 will be allowed to sell its own advertising time but will retain its distinctive programme remit, namely:

'. . . to cater for tastes and interests not served, or under-represented, by other parts of the independent sector; to encourage innovation and experiment in form and content of programmes; to devote a suitable proportion of its airtime to educational programming; to devote a suitable proportion of its airtime to high quality news and current affairs programmes including during main viewing hours; and to maintain a distinctive character of its own'.[24]

The White Paper states that Channel 4 will operate in a more independent fashion. It then goes on to list three 'illustrative rather than exclusive' 'constitutional models' for Channel 4. The first is a fully

---

[23] Cm. 517, para. 6.23. [24] Cm. 517, para. 6.23.

privatised Channel 4 which the White Paper concedes would mean that its complementary programme schedule to ITV would have to be abandoned. This would be a more competitive Channel 4 with a larger audience. The second option turns out to be the *status quo* – a non-profit subsidiary of the CTA with a guaranteed minimum level of income. The third model is to link Channel 4 to the new Channel 5 in much the same way as it is now linked to ITV. It is not at all clear how this tinkering and the statement that some models imply abandoning Channel 4's distinctive programme remit advance the coherence and consistency of the Government's policy.

COMPETITION AND PROGRAMME QUALITY

Underlying the White Paper is the belief that in a real yet undefined sense there is a conflict between competition and quality: that unrestrained competition between a large number of channels will lead to an undesirable decline in programme standards.

There is a relationship between competition and programming but it is not the one which is commonly alleged. In a market system where television is financed by advertising and where the number of channels is small, competition will not maximise consumer welfare. The reason for this is straightforward and arises from the fact that broadcasters have no direct contractual link with viewers. They sell one service – time to advertisers – but their performance is evaluated in terms of the welfare of another group which obtains the service free of charge. It is therefore not surprising that television funded by advertising will not provide the range and choice of programmes that viewers ideally want. If there is competition between several channels then the worst excesses of commercial television appear – common denominator programmes (endless chat and game shows) and wasteful duplication of programmes (all showing the same type of programmes at the same time).

A Simple Model of Wall-to-Wall Dallas

The claim that limited competition among channels funded by advertising can lead to 'wall-to-wall Dallas' has been one long modelled by economists.[25]

Consider the case of a television system totally funded by advertising revenue. Assume also that there are three programme categories: A = mini series such as Coronation Street or Eastenders; B = Game Shows and C = serious drama such as the oft-quoted example of *Brideshead Revisited*. The total potential audience is 100 viewers. Each individual has

---

[25] Roger G. Noll, Merton J. Peck and John J. McGowan, *Economic Aspects of Television Regulation*, Washington DC: The Brookings Institution, 1973; Bruce M. Owen, Jack H. Beebe and Willard G. Manning, Jr., *Television Economics*, Lexington, Mass.: D.C. Heath and Company, 1974.

a clear preference for one type of programme and if it is not shown he or she switches off the TV set. Assume that the potential audience divides between the programme categories A, B, and C in the proportions 80, 18, and 2 respectively.

To model the advertiser-supported channel it is assumed that the operator seeks to maximise his audience share and that if more than one channel shows the same programme they divide the audience equally between them. Each channel seeks to maximise its audience share because this maximises revenue.

Now consider the effect of introducing more channels. If there is one channel only programme A would be shown. If a second channel were introduced it would also show programme A because this would maximise its audience. Each would gain an audience of 40 which is larger than the audience if the second channel showed programme B (i.e. 18 people). A third channel would fragment the audience further but would still maximise audience share by showing type A programmes. In our example it would need five channels before one found it could maximise its audience by showing a different type of programme, namely B. And in order for the minority taste programme C to maximise the audience of at least one channel there would need to be more than 48 channels!

Thus competition in a setting of a small number of channels generates pressures for the same mass appeal programmes on all channels. The uncomfortable conclusion is that competition is wasteful. If we have three channels, the costs of programming and transmission could potentially triple without any enhancement in genuine choice for viewers.

The conclusion that has been drawn from these models for British broadcasting policy is that more competition financed by advertising would lead to less real choice.

Critical Mass Competition

However, before we accept this conclusion we must examine in more detail the relevance of this analysis to the British system of television or indeed any other. It does not support the proposition that competition is bad, only that artificially limited competition reduces viewer welfare. More channels lead to more choice, not less.

As the number of channels increases there will eventually arise an opportunity for at least one channel to increase its market share by showing a different type of programme to the others. There is a critical level of channel competition after which diversity becomes the profit-maximising strategy for some channels. This typically would take the form of several (three or four) mass audience channels (or networks) and a fringe of channels catering for minority or special interest audiences.

The point at which this will occur cannot be determined *a priori*. It depends on the distribution of the preferences of viewers. Thus an audience which is more heterogeneous in its tastes, say ethnically, with clearly defined groupings, would tend to have more diverse television programming with fewer channels than a relatively more homogeneous audience. This is why one tends to see more ethnic programmes and channels in the USA and other countries with large immigrant populations.

The reality of advertiser-funded broadcasting is that with less than a dozen advertiser-supported channels we begin to experience diverse not duplicative programming.

A MARKET FOR FREQUENCIES

The case against competition in broadcasting has always rested on a technical matter, namely that there are insufficient channels to create a truly competitive market. This was bolstered by the claim that even if competition was possible it would lead to unmanageable radio interference as the airwaves became overcrowded. This is sometimes called the scarcity rationale for government intervention and regulation. Scarcity, it was claimed, ordained monopoly or duopoly in broadcasting, and this in turn required heavy government regulation if not provision to prevent control over the media.

The original reason for establishing the BBC's monopoly was to deal with this technical constraint. If one organisation was responsible for broadcasting it could manage the radio spectrum. Thus monopoly was seen as the administrative solution to the possibility of radio interference which would result if many radio stations were permitted to broadcast.

But the simple fact remains that in other countries many more television and radio stations co-exist without technical difficulties. It therefore follows that nature has not placed a limit on the availability of spectrum for broadcasting.

Merriman and Government Inefficiency and Secrecy

There are two remarkable aspects of this area of broadcasting policy which really require exposure.

The first is the secrecy and the lack of public knowledge which surrounds the availability and allocation of frequencies. It was not until very recently that information became publicly available on these important matters. Indeed, the allocation of the spectrum table was until recently a classified official secret. The Peacock Committee asked many times how many television channels could be made available and received no answer. Had it known that a fifth and possibly sixth national channel could have been accommodated there is little doubt that its recommendations would have been more radical. Since the scarcity of spectrum is one of the principal reasons for state control of broadcasting, the Government's failure to inform the public is disturbing.

A review of UK spectrum policy was begun by the Merriman

Committee.[26] It delivered a scathing assessment of the Home Office's administration and procedures for assigning frequencies to new services. The Home Office, it stated, had grossly mismanaged spectrum policy, leading to waste and irrational decisions as to how spectrum should be allocated to competing uses. The Report's findings delivered a timely reminder of government failure in a policy supposedly designed to deal with the shortcomings of the market-place.

Market Allocation

The real source of the technical problems which surround the use of the spectrum by many users arises not from competition but the absence of clearly specified property rights in frequencies. The Government's task should be to define these rights and protect them from unwarranted interference. Once these rights have been established frequencies can be traded and treated like any other marketable commodity.

The present method of allocating frequencies is to assign them according to need and administrative criteria and not through the use of the pricing system or based on any economic criteria. This practice of giving frequencies away free of charge to commercial and government users not only awards them a valuable gift but provides no pressures for the economical use of frequencies.[27] If something is free and unpriced it tends to be over-used and wasted. The failure to price frequencies does not encourage users to invest in technology which would make more efficient use of the spectrum in the engineering sense, and if the right is a generally available one, such as CB radio, the allocated frequencies soon become overcrowded. Moreover, the failure to price frequencies leads to considerable inefficiency. Broadcasters and other users do not have the incentive to husband this scarce resource by investing money in packing more television channels on a given band width.

In essence there is no difference between land, and the problems of allocation and use it gives rise to, and the management of the spectrum.[28]

The White Paper now tells us that there is room for a fifth and possibly a sixth television channel. What it does not tell us is how the Government arrived at this conclusion. In the absence of a method of valuing the use of frequencies for different purposes it is impossible to determine whether five or six channels or what the overall availability of spectrum to broadcasting should be. The matter should be thrown out to the market to decide how many channels and whether they should be national or local.

---

[26] Cmnd. 9000, *op. cit.*

[27] C. G. Veljanovski, 'Broadcasting - Auctions, Competition and Policy', *Economic Affairs*, August/September 1988, pp. 33-37.

[28] M. L. Spitzer, 'Controlling the Content of Print and Broadcast', *Southern California Law Review*, Vol. 58, 1985, pp. 1,349-1,405.

AUCTIONING FRANCHISES

ITV contractors are licensed by the IBA in a competitive bid process. The competition is not in terms of the payment of money but programme promises and a range of other ill-defined considerations. The IBA's method of franchising has been the object of considerable criticism and the White Paper puts forward a radical reform. Instead of awarding franchises free of charge – generating the statement that these monopoly franchises were a licence to print money – potential applicants must, after they pass a quality hurdle and satisfy the ownership conditions, bid a sum of money. The franchise is then awarded to the highest bidder.

The Deficiencies of the Present Method

The IBA portrays its franchising procedures as a coherent and rational process and one that has yielded considerable benefits. The reality of the present ITV and ILR franchising process is very different. Although competition for franchises is encouraged, the procedures for selection have all the characteristics of a patronage system administered by a wilful ruler.[29] The IBA neither states its criteria nor gives reasons for awarding a franchise, and there is little real prospect of applicants gaining judicial review of its decisions.

One would be hard-pressed to think of another regulatory agency which exercises its discretion in such an arbitrary cloak-and-dagger fashion as the IBA. It is nearly impossible to discover any consistent set of clearly stated criteria which applicants can identify as crucial to winning a franchise. The IBA now admits that it did not give reasons for the award of a franchise in order to prevent a legal challenge – that is, to make its decisions judgement proof.[30]

Peacock Auction

The Peacock Committee was not particularly worried about the franchising process as a fair and effective regulatory scheme. It recommended that ITV and DBS franchises should be auctioned to the highest bidder and where this was not done that the IBA should be required to give its reasons.[31] This was proposed to deal with the cost inefficiencies of the ITV contractors. The Committee expressed concern about the efficiency and cost problems of the ITV contractors and the present method of taxing their profits. Many believe the Exchequer Levy,

---

[29] P. Lewis, 'IBA Programme Awards', *Public Law*, 1975, pp. 317-340; S. Domberger & J. Middleton, 'Franchising in Practice: The Case of Independent Television in the UK', *Fiscal Studies*, Vol. 6, 1985, pp. 17-32; A. Briggs & J. Spicer, *The Franchise Affair*, London: Century, 1986; R. Baldwin, M. Cave & T. H. Jones, 'The Regulation of Independent Local Radio and Its Reform', *International Review of Law & Economics*, Vol. 7, 1986, pp. 177-191.

[30] *Independent Television in the 1990's*, London: Independent Broadcasting Authority, 1988.

[31] Peacock Report, para. 655.

which is a profits tax, encourages cost-padding and weak bargaining with unions. By requiring the contractors to bid for the franchise the

> 'successful bidder would then have monopoly profits creamed off in advance of operating the franchise, and the subsequent earning of profits would depend on close attention to economy in the use of resources'.[32]

That is, competitive tendering would act as a tax on Monday's profits rather than the present Exchequer Levy which is a tax on Friday's profits and then only after the ITV contractors have taken steps to minimise their tax liability by inefficient expenditures. Peacock advocated the auction as a *substitute* for the Levy and to improve the efficiency of commercial television, not as a method of raising revenue for the Treasury.

Another major attraction of Peacock's auction system is that it greatly limits the discretion of the IBA to interfere with the ITV contractors in ways unrelated to and which do not further their public service role. The fettering of the IBA's discretion and capricious decision-making should be one of the principal features of any reform of the franchising process.

White Paper Franchising Procedure

The White Paper proposes that franchises for ITV and the proposed Channel 5 will be sold to the highest bidder. Yet the White Paper's proposed system of franchising consists of the following components:

o   initial programme quality hurdle

o   ownership restrictions

o   the award of the franchise to the highest bidder

o   a progressive tax on net advertising revenue

o   10-year franchises, renewable for 10 years

o   television companies subject to take-over mechanism.

The idea clearly is for the Treasury to get the monopoly profits from restricted competition in broadcasting channels and not for these profits to act as a beacon to support more channels and more choice for viewers. Moreover, the franchise scheme is complex and bound to lead to uncertainty and problems since the commercial broadcaster will be hit from a number of directions. In a world where everyone is perfectly informed it would not matter how television companies are taxed. But in the real world where there are considerable uncertainties it does matter; the White Paper's franchising scheme shifts a considerable amount of this uncertainty onto the companies without giving them the commercial freedom required to operate in an increasingly competitive market-place.

A scheme of franchising which is more consistent with the pro-

---

[32] Peacock Report, para. 655.

competitive philosophy of the White Paper and Peacock would be simply to sell the franchises and then allow them to be traded among potential broadcasters.

CONCLUSION

British broadcasting will never be the same. The advance of technology and demand of viewers for more choice will lead to more channels and a greater diversity of technologies used to deliver programmes to the viewer and listener. What the final outcome of this upheaval will be is anyone's guess. But if a richer and more varied service is to be provided it is the consumers and providers interacting in the market-place who must decide rather than governments or regulators. This does not imply a *laissez-faire* system where anything goes. Broadcasters must operate within the legal framework which governs taste and decency and the protection of privacy. But beyond these minimum constraints the market should decide. This is the half-belief of the White Paper. Yet underneath remains the conviction that broadcasting is much too important to be left to the market.

For some the White Paper draws the line too far in favour of censorship and intervention; for others it is the manifesto of a cultural Visigoth intent on destroying the best broadcasting system in the world.

2

THE CASE FOR
THE CONSUMER MARKET

Samuel Brittan

Assistant Editor,
Financial Times

LET ME TAKE as my starting point the conclusions of the Committee on Financing the BBC (The Peacock Committee), which reported in 1986 and of which I was a member. Although triggered off by the question of the BBC licence fee, much larger issues were raised.

PRINCIPLES AND CONCLUSIONS OF THE PEACOCK REPORT

Early in the final chapter of the Report, the Committee stated its agreement with those witnesses who, in criticism of what they thought were too narrow terms of reference,[1] maintained 'that before we can devise guidelines for the finance of broadcasting, we have to specify its purposes'. The Report's own central finding (para. 592) was that

'British broadcasting should move towards a sophisticated market system based on consumer sovereignty. That is a system which recognises that viewers and listeners are the best ultimate judges of their own interest, which they can best satisfy if they have the option of purchasing the broadcasting services they require from as many alternative sources of supply as possible.'

The fundamental aim of broadcasting policy was stated to be 'enlarging the freedom of choice of the consumer and the opportunities to programme-makers to offer alternative wares to the public'. Then followed two paragraphs that alone justified all the labour expended on the Report (paras. 548 and 549):

---

[1] The Committee's terms of reference are reproduced in Box 1, below, p. 27.

'Our goal is, of course, derived from aims much wider than any applying to broadcasting alone. They are embedded, for example, in the First Amendment to the US Constitution (15 December 1791). This lays down *inter alia*:

> "Congress shall make no law ... abridging the freedom of speech or of the Press ..."

It is often taken by US writers to mean both that broadcasting monopolies are to be prevented and that government intrusion of a negative, censorious kind is to be avoided.

'Another way of looking at the matter is *via* the parallel with the printing press, which was subject to many kinds of regulation and censorship in the first two and a half centuries of its existence. The abolition of prepublication censorship by Parliament in 1694 – leaving the printed word to be regulated by the general law of the land – was described by Macaulay as a greater contribution to liberty and civilisation than either the Magna Carta or the Bill of Rights.'[2]

Later we said (para. 696):

'The end of all censorship arrangements would be a sign that broadcasting had come of age, like publishing three centuries ago. Prepublication censorship, whether of printed material, plays, films, broadcasting or other creative activities or expressions of opinion, has no place in a free society and we would want to advise Government and Parliament to embark forthwith on a phased programme for ending it.'

The Committee did not apply the slogan 'anything goes' to broadcasting any more than it is applied to print publishing or the theatre. Recommendation 18 stated that 'the normal law of the land relating to obscenity, defamation, blasphemy, sedition and other similar matters should apply to broadcasting'. Exemptions, in favour of broadcasting, the main example of which is the 1959 Obscene Publications Act, will therefore have to go, as regulation fades.

The organisation of British broadcasting, as it has existed for most of its life, flies in the face of the goals just stated. The main features of the British broadcasting system have been that the BBC has had a monopoly of tax finance (the licence fee is, of course, a hypothecated household tax), and the ITV and Independent Local Radio (ILR) companies have had a monopoly of advertising finance.

Not only has broadcasting been a duopoly, it has been a highly regulated one. The BBC has had the right to interpret its responsibility to 'educate, inform and entertain' and the Independent Television (ITV) companies have been regulated by the Independent Broadcasting

---

[2] Macaulay, *History of England*, Chapter XXI: 'While the Abbey was hanging with black for the funeral of the Queen, the Commons came to a vote which at the time attracted little attention, which produced no excitement, which has been left unnoticed by voluminous analysts, but which has done more for liberty and civilisation than the Great Charter or the Bill of Rights.'

BOX 1

The Task of the Peacock Committee

The Home Secretary announced on 27 March 1985 that this Committee was to be established with the following terms of reference:

(i)   To assess the effects of the introduction of advertising or sponsorship on the BBC's Home Services, either as an alternative or a supplement to the income now received through the licence fee, including:

    (a)   the financial and other consequences for the BBC, for independent television and independent local radio, for the prospective services of cable, independent national radio and direct broadcasting by satellite, for the press and the advertising industry and for the Exchequer; and

    (b)   the impact on the range and quality of existing broadcasting services; and

(ii) to identify a range of options for the introduction, in varying amounts and on different conditions of advertising or sponsorship on some or all of the BBC's Home Services, with an assessment of the advantages and disadvantages of each option; and

(iii) to consider any proposals for securing income from the consumer other than through the licence fee.

Source: Peacock Report, Cmnd. 9824, London: HMSO, 1986, para. 1.

Authority (IBA) – another government-appointed body. The right of anyone to publish material, or produce a work of art, so long as he can attract consumer support or finance himself in any other way and observe the law of the land, has simply been absent from British broadcasting. The First Amendment provision that Congress may make no law abridging freedom of speech is in flat contradiction to the British system as it has developed.

Much worse than the method of financing the BBC – which may have been a regrettable necessity for a time – has been the general assumption that broadcasting, unlike the Press and the theatre, needs to be regulated, that is, censored. Cries of censorship are usually confined to particular programmes which displease the Government. But the whole process of the IBA, both its continuing vetting of schedules and programmes and its long-term power to withdraw franchises from contractors who displease, has amounted to censorship.

Members of Parliament who identify freedom of speech and freedom of artistic expression with soft porn are merely revealing something about themselves. Many other matters are involved. Examples of broadcasting suppression include decisions not to broadcast a programme on Count Tolstoy's book about British involvement in the forced repatriation of anti-Communist Russians and Yugoslavs and a critical programme on the role of the IBA itself. In an earlier period, Churchill's warnings on the dangers of Hitler were kept off the air to please the party Whips.

A free market in ideas implies, however, a market in a more mundane sense. It is precisely because we are not dealing with baked beans or package holidays but with the communication of ideas, and the dissemination and analysis of news and artistic endeavour, that freedom of entry by producers and freedom of choice by consumers to the maximum feasible extent are so vital. There is no need to enter into a metaphysical debate whether the consumer is the best judge of artistic quality or the best judge of which programmes will benefit him, or his capacity for citizenship. The point is that no one person or group, or committee, or 'establishment' can be trusted to make a superior choice.

A competitive market does not just mean providing the consumer with 'what he wants'. The Report noted that the market is a 'discovery mechanism for finding out by trial and error what the consumer might be enticed to accept (as well as the least-cost method of supplying it) and for trying out new and challenging ideas'. Indeed, we cited the late Sir Huw Wheldon's criticism of the false dichotomy between giving the viewer what he or she wants and what he or she ought to have. According to Wheldon, the producer or creator provides what is 'in him to give'. The proviso in a market economy is that a sufficient number of consumers must be persuaded to take it.

Incentives to Inefficiency

Apart from its restrictive effects on freedom and choice, the British duopoly has been a byword in high costs and restrictive practices. The view that costs have been unnecessarily high is supported both at the anecdotal level and that of elementary economic theory.

Indeed, many outsiders who have taken part in broadcasts, whether in the BBC or ITV, have been amazed by the large crews and other staff involved and by a network of 'Spanish practices' rivalled only by Fleet Street in its heyday. The most astonished have been people with experience of non-British networks.

This is what one would expect from the duopoly. The BBC could not be displaced by lower-cost suppliers of similar output; and IBA franchise-holders have not been under competitive pressure from rivals – at least not until very recently. As the Peacock Committee remarked (para. 585), 'No amount of scrutiny by accountants or consultants can be a substitute for the direct pressures of a competitive market'.

But are not these distortions fading with the imminent explosion of broadcasting choice resulting from cable and satellite? The first answer is that the future takes time to occur. Some 50 per cent of all homes could still be dependent on the present four mainstream channels up to the end of the century. So *ad hoc* temporary measures - like quotas for independents - are still required.

But more fundamentally, and contrary to what is often supposed, commercial rivalry among advertising-financed channels does not represent a genuine consumer market.

Advertising and the Consumer

The popular view that Peacock opposed forcing the BBC to take advertising because there was 'not enough advertising revenue to go round' is wrong. The econometric studies did not - and could not - have decided the argument either way. Given the subsequent upsurge in advertising revenue and rates it is as well that we did not base our findings on elasticity pessimism.

The Report stated (para. 617):

'The main defect of a system based on advertising finance is that channel owners do not sell programmes to audiences, but audiences to advertisers. So long as the present duopoly remains in being and competition is limited to a fringe of satellite and cable services, the introduction of advertising is likely to reduce consumer choice and welfare. It could do so both by driving the BBC into a ratings war and by putting financial pressure on ITV companies which would make it more difficult for them to provide minority programmes. The result could be an inadequate supply of programmes which many of us watch some of the time and some of us watch most of the time, but which do not achieve top audience ratings'.

These conclusions would stand over a very wide range of estimates for the price and income elasticity of demand for advertising.

Advertising-financed broadcasting does not accurately reflect consumer requirements - at least, while the number of channels is severely limited - because:

(a) the ratings will inevitably dominate and minority tastes will be under-represented (and we all belong to minorities some of the time), and

(b) even the ratings do not measure intensity of preferences - whether a viewer is keenly interested in a programme or barely conscious of what is in front of him.[3]

Maybe if audiences were highly segmented the conclusion would not follow and there could be a television equivalent of the *Financial Times* or

---

[3] B. M. Owen, J. H. Beebe, and W. G. Manning, *Television Economics*, Lexington, Mass.: Lexington Books, 1974.

Guardian. But audience research has shown that the social profile of *Panorama* viewers is not very different from that of *Dallas* viewers; there are just fewer of them. Advertisers have not, up to now, been prepared to pay more per viewer minute for one type of programme than another, whatever the future may hold.

A further conclusion is that with a sufficiently large number of channels the difference between pay-per-view and advertising finance diminishes. (If there are many dozen channels, the typical channel cannot expect more than a small proportion of viewers. It may therefore do just as well to go for minority or specialist audiences as compete in the transmission of soap operas.)

There is no general theory on quite how large 'sufficiently large' is. Experience in the USA and Italy suggests that the number is quite high. Nor is it likely that advertising-financed channels could finance all the higher-cost programmes which might be viable under pay-per-view or pay-per-channel. (A full analysis would also have to take into account the disutility to the viewer of the large amounts of advertising time necessary to pay for minority programmes – a subject crying out for research.)

The existence of a tax-financed BBC and the IBA regulation of commercial television were both justified by the Peacock Report as second-best attempts to replicate artificially the programme structure of a broadcasting market with pay-TV – together with some public service, in the sense described below.

'Mimicking the market' cannot, however, be satisfactory in the long run. The traditional system has suffered from weak cost control, the absence of true market signals for which no amount of audience research can be a substitute, and vulnerability to political and other pressures. True market signals require both consumer charging systems and more channels.

Public Service

Some broadcasters will wonder how I could have gone so far in this chapter without mentioning the magic words 'public service'. These are indeed puzzling and embarrassing words for liberal economists who assume that all provision for the consumer on a competitive basis in a non-distorted market is a public service. Broadcasters do not help by using the term to describe anything the BBC (or even ITV) chooses to do. But a useful, if narrower, meaning can be elicited by dwelling on the distinction between paternalism and patronage.[4] Paternalism is embodied in Lord Reith's dictum: 'Few know what they want and fewer still what they need'.

Patronage is completely different. Under a patronage system, consumers express their desires in the market-place, in the Arts and entertainment as in other spheres. Market-financed activities are,

---

[4] Alan Budd, 'Is Broadcasting Different?', *Public Money*, November 1986.

however, supplemented by support for selected activities by rulers or rich individuals, such as the Medici family's patronage of Michelangelo or the Esterhazy patronage of Haydn. (Most of London's statues and monuments are the result of patronage.) While both private and corporate patrons still have a role to play, much of the burden of supplementation today falls on the public purse.

A democratic justification is that viewers and listeners may themselves be willing to support activities in their capacity as voting taxpayers which they are not prepared to pay for directly as consumers in large enough numbers. For instance, many citizens who rarely go near our National Galleries value their existence and are prepared to contribute as taxpayers to their upkeep.

The application to broadcasting made by the Peacock Report (para. 566) is that public intervention should be of a

> 'positive kind and transparent, to help finance additional production, rather than of a negative, censorious kind, oblique and undetectable, which even the best systems of regulation risk becoming, and also that such patronage should account for a modest proportion of total broadcasting'.

A 'Public Good'

There is one argument against pay-per-view or pay-per-channel to which Peacock in the end gave less weight than some other writers and broadcasting economists. In strict theory, a charging system would lead to 'too little broadcasting'. For the great bulk of programmes, the cost of provision is independent of the number of viewers. Once a programme has been made, the marginal cost both to society and to the broadcaster of additional viewers and listeners is negligible. A switch to Pay-TV would therefore exclude some viewers for whom the programmes have value, without saving any real resources.

Charles Jonscher[5] has indeed shown that from a public good point of view advertising finance has similar characteristics to the licence fee; for it too finances a public good without the excluding effects of direct consumer pricing. Indeed, *if*

(a) advertising breaks are sufficiently brief (or entertaining) so as not to interfere with viewer enjoyment, *but*

(b) advertising has no beneficial effects in informing consumers, or in achieving efficient production volumes, and is thus a pure burden on consumers, paid for in the price of final products, *then* the licence fee and advertising finance have identical welfare effects. If (a) is satisfied, but advertising has net economic benefits, then advertising will be *superior* to a licence fee.

---

[5] Booz, Allen, *Subscription Television: A Study for the Home Office, Final Report, May 1987*, London: HMSO, 1987.

Thus Jonscher endorses a combination of the licence fee and advertising finance. His advocacy of new subscription services is a second-best recommendation, based on the postulated political difficulty of raising the licence fee to the level he regards as economically desirable.

The main criticism of the Jonscher analysis is of the welfare economics on which it depends. If this is open to question so is the endorsement of both tax-financed broadcasting and the advertising-financed equivalent. The underlying objection was put very succinctly by Sir Alan Peacock, 10 years before the broadcasting report which bears his name:

'The existence of market failure leads welfare economists all too readily to assume that there is an efficient and costless form of government action always at hand to rectify the market's deficiencies . . . Seldom are the costs of the control methods themselves evaluated: and the kinds of distortion inevitably associated with bureaucratic control are conveniently forgotten. [Welfare economics] is a curious blend of often penetrating observation of the workings of the market system with an astonishingly naive view of the political and bureaucratic process'.[6]

The relevance of these strictures is clear in relation to tax-financed broadcasting systems. Not only is there no guarantee or even likelihood that the political process will discover, still less introduce, an optimal licence fee; but guaranteed state finance provides an incentive to pad out costs and to give undue weight to producers' rather than consumers' tastes. This last point is particularly important in the case of broadcasting which is not a homogeneous product, like electricity, that can be supplied in 'optimum' quantities. Rather, it is a diversified service where the choice of what to transmit is as important as the quantity received.

In the case of advertising finance, other distortions have already been mentioned, arising from selling audiences to advertisers rather than programmes to audiences. This process is likely to result in an under-representation of minority or specialist tastes, judged not by Reithian but by normal standards of consumer sovereignty.

Jonscher is, of course, well aware of these distortions and relies on IBA-type regulation to protect us from them and make ITV 'more like BBC1 than US television'. But the IBA is another state-appointed body and has functioned through censorship, both via its power over schedules and programme content, and via the power to award franchises.

If the state is to pay the piper, or regulate the piper's activities, it will eventually seek to call the tune – to the amazed indignation of the broadcasting fraternity which thinks it can have the benefits of state finance or regulation without paying the costs.

---

6 Alan Peacock, *The Credibility of Liberal Economics*, Occasional Paper 50, London: IEA, 1977.

Conditions for an Effective Market

The conclusion I would draw from Charles Jonscher's Booz Allen Report is that there are three known methods of payment for television: advertising, Pay-TV and tax finance. Each has drawbacks. Advertising finance has a bias towards the mass market and is not sensitive to intensity of preferences. Pay-TV runs into public good problems – that is, viewers are excluded who could be supplied at little extra cost. Tax finance has all the well-known problems of government subsidy and public-sector involvement. The way to overcome these drawbacks in the broadcasting market is to use a mixture of all three methods.

This pluralism is implicit in the Peacock Report; but with hindsight I wish it had been more explicit. It would then have been clear beyond doubt that pay services were meant to provide opportunities additional to advertising and tax-financed channels, and not to replace either of them.

The following preconditions for a genuine consumer market are set out in the Report:

1. Viewers must be able to register directly their preferences and register their intensity.

2. There must be freedom of entry for any programme-maker who can cover his or her costs or otherwise finance production.

3. Operators of transmission equipment, where monopoly is likely to prevail, must have common carrier obligations and accept regulated prices.

As the third condition suggests, some members of the Committee (myself included) were impressed by Peter Jay's vision of a fibre-optic network which would enable an indefinite number of channels to be received by householders who could pay directly per view or per channel for what they chose to receive. But the Committee was careful to avoid endorsing any one specific transmission technology.

It did, however, envisage three stages, stretching into the next century, over which a broadcasting market would be implemented:

1. Index-linking of the BBC licence fee.

2. Direct subscription to the BBC to replace the main part of the licence fee.

3. Multiplicity of choice with pay-per-view, as well as pay-per-channel, available.

Index-linking of the licence fee was recommended for the early years for three reasons. Firstly, it would furnish a systematic and agreed formula to provide for BBC finance in Stage 1 and avoid the sudden leaps of the old system. Secondly, index-linking would

'put some pressure on the BBC to exploit its revenue-earning potential

BOX 2

Peacock Committee: Recommendations for Stage One

Recommendation 1: All new television sets sold or rented in the UK market should be required from the earliest convenient date, and in any case not later than 1 January 1988, to have a peritelevision socket and associated equipment which will interface with a decoder to deal with encrypted signals.

Recommendation 2: BBC television should not be obliged to finance its operation by advertising while the present organisation and regulation of broadcasting remain in being.

Recommendation 3: The licence fee should be indexed on an annual basis to the general rate of inflation.

Recommendation 4: To permit the BBC to be the managing agent in the collection of the licence fee, the Post Office should be released from its responsibility as agent to the Home Office for collection and enforcement procedures associated with the licence fee. The BBC should become responsible for inviting proposals for collection and enforcement procedures and for identifying the most efficient and economic collection and enforcement system. (The Post Office, of course, could tender for the role of agent.)

Recommendation 5: On the understanding that the proceeds would be used to reduce the cost of the television licence and not to increase the total sum available for broadcasting, a separate licence fee of not less than £10 should be charged for car radios.

Recommendation 6: Pensioners drawing supplementary pension in households wholly dependent on a pension should be exempt from the licence fee.

Recommendation 7: The BBC should have the option to privatise Radios 1, 2 and local radio in whole or in part. IBA regulation of radio should be replaced by a looser régime.

Recommendation 7a: Radio 1 and Radio 2 should be privatised and financed by advertising. Subject to the Government's existing commitments to community radio, any further radio frequencies becoming available should be auctioned to the highest bidder. IBA regulation of radio should be replaced by a looser régime. (Supported by five out of seven members of the Committee.)

Recommendation 8: The BBC and ITV should be required over a 10-year period to increase to not less than 40 per cent the proportion of programmes supplied by independent producers.

Recommendation 9: The non-occupied night-time hours (1.00 am to 6.00 am) of the BBC and ITV television wavelengths should be sold for broadcasting purposes.

Recommendation 10: Franchise contracts for ITV contractors should be put to competitive tender. Should the IBA decide to award a franchise to a contractor other than the one making the highest bid it should be required to make a full, public and detailed statement of its reasons. (Supported by four members of the Committee.)

Recommendation 11: Franchises should be awarded on a rolling review basis. There would be a formal annual review of the contractor's performance by the Authority.

Recommendation 12: Consideration should be given to extending the franchise periods, perhaps to 10 years.

Recommendation 13: DBS franchises should be put to competitive tender.

Recommendation 14: Channel 4 should be given the option of selling its own advertising time and would then no longer be funded by a subscription from ITV companies.

Recommendation 15: National telecommunication systems (e.g. British Telecom, Mercury and any subsequent entrants) should be permitted to act as common carriers with a view to the provision of a full range of services, including delivery of television programmes.

Recommendation 16: The restriction of cable franchises to EEC-owned operators should be removed.

Recommendation 17: All restrictions for both Pay-Per-Channel and Pay-Per-Programme as options should be removed, not only for cable but also for terrestrial and DBS operations.

Recommendation 18: As regulation is phased out the normal laws of the land relating to obscenity, defamation, blasphemy, sedition and other similar matters should be extended to cover the broadcasting media and any present exemptions should be removed.

more forcefully and to think more carefully before embarking on peripheral activities far removed from its core obligations'. (para. 621)

The third and most important reason was that it would

'bring a measure of insulation of the BBC from political influence. The evidence suggests that the need to renegotiate the licence fee does at least occasionally influence the Corporation in its general policies and its attitude to particular programme suggestions. Indexation will not eliminate the paymaster relationship, but will put it more at arm's length'. (para. 624)

Independent Quotas

A key Stage 1 recommendation[7] was that the BBC and ITV should be required to take a quota of programmes from small independent producers. These producers had emerged mainly as a result of Channel 4's mandate to buy its programmes from outside. The recommendation had a twin justification. One was to impose some check on broadcasting costs, which greater competition between in-house and independent producers would bring. As the Report stated (para. 647), 'Witnesses from the ITV contractors have stressed that the requirements for in-house production are at the root of union restrictive practices'. Secondly, and of greater importance, the Committee (para. 647) thought it 'extremely unhealthy, for reasons of freedom of speech and expression, that independent producers should face what is virtually a monopoly buyer in Channel 4'. Moreover, the recommendation 'would have the great advantage of encouraging new small-scale units in preparation for the more competitive markets to come'.

Another attempt to put pressure on inflated costs was the recommendation by four out of the seven members that ITV franchise contracts should be put to competitive tender. We noted that the inflation of costs had its main origin in the ITV sector:

'Inevitably the profits theoretically obtainable from a monopoly franchise in a large and prosperous region are shared between the contractors and the unions, with the taxpayer – the real freeholder of the franchised public asset – coming a poor third through the levy.' (para. 645)

The combination of the levy system (which is on profits) and the discretionary allocation of franchises does not offer enough incentive to economise on costs. As monopoly profits would be creamed off in advance under the tender system, the need for the present levy on profits would go.[8]

As before, there was also a more political thought in the Peacock

---

[7] All the Peacock Committee's Stage One recommendations are reproduced in Box 2, pp. 34-35.

[8] The reference of restrictive practices in film and broadcasting to the Monopolies and Mergers Commission announced in 1987, although valuable, is secondary to direct policy measures, such as the ones discussed above in the main text.

reasoning, namely to introduce an element of 'due process' into what has been a highly arbitrary exercise of power by the IBA, which has allocated franchises entirely at its own discretion on a basis it has never deigned to explain.

Freedom for Radio

Radio was certainly not overlooked by Peacock, but it did receive less attention. One reason was that the prospects for advertising revenue, the issue which led to the Committee being set up, were clearly much brighter in television than in the ailing ILR system. In addition, the various methods of extending consumer choice, such as cable, satellite and direct consumer payment, were envisaged in relation to television; and it was not clear if they could be extended to radio.

The Committee did declare finally (para. 640) that:

> 'The case for continued regulation of radio, even in Stage 1, is much weaker than for television. The ordinary listener can with his existing equipment already receive a far greater number of radio than television signals – and the discrepancy is even larger when overseas stations are taken into account. Moreover, Radios 3 and 4 (which cover music and speech) and BBC Local Radio already supply the additional 'range and quality' which commercial stations may not, at present, be able to provide profitably. Regulation of the (commercially hard-pressed) commercial sector does little for the listener.'

The Committee's recommendation that 'any further radio frequencies becoming available should be sold to the highest bidder' is more important than the more publicised and rejected majority proposals to privatise Radios 1 and 2. So, too, is the unanimous recommendation that IBA regulation of radio be replaced by a looser régime, such as that operated by the Cable Authority.

The case for a looser régime was subsequently endorsed by the Government Green Paper on radio,[9] and other official pronouncements. Radio is to be taken from the IBA and put under a new authority. Competitive tenders have been accepted for national commercial channels, but curiously not for local radio.

Pay Television

The most far-reaching specific recommendation was the one designed to pave the way for the fuller broadcasting market of the future, admittedly largely for television.

One precondition for a full broadcasting market is that all the many legal obstacles 'restricting both pay-per-channel and pay-per-view programmes as options for terrestrial broadcasting, as well as Direct Broadcasting by Satellite (DBS) and cable should be removed'. Another

---

[9] Home Office, *Radio – Choices and Opportunities*, Cm. 92, London: HMSO, 1987.

recommendation called for the removal of restrictions to allow national telecommunication systems, such as British Telecom and the new competitor, Mercury, 'to act as common carriers with a view to the provision of a full range of services, including the delivery of television programmes'. We had in mind the possibility of Telecom acting as a common carrier to provide a fibre-optic network which would transmit both telephone messages and an indefinitely large number of television channels.

Subscription to the BBC was recommended 'well before the end of the century' as a step towards consumer choice by which viewers would voluntarily pay for BBC television instead of being forced to do so through the tax system.

Contrary to what is often supposed, the Committee did not say that pay-per-view should be the only, or even the main, form of payment in the full broadcasting market – merely that it should be available. Paragraph 600 of the Report commented:

> 'It is a common misunderstanding to suppose that in a fully developed broadcasting market most people would spend most of their time facing a bewildering set of dials, trying to make up their minds between thousands of alternative programmes. Of course, many people for much of the time will prefer to economise on the effort of choice by paying for packages of programmes or whole channels, just as at present people buy collections of published material in the form of newspapers, magazines and journals, as well as individual books. So it would be with multiplicity of choice in broadcasting.'

The point is that just as some readers want books or pamphlets as well as newspapers and journals, so viewers and listeners should be able to buy individual programmes at varying cost per unit of time to supplement their channel reception if they so wish.

Media experts are fond of telling us that the public demand is only for pay-per-channel; but such judgements are premature. Pay-per-view is only now beginning to become available in the US broadcasting market, which is not nearly as advanced as is often supposed. The demand for pay-per-view will only become clear after the opportunities and limitations of the video cassette have been discovered and reached.

Arts Council of the Air

The aim of a sensible broadcasting policy is *not* to maximise quality. That is the part of the case for a broadcasting market that many people find difficult to grasp. The furniture industry does not try to maximise the quality of the average chair, and publishers certainly do not try to maximise the quality of the average book. Consumer associations and book reviewers try to promote their view of desirable standards; but in the end the customer is judge and jury. It is the *process* of personal choice that is itself desirable, and not what I or any other commentator personally happens to think of the results.[10]

There is a harmless sense in which 'more means worse'. When the printing press superseded the handwritten manuscript, the number of publications multiplied, and their average quality declined. But, because of the great expansion of published works, the absolute number of high-quality publications and their total readership both increased a great deal. It would be absurd to ignore the spectacular rise in the sale of paperback classics, on the grounds that popular tabloids sell in even greater numbers.

The concern of public policy in broadcasting (as in print publishing) should be not to regulate the whole market, but to do what it can by supplementary finance to see that the amount and range of high-quality material (however defined) are not squeezed out by economic change, but are, if possible, enhanced.

That is why Peacock paid so much attention in Stages 2 and 3 to the role of public service broadcasting, in the sense of high-quality or minority programmes in the Arts, current affairs, science and other specialist or minority areas. Some programmes could become commercially viable once there is a multiplicity of choice and pay-per-view is available. But the Committee did not wish to rely on this, and was conscious of the risks from the intermediate phase just ahead when regulation may have withered, but channels are still limited. The Committee therefore suggested a Public Service Broadcasting Council (or 'Arts Council' of the Air) which would be able to make grants to both the BBC and private enterprise broadcasters. It is discussed in detail by Sir Alan Peacock in Chapter 3.

POST-PEACOCK DEVELOPMENTS

Initial Government Reaction

According to Press reports at the time of publication in July 1986, the Thatcher Government was so disgusted with the recommendation not to press advertising on the BBC that the Peacock Report was shelved.

This was far from being the case. A Cabinet Committee under the Prime Minister was established to consider the key issues. According to one leading broadcasting journalist the Report scored a 'strike list' of about two-thirds on recommendations eventually accepted in the Broadcasting White Paper published in November 1988.

Unfortunately, the selective way in which the Government picked up specific proposals from the Report, while failing to accept its basic import, was unpromising. *To the extent that the Government endorsed some*

---

[10] A notable example of the opposite argument, written from the point of view of broadcasting interests, is the House of Commons' Home Affairs Committee Report, *Broadcasting in the 1990s: The Challenge of Maintaining Standards*, London: House of Commons, 1988.

Peacock recommendations it is the letter that was accepted, and the spirit that was rejected. (As the proposed fifth channel is likely to be financed exclusively by advertising, even the letter, in its up-to-date form, has now been rejected.)

In putting forward the idea of a free broadcasting market without censorship, Peacock exposed many of the contradictions in the Thatcherite espousal of market forces. In principle, Mrs Thatcher and her supporters are all in favour of deregulation, competition and consumer choice. But they are also even more distrustful than traditionalist Tories of policies that allow people to listen to and watch what they like, subject only to the law of the land. They espouse the market system but dislike the libertarian value-judgements involved in its operation – value-judgements which underlie the Peacock Report. The 1988 White Paper thoroughly muddles the issue by trying to equate censorship of officially disapproved programmes with consumer protection, which is an entirely different matter concerned with false claims and misleading packaging.

The whole idea of a First Amendment-type protection for freedom of speech has been turned down and policy is moving in an opposite and censorious direction.

Unfortunately, the opposition to the Government from the broadcasting fraternity is nearly all of a paternalist, interventionist kind. Thus I find it difficult to summon up any enthusiasm either for the Government's broadcasting policy or for the mainstream opponents of that policy.

Early Policy Announcements

The most important specific Peacock proposals to be accepted were the index-linking of the BBC licence fee and quotas for independent producers on both BBC and ITV.

An index-linked licence fee is immeasurably preferable to a yearly or even three-yearly haggle between the BBC and the Government. The fear of putting the licence fee increase at risk by displeasing the Government should be, if not removed, at least very much reduced.

At the same time there is powerful pressure to hold down costs and concentrate resources where the Corporation has an advantage, rather than to attempt to be 'in' on every development. In view of this constraint on rising costs, the failure to privatise the popular Radio 1 and Radio 2 channels is of modest significance. The onus is now clearly on the BBC itself to eliminate inessential or peripheral activities.

Again, the rejection of the licence fee for car radios was a minor matter, arguable either way. The more important change is that the BBC has been given responsibility for the collection of the licence fee. The Government's predictable rejection of the licence fee exemption for pensioners on supplementary benefits was unfortunate, but more on social policy than broadcasting grounds.

Quotas of any kind jar against liberal market thinking. They can indeed have no permanent place in a competitive broadcasting market. But so long as the bulk of the population remains dependent on four terrestrial channels, run by the BBC-ITV duopoly, pressure to take independent output does increase the number of programme-makers, and the opportunities open to them. Already, the requirement to take an eventual 25 per cent of programmes from independents has changed mainstream broadcasters' attitudes to their whole cost and management structure. In a speech to the Coningsby Club on 22 June 1988, the Home Secretary, Douglas Hurd, went so far as to question the assumption that programme-making and channel operation should be in the same hands. Restrictions on contracting out are accordingly to be removed for ITV contractors. He also reminded the BBC and ITV contractors that they had no prescriptive right to the hitherto unoccupied night hours. The White Paper indicated that the BBC would lose the night hours on one of its channels and announced separate night-hour licences for ITV.

On the contentious issue of ITV franchises, the Government paved the way for a change in the basis of awarding by extending existing franchises for a three-year period up to 1992. The White Paper announced competitive tenders for the main ITV franchises, subject to safeguards for range and quality – safeguards which Peacock agreed would be necessary in the short to medium term until a full broadcasting market was established.

Unfortunately the type of tender announced was different from what the Peacock Report had suggested. The Peacock idea was that the tender payments (which could have been a proportion of revenue) would extract the economic rent for the taxpayer and make the ITV levy unnecessary. Instead the White Paper proposed a belt-and-braces approach, with a progressive revenue levy on top of the tender payments. The Committee had said that clear and explicit reasons would have to be given for awarding the contract to anyone other than the highest bidder. The Government suggested instead a two-stage bid, in which the highest bidder would automatically win the second stage, even presumably if he offered £5 more than the runner-up. Moreover, the competitive tender need only occur once. For if the new Independent Television Commission were satisfied, the existing holder could apply to have his licence renewed, after paying a formula-based renewal fee, towards the end of the initial 10 years' licence period. This looked like a successful counter-attack by the Home Office, which never liked the tendering idea.

As for Channel 4, the Government rightly came down in favour of retaining its special remit to cater for minority interests and innovation, while continuing on the publishing house model to purchase much of its programmes from independent producers. On the other hand, it favoured severing the links with the ITV contractors who have up to now sold Channel 4 advertising and who have financed it by levy. Three alternative options were suggested for securing the Channel's independence while sustaining its income.

The DBS Saga

The Peacock recommendation for competitive tenders for the UK DBS franchise suffered a much sadder fate. The recommendation was essential to the consistency of the Report. But by July 1986, the IBA was well on the way to making a discretionary award. And soon afterwards, the contract for three out of the five channels on the British satellite was awarded to the British Satellite Broadcasting company (BSB). One of the BSB channels is to be financed on a subscription basis.

The whole DBS saga was, however, the epitome of everything that is wrong with the official industrial policy of selecting favoured ventures or companies. The award to BSB was the third attempt to launch a British high-powered satellite. One earlier attempt had failed because of official insistence on an all-British satellite. As a result the Government had become trapped into backing BSB against alternative means of transmission instead of ensuring a level playing field.

I remember, when sitting on the Committee, being suspicious of the rather too neat presentation of three kinds of possible transmission: (a) traditional off-air or terrestrial; (b) low-powered satellite channels transmitted via cable operators; and (c) high-powered satellites, from which the ordinary viewer could receive transmissions directly by means of a dish.

The thought occurred: 'Couldn't there also be a medium-powered satellite?'. And soon enough, to Whitehall's obvious embarrassment, came the announcement of a 16-channel medium-powered satellite, Astra, operated from Luxembourg. At least eight of these channels were likely to be in English, and in 1988, Mr Rupert Murdoch arranged to take four of them.

Another transmission system, the microwave MultiVideo Distribution System (MVDS), was also initially played down. Nevertheless, MVDS is a useful way of taking conventional television pictures and relaying them via a low-powered transmitter. Mr Andrew Glasgow of Marconi Communications has claimed that up to 30 channels could be transmitted by MVDS within a 30-kilometre radius to between 80 and 90 per cent of the UK population. The price of domestic receiver equipment would, he said, be much cheaper than the equipment for receiving DBS. The system, if permitted, could be especially attractive to companies now in cable who would reach far more homes within a similar franchise locality by MVDS. Fortunately, early hints that the Government would prevent or limit MVDS proved a false alarm and the White Paper offered cable operators freedom to choose their own transmission method.

In considering such matters, there is a very important if subtle distinction to be made between government intervention to remove a distortion or facilitate the development of a market (where more official activity would be desirable) and the practice of usurping entrepreneurial or technological judgements. In the latter areas less activity would be desirable.

Peacock's 17th recommendation to remove all restrictions on Pay-TV was accepted. Mention has already been made of Peacock's interest in the possibility of a nationwide optical fibre grid. This is a high-quality cable which would enable an indefinitely large number of broadcasting and other messages to be transmitted, and two-way signals to be sent to and from households. Sir George Jefferson, then Telecom Chairman, had told the Committee that Telecom would be interested in replacing the copper wiring of household telephones with fibre optic, if it could act as a common carrier for a full range of services, including broadcasting.

Peacock's Recommendation 15 was designed to remove obstacles to organisations such as Telecom and Mercury from acting as common carriers. Unfortunately, Jefferson retired and Telecom management, not surprisingly, had cold feet about wanting to be a common carrier. But that was no excuse for the Department of Trade and Industry Steering Group rejecting 'for the time being' Recommendation 15, on the ground that it did not want to strengthen the Telecom-Mercury duopoly. The DTI failed to give adequate weight to the far greater competition that would become possible between channels and programmes if a fibre optic network were ever established by a regulated common carrier.

New Developments

The broadcasting scene, two years after the Peacock Report, was well described by Hurd in his Coningsby Club speech:

> 'Every week it seems our deliberations are interrupted by ingenious entrepreneurs and passionate evangelists bustling through the door with a new consultant's report, or a new technical marvel which they say transforms the whole scene'.

The different interests involved were, Hurd remarked, 'well-heeled, articulate and adept at identifying their own well-being with the public good'.

The most worthwhile new thinking on broadcasting arose as a byproduct of the previously mentioned Report by Charles Jonscher and associates on subscription. It was intended as a sequel to the Peacock Committee's recommendation of subscription as an eventual replacement for the BBC licence fee.

Jonscher and his associates concluded that Pay-TV was technically feasible and that the required decoding equipment would cost the consumer very little provided that (a) it was built into new television sets and (b) the Government established a common standard so that the same equipment could be used for all subscription services, whether cable, satellite or terrestrial.

Jonscher came out against subscription replacing the licence fee for

BBC mainstream transmission partly on the previously discussed 'public good' grounds and partly because he believed that subscription revenue would be far too low to finance the present BBC channels. He considered, however, that Pay-TV should be used to finance extra BBC services (e.g., for downloading on to video recorders in the 'silent hours') and for some late-night and weekend BBC2 transmissions.

But the main early recommendation for Pay-TV was to finance new terrestrial channels. In making the case for the latter, Jonscher demolished decades of mythology about spectrum shortage, but also embarrassed the Whitehall establishment which was committed to the British DBS and did not want to see it threatened by 'premature' competition.

The Government was inclined to make haste slowly on new terrestrial channels because of its commitment to BSB, due to come on air in 1989 – even though a dish aerial is likely to be more expensive than the terrestrial equipment required to receive a fifth channel. The Government is to authorise a fifth channel by 1993 after BSB has had a four-year start. This is expected to cover 65-70 per cent of the population. The Government is to study the feasibility of a sixth channel with 50 per cent coverage.

Research such as Jonscher's suggested that the main market for Pay-TV was for premium services, such as newly released films and major sports events. Although Arts channels have not yet prospered on the existing European cable networks, their full potential on a continental basis has yet to be exploited.[11]

The next choice to be made is how a fifth channel is to be financed. The Government has opted for a competitive tender for Channel 5, with the bidders deciding whether to use Pay-TV or advertising finance. The choice is thus highly likely to be for advertising. This is not the market policy it appears on the surface. For reliance on advertising involves unfavourable externalities and distortions which public policy ought to correct when it can easily do so, as in this case.

France already has a pay-television channel, Canal Plus, which is terrestrial, unlike US pay channels, such as Home Box Office. Canal Plus is the second largest pay channel in the world. It had more than two million subscribers in 1988, and was expected to make a profit of well over £50 million.[12] The Canal Plus subscription rate was £16 per month whereas UK studies tended to assume a lower rate of around £8 to £10, and a higher penetration target. The capital costs of transmission for a fifth channel operator would, in any case, be far less than for DBS, and the decoding equipment for the channel would be much less expensive than the dish required to receive transmissions from the high-powered satellite.

---

[11] Brian Wenham has suggested that a Music Live Channel calling on Western European opera houses and concert halls might find an audience of more than two million subscribers who would be happy to pay £100 per annum or more. (*Broadcasting: Questions for the 1980s*, Cabinet Office, Office of the Minister of the Civil Service, June 1988.)

[12] Alan Budd, *A Fifth Television Channel*, London: LBS, 1988.

Government Thinking

The debate on new channels took a fresh turn in the summer of 1988 when Lord Young, the Trade and Industry Secretary, came out with a strange proposal to put BBC2 and Channel 4 on the two channels of the British DBS not occupied by BSB. The idea was to transfer the two 'cultural' channels on to the satellite where they would be available only by subscription. The proposal met with strong opposition and was soon withdrawn. But as the underlying thinking remains, it is still worth discussing.

The notion of putting BBC2 and Channel 4 on DBS was a travesty of the whole subscription and Pay-TV case. While there is an argument for Pay-TV for minority channels, there is no case for forcing viewers to use the expensive high-powered satellite system when much cheaper terrestrial Pay-TV is possible.

One idea behind the Young project was to release terrestrial frequencies to provide several extra advertising-financed channels. The Government was over-influenced, as the White Paper showed, by lobbies of advertisers who complained about the 'cost' of advertising time. This so-called excess cost consisted of two elements. One was a genuine resource cost arising from inflated television costs, due to the ITV monopoly of advertising finance. The second was an allocational loss arising from the price (not the cost) of advertising being higher than it would be in a market with more suppliers. As a result, 'too little' was being spent on television advertising relative to other forms of business expenditure.

The first cost will come down with the proliferation of new media, which has already cast its shadow and has led to cost-cutting drives among the ITV contractors. The process will be hurried on by the competitive tender for commercial television franchises. The second allocational effect is of a highly rarefied kind, normally occupying the attention of theoretical welfare economists rather than Cabinet. It is of the second order of smalls.

The reason why advertisers and their Cabinet supporters became so interested in more advertising-financed channels was a straightforward, but misplaced, commercial interest in paying less for each advertisement. 'Misplaced' because the campaigners failed to see that if the number of advertising channels is doubled, each advertising minute is likely to reach only half as many viewers. The only way to reduce the cost per viewer minute would be either to make major inroads on the BBC's half of the television audience or to increase the permitted number of advertising minutes, which could easily reduce viewer satisfaction. The White Paper hinted at a likely move to increase advertising minutes without any viewer research.

The whole episode showed the ever-present danger that a Conservative Government would confuse a market-promoting policy with one of initiating deals with, or between, particular commercial enterprises – the

45

notorious policy of picking so-called winners. The danger was enhanced by the preference, especially in the DTI, for business rather than economic advisers.

The Coningsby Club speech by Douglas Hurd, already mentioned, was apparently more in line with Peacock thinking. Mr Hurd reminded his audience that he had accepted the recommendation against imposing advertising on the BBC, and that the licence fee had been linked to the Retail Prices Index (RPI), 'which imposes in practice a substantial financial squeeze'. He then went on to say that the licence fee could not

> 'be regarded as immortal. As choice multiplies and the average viewer has more and more channels to choose from, it will become less and less defensible that he should have to pay a compulsory licence fee to the BBC, irrespective of the extent to which he watches its programmes ... subscription enables the viewer to pay precisely for what he wants; and I am sure that this is the direction in which the BBC should move'.

In a world of numerous rival channels it will, indeed, become more and more difficult to justify forcing the taxpayer to pay through the licence fee for the BBC's massive network of television and radio services, covering everything from light entertainment to the occasional genuinely cultural programme, whether or not he wants to watch it.

The 1988 White Paper came out in favour of a shift from the licence fee to subscription. It was vague about the timing, but announced that the licence fee would rise by less than the RPI from April 1991 onwards – far earlier than anything the Committee had in mind.

Reduced Urgency of BBC Subscription

To be blunt, developments since the Report have reduced the urgency of subscription to the BBC as a step to a full broadcasting market. In paragraph 607 the Committee gave five reasons for BBC subscription:

1. It would accustom viewers to paying for television directly rather than through the licence fee or advertising.

2. There would be less reason for viewers to resent payment of a voluntary subscription than a compulsory licence fee.

3. The Committee was optimistic about the BBC's ability to attract subscription revenue.

4. Subscription to the BBC might be a stepping stone towards a wider use of pay-per-channel, and eventually pay-per-view.

5. Subscription would reduce the political dependence of the BBC on the Government of the day.

Arguments (5) and (2) retain their force, in that order. The Jonscher research, suggesting that Pay-TV could not finance the BBC's present output, does, however, affect Argument (3). Without being starry-eyed about market research, the Jonscher work goes at least a little way towards undermining the original optimism.

The most important developments, however, affect Arguments (1) and (4). With the possibility of more terrestrial channels financed by Pay-TV, and with the BSB committed to one Pay-TV channel (and with other possibilities on the horizon), subscription to the BBC is no longer so important as a way of introducing the viewer to direct payment for his or her programmes.

The Peacock Report itself had in mind 'the later 1990s' for the transition to subscription for the BBC, which would allow a reasonably long run for the index-linked licence fee. The Committee, in contrast to the Government's White Paper, called for a political decision to be made first on the minimum proportion of households which had to have the decoding equipment before the transition could be made.

There is thus everything to be said for playing the issue long. The BBC needs to soften its dogma about universal reception, and experiment with Pay-TV services, not merely in the now silent early-morning hours, but at other times too, as Jonscher suggested. The Corporation obviously cannot afford a full morning to night high-quality BBC2. It would therefore surely do better to substitute programmes which would attract the paying viewer for some of its present fill-in, daytime items. The change would save expense and provide revenue to improve the quality of the main evening transmissions.

The Government, for its part, needs to be very sure that it has secured the financing of the informative and minority programmes (public service in the stricter sense) which may not be profitable in the market-place, but which people would still want in their capacity as citizens and voters. All the kite-flying and jostling for position have shown how urgent it is to make an early start on the Arts Council of the Air before too many minority programmes are squeezed out of terrestrial transmission.[13] But again the Government dodged its responsibilities by postponing the issue until 1996, when the BBC Charter is due for renewal.

Some residual licence fee or other tax will probably always be necessary to finance such programmes, whether through the Arts Council of the Air or directly. Before running down the BBC by enforcing subscription, the Government needs to establish this Council and also ensure that there really is a multiplicity of channels available to most viewers, and not merely for a few satellite or cable enthusiasts.

If the BBC did not already exist, it certainly would not be invented. But we are not establishing a broadcasting system in a new country. The BBC

---

[13] The Council could make a start on a small scale by providing guarantees to makers or sponsors of selected programmes, in the same way that commercial firms have guaranteed but not directly financed major exhibitions at public art galleries.

itself must surely realise how difficult it would be to justify the present scale of licence fee in the next century, either as a promoter of popular programmes, or of minority specialist or public-interest programmes. Yet as long as there are plenty of other channels, the existence of the BBC does not interfere with a competitive broadcasting market. The urge to privatise it, or run it down prematurely, is symptomatic of a misconceived approach to market economics more concerned with destruction than creation.

A Fibre-Optic Network?

The vision of a fibre-optic network, with a near infinity of channels on which any would-be broadcaster could hire time, suffered a setback following Telecom's loss of interest. Technical developments also reduced some of the urgency. It became clear that two-way addressable decoders giving pay-per-view facilities could be provided without the expense of a fibre-optic network.

In addition, the probable increase in the number of new channels was even greater than Peacock envisaged; and there was likely to be a good deal of channel space available for any group wanting to transmit programmes. The most promising early step might have been BSB's suggestion that one of the two unallocated channels on the UK DBS should be used as a common carrier on a pay-per-view basis.

But the Government showed a wooden and flat-footed understanding of a market economy by rightly announcing in the White Paper that the remaining two channels would be put to competitive tender, but omitting provision for anything like the BSB idea.

If broadcasting is ever to be like print publishing, broadcasters need to have the same opportunities to place their wares in the market-place without running into any potential shortage of channels. At present the only known way of achieving this fully is through the virtually unlimited capacity of a fibre-optic network available on a common carrier basis.

Peter Jay originally suggested public-sector control or operation of such a network on a public utility basis because the common carrier would be able to charge a monopoly rent. But if demand for the services is insufficient to secure a normal return, let alone a monopoly return, the problem is reversed. There may be spillover benefits which would justify a subsidy but, pending a full cost-benefit analysis, it is not obvious what they are. (The French Government's decision to go slow on its original plans for a fibre-optic network has deprived other countries of much useful information which would have been obtained at the expense of the French taxpayer!)

A fibre-optic network is most likely to be a commercial runner if broadcasting services can be combined with other facilities, including banking and shopping. But we still need to make sure that opportunities are not stultified by government prohibitions or commitments of the kind mistakenly endorsed by the DTI Steering Group.

CONCLUSION

To a liberal, the most striking aspect of broadcasting is the absence of the tradition of free expression – a tradition to be found, for instance, in the print media and, since the abolition of the Lord Chamberlain's censorship, in the theatre.

The main political camps are equally unprepared for a free broadcasting market, subject only to the law of the land. The Left and the broadcasting establishment are both supposedly against censorship and political interference. But they are hostile to the market which alone can provide an opportunity for viewers and listeners to make their own choices. They rely on governments to regulate broadcasting closely, but to exercise a self-restraint in the use of their power, the like of which has never been known in the history of the world.

The radical Right cries out for competition and choice, so long as people do not choose to watch programmes regarded by their political friends as offensive and so long as broadcasters do not rock the political boat. The Peacock recommendation that was most decisively rejected by the Thatcher Government was that which looked forward to the phasing out of all regulation and the use of the normal 'law of the land' to cover matters such as obscenity, defamation, sedition or blasphemy.

There were numerous ministerial references to the need for regulation with a lighter touch; and this was given as one reason for replacing the IBA with a new quango to be called the Independent Television Commission (ITC). But on the basic 'First Amendment' issue of not restricting freedom of speech or artistic expression and no pre-publication censorship, Government policy moved backwards.

There were numerous attempts to lean on broadcasters to stop some programmes, and other programmes incurred well-publicised prime ministerial disapproval. On any individual programme (as in any one of the 'secrets' trials) the Government might have had a case on national security grounds. But the length of the list of such programmes suggests either that national security was extended to anything of which the Government disapproved, or that the Government still regarded the BBC (and perhaps ITV) as the voice of the nation rather than as competitive organisations in a market-place.

New-Style Authoritarianism?

The Broadcasting Standards Council, established in 1988, was the first expression of the new-style authoritarianism. The endearing qualities of its first Chairman, Lord Rees-Mogg (who said on appointment that he was re-reading Locke and Mill), could lead to an altogether false sense of reassurance. For who knows who will succeed Rees-Mogg? Or whether the Council will be given legal powers? Or its ambit extended beyond 'violence and sex'? The body is inherently objectionable.

It is little consolation that restrictive intentions are just as prevalent in other European countries, as shown by the attempts to formulate a common broadcasting policy in the Council of Europe and the European Community. The emphasis elsewhere in Europe is particularly on protection, by quotas or similar means, against programmes originating in other areas, especially the USA. This is an aspect of the inward-looking and protectionist tendencies which emerge when Eurocrats are left to themselves.

The new technology will, fortunately, increase the difficulties of governments trying to police the air. Satellite transmission from distant places will be less at the mercy of London censors than the BBC or the mainstream ITV companies.

But it would be over-sanguine to rely on technology for salvation. The broadcasts designed for Britain from the announced DBS systems (whether on the BSB satellite or Astra) will be beamed from this country and subject to UK Government control. The cable companies could lose their licences if they take services which persistently ignore Thatcher, Rees-Mogg and their successors. Determination and powerful equipment will be required by viewers who want to see programmes beyond the official pale.

The most Orwellian section of the White Paper is indeed the last page, threatening draconian penalties for anyone who advertises on, or sells supplies to, or advertises the services of, a satellite service which offends the Government's idea of propriety.

Like other controls, broadcasting controls will not be completely effective; yet they still represent a major interference with choice and freedom. Constant vigilance will continue to be the price of liberty in broadcasting, as in all other walks of life.

3

THE FUTURE OF PUBLIC SERVICE BROADCASTING

Alan Peacock

Executive Director,
The David Hume Institute

BACKGROUND TO THE 'NEW ERA' OF BROADCASTING

WITHIN A VERY SHORT TIME there are likely to be enormous changes in the structure and financing of television broadcasting which may be listed as follows.

A Wider Choice of Channels

Viewers will be able to choose from a much larger number of channels. In addition to the present four terrestrial channels, the Government may permit the use of the radio spectrum for at least one more national terrestrial channel. At least a dozen channels will be available for direct satellite transmission to domestic receiving dishes within less than two years, and the price of dishes is falling rapidly. Cable stations already offer 15 channels. Thus there will be relatively few people in the UK who will not be able to view at least three times as many channels as they do at present, and within a remarkably short space of time. Indeed, hotels and public buildings in urban areas already offer a bewildering variety of choice by conventional British standards.

Direct Charging

The removal of spectrum shortage as a limiting factor on transmission is being accompanied by the prospect of being able to charge the consumer directly for television channels and programmes. The rapidly falling cost of adapting sets, so that only those viewers willing to pay can receive

51

signals, will allow even satellite channels to charge for services. Cable systems can already operate effective subscription services.

Increased Competition

The availability of more consumer choice will increase competition. If independent television companies are to earn rates of return sufficient to attract investors, they will have to sell more advertising (possibly at the cost of press advertising), and seriously consider alternative revenue sources such as the use of subscription or pay-per-view (e.g., for programmes targeted at specialised audiences), development of sponsorship, overseas sales of programmes buttressed by co-production arrangements, and diversification into other lines of business such as production for video transmission. Alternatively, they will have to cut costs by improving working practices, changing management structure, and so on.

Strategy of Independent Companies

The Government is noticeably sympathetic to the creation of a more competitive market in television services. In fact, contrary to initial expectations, it has welcomed the Report of the Committee on Financing the BBC (RCFB) and proposes to implement several of its short-term recommendations. Independent companies cannot now assume that it will be possible to induce the Government to stay its hand in laying the foundations for more competition. That being so, they are likely to adopt the following strategies: (a) ask for as much time as possible to adjust to the changes; and (b) bargain for a minimum of regulation, particularly those regulations which require companies to fulfil so-called public service broadcasting (PSB) obligations which entail uneconomic programming.

*   *   *

What exactly 'public service broadcasting' will come to mean in this new era of expanded choice of programmes is an open question. The extensive review of the meaning of the term undertaken by the Committee on Financing the BBC (1986) led them to conclude, in paragraph 575, that there appeared to be as many interpretations as contributors to the debate. For example, *The Public Service Idea in British Broadcasting*, a publication produced by the Broadcasting Research Unit in 1986, which claims to have the blessing of the major pundits, enumerates no less than eight 'principles':

1. Geographic universality of reception from the four terrestrial channels.

2. Catering for all interests and tastes.

3. Catering for minorities.

4. Concern for 'national identity and community'.

5. Detachment from vested interests and government.

6. One broadcasting system to be directly funded by the corpus of users.

7. Competition in good programming rather than for numbers.

8. Guidelines to liberate programme makers and not to restrict them.

An *ex-cathedra* statement of this kind, however well-intentioned its authors, immediately runs into problems of definition of terms and invites the suspicion that it offers *ex-post* justification for whatever broadcasters provide us with. It also makes no reference to the problem of 'trade-off' of one objective against another, given that broadcasting resources are limited. Moreover, the absence of any reference to the preferences of viewers (though identified as funders of the system – 'the corpus of users') is clearly far from satisfactory to anyone who, like the author, makes the initial value-judgement that the purpose of a broadcasting service, like any other service, is to maximise the satisfaction of the consumer.

The rest of this chapter considers the case for retaining a public service element in the broadcasting system, but under the strict assumption that the system must be 'consumer-driven'. The next section discusses the case for public intervention in the broadcasting system on the basis of consumer sovereignty. The third section explains why public intervention of the traditional kind is neither desirable nor possible in the 'new era'. The fourth section outlines a system of PSB more attuned to the preferences of viewers, and a final section considers the more important implications of that system.

PSB AND CONSUMER SOVEREIGNTY

A common characteristic of conventional definitions of PSB is the rejection of consumer choice through the market as the guiding principle in the provision of broadcasting services. Correspondingly, it requires close regulation of programme balance and content. The basic proposition in conventional PSB thinking is that while broadcasting is designed to benefit viewers and listeners, they neither know what they want nor where their interests lie.

Main Conclusions of RCFB
RCFB put forward the revolutionary view (to broadcasters, at least) that the main objectives of PSB are compatible with a competitive market in a broadcasting system financed in a variety of ways. Moreover, this need not require regulation of programme balance and content, other than that which would apply to publication and performance in general, e.g. in the form of laws governing obscenity and libel.

Contrary to much that RCFB was supposed to have recommended, the Committee agreed with those who argue that listeners and viewers frequently do not know what they want, or might enjoy, but this is not to say that they should be deprived of choice in programmes. They can actively seek for information about the choices open to them, and in the process of making choices their tastes may change. Correspondingly, programme producers in the new era will be offered the challenge of seeking to persuade consumers to widen their experience. These same producers will also need to attract consumers in sufficient numbers to ensure their own survival in the market-place.

Nor did RCFB accept that the expression of consumer sovereignty required the abandoning of public intervention designed to ensure the continuation of important elements of PSB. The Report supported programmes which require the active attention of listeners and viewers, which extend knowledge, promote culture, embody critical attitudes to our society, and involve experiment in methods of presentation. If these require public support, then so be it. But this support need not mean that listeners and viewers become the unwilling instruments of cultural experiments. RCFB preferred to think that they do and will actively support provision of programmes which would not survive if they had to be directly paid for. The maintenance of universal access to programmes of national concern may mean that those who live in isolated and sparsely populated communities and those who are very poor would have to have their broadcasting paid for by society as a whole in some form or other. In short, only a naive view of making the consumer the ultimate arbiter in determining the scope and content of broadcasting would assume that commercially viable programmes would alone be produced. At the same time, where public support is required, it must be transparent.

It would be right to conclude that this description of PSB is narrower than that contained in the UK Broadcasting Acts, in so far as those Acts can be given any specific interpretation. As things stand at present, the Act allows television companies to claim that almost anything they show has a public service element in it, including rubbishy 'sit coms' – so long as engineering standards are maintained and the decor looks good.[1]

Other Options for PSB

The recognition of a public concern for programmes which require 'active attention' does not in itself make a case for any form of intervention, provided that consumers have freedom of choice and a wide range of choice. It might therefore be argued that our 'new era' with a much wider range of choice will give the consumer the power to force producers to cater for a greater variety of tastes. Even if programmes are not

---

[1] *Report of the Committee on Financing the BBC (RCFB)*, Cmnd. 9824, London: HMSO, 1986, paras. 30-32.

commercially viable, it is only necessary to remove any obstacles to private initiatives setting up their own PSB stations, or to buy time from commercial stations so that public service programmes can be shown.

There is a possibility that public service programmes could be shown by local television stations operating on microwave frequency bands, financed by voluntary subscription and some advertising or sponsorship and operating as non-profit-making concerns. However, it seems probable that such stations would appeal only to a relatively small and well-off cultural élite who would have little difficulty in persuading each other to reveal their preferences even if programmes could be received without direct payment. This may also be an area in which subscription television might take off or where existing local cable stations could supply public service programmes on separate channels for extra payment of some kind.

However, the purpose of public service programmes, as we have described them, is to widen the opportunity for 'active listening' which assumes that some inducement has to be offered to viewers to extend their range of interests and concerns. Voluntary payment to ensure that 'active listening' programmes would be supplied runs into the 'free rider' problem. One's willingness to pay depends on whether or not others are willing to pay and also how much they would pay. The process of persuading individuals to reveal their 'true' preferences could be very costly if we consider nation-wide PSB, and the cost would rise progressively with the number of individuals from whom agreement had to be sought. Assuming a national interest in 'active listening', some means has to be found to influence the programme content and structure of television companies.

In short, the acceptance of consumer sovereignty means that it is the recognition of the uncovenanted, intangible benefits of PSB which have previously justified public intervention in the broadcasting system. As that system is moving nearer to a situation where consumers have an expanded range of choice and producers have to compete for their custom, this points towards some system of public financing of PSB services. Such a system is, however, far removed from existing or proposed methods of fulfilling PSB obligations. We must be clear first of all why the conventional ways of fulfilling these obligations would not be appropriate in the 'new era' of broadcasting.

PSB AND REGULATION

Broadly speaking, the present conception of PSB is of a 'balance' of universally available programmes designed to 'inform, instruct and entertain'. This balance is ensured by two bodies, the BBC Governors who cover the operations of the BBC and the Independent Broadcasting Authority (IBA) which covers the independent terrestrial television stations. The growing cable sector's obligations are primarily confined to protecting the viewers from programmes which offend public decency or encourage crime, and ensuring a 'proper' proportion of British material. It is expected that the IBA will adopt a 'lighter touch' with the three new satellite channels which will be fully operational in the early 1990s.

This system of regulation is both untenable and undesirable. More competition, in the form of new terrestrial channels and satellite channels (both British and non-British), and also from video tapes and discs, will put television companies under strong pressure to avoid showing non-commercial programmes. Regulation would have to become more inter-ventionist and dictatorial, which would be undesirable in itself. And there would be other undesirable features. Home-based companies might rightly complain if they were strictly regulated while their overseas competitors – cable companies, not to mention DIY video shows by consumers – had few if any PSB obligations. In addition, the BBC would be free to compete over the whole range of programming, cushioned by a massive subsidy in the form of its index-linked licence fee.

A possible solution would be to cancel all PSB obligations for independent companies when there was sufficient competition between them, and to confine PSB obligations to a licence-financed BBC. This hardly appeals to the IBA, for it would destroy one of its major functions – at a time when its other functions, such as the sole supply of transmission services to independent companies, are being called into question. It is, however, strongly supported by those with an interest in breaking into the television market.

The consumer interest is certainly not going to be properly served by conferring a cultural and educational monopoly on the BBC of the kind which operated before the establishment of independent television. Even if the BBC made every effort to represent alternative points of view on matters of education and culture, it would be perceived as a powerful controller of our thought processes. In any case, the consumer would not have a direct, continuous and immediate method of comparing such alternatives unless he was in a position to choose the programmes himself. Consumer sovereignty requires that there should be a range of alternatives amongst suppliers of public service programmes as well as purely commercial programmes.

PUBLIC FINANCING OF PSB: GENERAL CONSIDERATIONS

While the general case for public financing of PSB (as I have defined it) should be clear, it is all too easy to fall into the trap of comparing some imperfect and soon unworkable system of regulation with some idealised funding system. There would be many problems to be ironed out along the way.

Source of Funding

The conventional approach would be to meet the cost of funding out of general taxation, and this would have strong support from fiscal experts. Allocation from the central government budget would be appropriate, for the government could then weigh expenditure on PSB against appropriate alternative uses of funds. To allocate a given percentage of a particular tax would introduce rigidity into the system. On the other hand, an earmarked source of funding would be a better way of obtaining some indication of the preferences of the viewing public. It would concentrate debate on the public's commitment to PSB, particularly when proposals are put forward for altering the level of funding.

Public interest in such a debate might be all the livelier if the source of funding were linked to viewing. This was why the RCFB suggested that the licence fee should be retained but as a way of financing PSB for all channels and not for the BBC alone.[2] In addition, it would avoid the necessity of introducing some new and unfamiliar form of taxation. The receipts from the sale of franchises might also be devoted to PSB purposes.

A supplementary source of finance might be found in the extension of recent government-backed schemes for business sponsorship of the arts to cover sponsoring of public service programmes encouraged by some form of tax relief. The advantage of this kind of funding is that it encourages private initiatives in the provision of public service programmes rather than leaving all decisions on the level of PSB funding in the hands of a government Quango.

If it became possible to establish private non-profit-making local PSB television stations, one method of funding might be from payments (attracting tax relief) made by individuals as well as companies. The existing Payroll Giving scheme, sponsored by the Office of Arts and Libraries, allows employees to give up to £120 per annum to bodies with charitable status. This amount is deducted from their pay and they are given tax relief on it. The scheme could be extended to cover television stations with charitable status.

Tax relief, like direct expenditure by government, has, of course, an opportunity cost in the form of the alternative uses of the tax yield which have been foregone. Also, it would be more difficult to forecast the amount of relief granted when the initiative to take advantage of any tax relief scheme lies with the individual citizen or firm.

Control of Funding

The next question is: Who should control the funds available and decide on their allocation? A body similar to the Arts Council of Great Britain might be a possible model. The obvious fear about such a body is that it could

---

[2] *RCFB*, para. 689.

come very close to dictating preferences for public service programmes unless the following safeguards were built in:

1. As there is no scientific method of choosing between aesthetic and cultural judgements, the governing body must not be dominated by one set of interests, e.g., producer interests, and to ensure no particular view predominates, membership must circulate rapidly.

2. National and regional devolution of funding decisions would be necessary so that cultural differences would be properly identified.

3. Wherever possible, PSB contracts would need to be awarded on the basis of competitive tender.

4. Alternative means of funding, e.g., through tax relief as described above, would be essential.

Form of Funding

The final question concerns the disbursement of funds in a manner which promotes both economical use of resources and their efficient allocation between competing uses. The aim is to pursue consumer freedom within what must inevitably be a somewhat constrained choice of PSB types of programme.

Currently, bodies such as the Arts Council favour direct subsidies to producers. However, these direct subsidies can exercise a powerful influence on the forms of culture which are to be supported. They also encourage the formation of sectional cultural interests who work hard at developing a 'special relationship' with their sponsors. Direct subsidies can therefore have adverse effects on both technical and allocative efficiency.

The subsidised company can exploit the 'asymmetric information' problem facing the subsidising authority. For where can the latter obtain an accurate check on the company's costs of producing alternative levels of 'output' of their PSB activity? Searching for this information may be both costly and time-consuming, and could put a strain on the relationship itself. Officials in charge of grant awards are likely to be employed because of their knowledge of the 'culture business' and may be understandably unwilling to have their personal utility reduced by alienating their professional *confrères* who seek support. Technical inefficiency may therefore be difficult if not impossible to avoid.

A further effect of direct subsidies is that it is highly convenient for administrators to support continuing funding of a few companies whom they get to know well. With constraints on funding and the building in of an implicit 'permanent' commitment to entrenched grant receivers, a bias is soon introduced against new entrants with fresh ideas to present to the public. As I shall indicate shortly, it may be difficult to avoid direct funding because of the practical problems entailed in any alternative method. However, if direct funding were used, then at the very least competition for subsidy must be encouraged, both by competitive tendering, as previously suggested, and by limiting the length of any commitment to fund PSB services to, say, five years. After this period re-contracting arrangements would have to operate.

To those who support the competitive market as the best method of delivering goods and services, the most acceptable form of subsidy would be one which maximised the control of consumers over their demand, subject to the constraints of supporting PSB. This accounts for the considerable attention paid to developing voucher systems tied to particular forms of consumption, such as education and health. Such a system would not require the government either to provide or directly subsidise these services.

Could a voucher system or its equivalent be developed for PSB delivery? Probably not, because of two important practical difficulties. The first is that a voucher system presupposes that the services which can be purchased are priced. If Pay-TV were fully developed then vouchers could be submitted in payment or part-payment of subscription services for which consumers would be billed. Or if consumers had access to encoded services by tokens, free tokens could be issued representing entitlement to view public service programmes. Although the RCFB recommended that the optimal broadcasting system would be one in which all stations used subscription as the major source of finance, it seems unlikely that a comprehensive competitive pricing system in broadcasting will be developed in the foreseeable future.

The second problem is that there is no guarantee that vouchers or tokens would be used for the purpose for which they were designed. A fair proportion of the viewing public might seek to trade them for cash with those who have a more continuing interest in active listening – likely as not, the educated and well-off. This problem is circumvented in the case of school education where consumption is compulsory. Compulsory consumption of PSB would, of course, be both undesirable and im-practical, though it might be possible to prevent transferability of voucher or token rights by a numbering system which linked these rights to the viewer's personal subscription account number or encoding number.

MOVING TOWARDS A NEW SYSTEM OF PSB

A government faced, as is the present one, with the unscrambling of a highly regulated, duopolistic system of broadcasting, is likely to be understandably cautious about moving towards a new system of PSB. A move towards such a system might embrace several features, outlined below.

Universality

PSB clearly requires that the universality rule should be retained in some form. The long tradition of public control of broadcasting has conditioned us to expect that all terrestrial television stations should be transmitting to all citizens as a matter of right. For the government to reduce the universality commitment would in itself be unpopular in the extreme and would militate against a policy of trying to encourage 'active listening'. However, the universality rule should not be applied to additional terrestrial stations, at least not in any rigorous fashion that forces any such station to provide the same service at the same cost to all viewers, irrespective of where they happen to live.

PSB Contracts and Grants

If the existing four channels were obliged to meet the universality requirement, whilst facing increasing competition from other methods of programme delivery, there would be a strong case, initially at least, for giving them preference in the award of PSB contracts. This would be in recognition both of their universality obligation and their experience of and commitment to public service programming.

A complementary arrangement would be to offer more PSB grants to independent producers and to insist that scheduling arrangements were made to show their programmes. Alternatively, a condition of receipt of PSB contracts would be an obligation to continue to buy a specified percentage of programmes prepared by independent producers.

Regional Diversity

PSB should have a regional/national (Scotland and Wales) dimension, thus recognising cultural differences. This could be done by awarding contracts directly to regional companies or to independent producers seeking regional outlets.

Effects on the BBC

The above features assume that if the licence fee became the source of revenue for PSB funding, then the BBC would have to seek other methods of funding. Alternatively, other companies would have to finance public service programmes themselves, some of which might appeal to advertisers. Or they could rely on sponsored programmes which, as suggested, might attract tax relief. Increasing the rate of growth in the licence fee is probably out of the question! Unless the BBC were to be in the privileged position of being the PSB 'flagship', which has already been argued against (above, pp. 55-56), the licence fee cannot be pre-empted for BBC use. In time, the BBC would become a television company like any other, competing for revenue from consumers (through subscription and advertising, if it so chose) as well as the PSB funding.

Access to BBC Programmes

To ease the transition, this scenario could be modified. The BBC might still retain a proportion of the licence fee, but this proportion would diminish over time. The Corporation would still have an enormous stock of programmes which it could license to other channels. At present, it faces copyright difficulties in exploiting this source of income to the full, and it is imperative, in the public interest, that access to these programmes be increased.

As the stock of recorded programmes has been largely financed by the licence fee (a compulsory tax on viewing), it should be placed in the public domain. Any television company should have the right of access to these programmes in return for a fee payable to the BBC during the transitional period. In time, the proceeds might be used as a further source of finance for PSB.

*   *   *

After his famous critique of the Mercantile System, Adam Smith warned his readers that the restoration of free trade would require great persuasive power:

> 'Not only the prejudices of the public but what is more unconquerable the private interests of many individuals irresistibly oppose it'.

How much more difficult it will be to gain acceptance of a free market, but one which meets PSB requirements, in a service which has never yet known competition in this country. Inevitably, the arguments in this chapter are as tentative as they are unfamiliar, but they do attempt to address issues which the British broadcasting system cannot avoid. Whether they have the persuasive power necessary to command acceptance is another matter!

POSTSCRIPT

Broadcasting in the '90s: Competition, Choice and Quality[3] – the Government's White Paper on Broadcasting – appeared after this contribution had gone to press. It describes the Peacock Report as 'particularly influential in recent debate on broadcasting', acknowledges the Government's debt to the Committee, and endorses its emphasis on viewer choice as the ultimate driving force of the broadcasting system. This must be very gratifying to the Committee, but it must also be noted that the White Paper does not attach the same importance to the Committee's views on the financing of PSB through a Public Service Broadcasting Council (PSBC). The Committee recommended that the

---

[3] Cm. 517, London: HMSO, 1988.

PSBC should begin operations well before the end of the century, implying that plans for its foundation should be prepared now. The White Paper regards discussion of public funding of PSB as 'premature' (para. 3.19) in advance of experience in the working of a multi-channel system incorporating satellite and cable as well as terrestrial methods of programme delivery. This is a classic example of the invocation of Cornford's 'Principle of Unripe Time'. One feels that a document as adventurous as the White Paper might have gone just a little further and announced the Government's intention of examining in detail the arguments for a PSBC of the sort advanced in this chapter.

4

THE PEACOCK REPORT –
SOME UNANSWERED
QUESTIONS

Alan Budd

Group Economic Adviser,
Barclays Bank

I START BY ACKNOWLEDGING that the Peacock Report is one of the great liberal documents of the age.[1] I fully accept its statements in relation to freedom in broadcasting and in particular its reference to the First Amendment to the US Constitution and its account of the ending of monopoly and censorship in British publishing. I share its conclusion that

> 'The fundamental aim of broadcasting policy should in our view be to enlarge the freedom of choice of the consumer and the opportunities available to programme makers to offer alternative wares to the public'.

Much of the opposition to the Report, particularly the intemperate reception by Members of Parliament and broadcasters, merely repeated (in more or less disguised form) precisely those producer interests that the Committee was at pains to attack. We need not concern ourselves with such arguments here. The questions I wish to raise are related to the following general problem: if one accepts the liberal aspirations of the Report does one necessarily agree with the Committee's recommendations? In particular, the Committee argues that there are technological developments which will enforce changes in broadcasting, especially in television. Those developments include the opportunities for a dramatic increase in the available number of channels. That in turn raises the following questions:

o   Are the Committee's (albeit tentative) forecasts correct?

---

[1] Home Office, *Report of the Committee on Financing the BBC*, Cmnd. 9824, London: HMSO, 1986.

o If they are, will proliferation of channels necessarily lead to improved consumer welfare?

o If the Committee's forecasts are wrong, should its recommendations be accepted?

I start with a brief summary of what I believe to be the main elements of the Committee's approach and conclusions.

THE PEACOCK PHILOSOPHY

The Peacock Report broke away completely from the paternalist, public service approach of the earlier reports on broadcasting. Its starting point was the sovereignty of consumer preferences combined with the belief that such preferences are best served by freely operating competitive markets. That starting point should not have surprised anyone who was aware of the views of Professor Peacock and Mr Samuel Brittan. The possibility that they might be 'captured' by the broadcasters would not have occurred to anyone who knew them personally.

The market-based approach endorsed by the Committee did not rule out the concept of public service broadcasting (PSB), but the Committee did not start with any presumption about it; the case for PSB had to be established and not assumed. The prior assumption is that broadcasting is an economic activity like any other and requires special attention only if there is evidence of market failure. But the unfortunate fact is that broadcasting, particularly television broadcasting, is beset by market failure.

As the Report says (para. 598):

> 'A satisfactory broadcasting market requires full freedom of entry for programme-makers, a transmission system capable of carrying an indefinitely large number of programmes, facilities for pay-per-programme or pay-per-channel and differential charges per unit of time. Such a system may be called the full broadcasting market akin to that which exists in publishing'.

Such a system bears no resemblance to current arrangements. In particular, supply is dominated by two organisations – the independent television (ITV) companies and the BBC – and consumers do not directly express their preferences by buying programmes. These two features create the 'comfortable duopoly' which so alarmed the Peacock Committee and conditioned many of its proposals. In the Committee's view the 'comfortable duopoly' causes inefficiency in the production of programmes (over-large, over-paid crews, etc.) and allows producers to concentrate on producing programmes to win prizes (which they mainly award to each other) rather than on meeting the wishes of viewers.

It may be noted that the Report is not completely consistent in its view of the effects of current arrangements. The tone of Chapter 4, 'The Comfortable Duopoly', is considerably more sceptical, not to say hostile, than that of Chapter 12. In Chapter 12 (paras. 581 and 582) praise is added to praise:

'The BBC and the regulated ITV system have done far better, in mimicking the effects of a true consumer market, than any purely *laissez-faire* system, financed by advertising could have done under conditions of spectrum shortage. To aid them in their task they have established systematic and frequent market research, covering audience appreciation as well as ratings, of a kind that no newspaper has available on a regular basis. In addition they have provided more demanding programmes (for instance in the Arts), which viewers and listeners might have been willing to pay for in their capacity as taxpayers and voters, but not as consumers.

'We would go further. The broadcasting authorities have not only mimicked the market; they have provided packages of programmes to audiences at remarkably low cost (measured by the licence fee and by the implicit cost to the consumer of ITV advertisements) and judged by the standards of other forms of leisure and entertainment and by international standards. We can also pay tribute to the way in which the packaging of programmes has satisfied and developed audience tastes. The intertwining of information, education and entertainment has broadened the horizons of a great number of viewers and listeners'.

And so on; after such praise one might ask why anything need be changed. There are two parts to the answer; the first relates to current conditions and the second to possible future conditions. The Committee seemed to believe that the current mix of programmes, good though it might be, owed much to luck and not enough to directly expressed consumer preferences. One can also, perhaps, detect an instinctive distrust of organisations like the BBC and the Independent Broadcasting Authority (IBA). It certainly feared, despite the remarks quoted above, that programmes were produced at excessive cost. Those fears, about lack of directly expressed consumer preferences and excessive costs, would justify changes in current arrangements; but the more pressing need for change arises from technical developments. As the Report says (para. 591):

'The true friend of "public service" programmes will realise that the present system for supporting them is unlikely to last far into the 1990s and that they will require for their future sustenance a combination of moves to a genuine consumer market and some direct support from the public purse'.

The Committee assumed that 'well before the end of the century' television broadcasting would no longer be dominated by the four terrestrial channels and that it would no longer be possible to influence programme content and standards (if that were thought desirable) by the current methods.

THE PEACOCK PROPOSALS

In the light of its concerns about current arrangements and its view about future developments, the Committee made proposals which would (a) reduce the inefficiencies associated with the present system, and (b) pave the way for the complete broadcasting market.

The proposals relevant to reducing inefficiency were:

o   The index-linking of the BBC licence fee.

o   The auctioning of ITV franchises.

o   The increased use of independent producers.

o   The option for Channel 4 to sell its own advertising time.

All these proposals are intended to take effect during the Committee's Stage 1. They are concerned with efficiency of production rather than efficiency of consumption. The first proposal can be seen as a way of protecting and de-politicising the BBC's revenue. But it may seem rather a tough way of doing so, since it freezes the BBC's revenue in real terms (apart from further shifts from black and white to colour licences) at a time when the real costs of broadcasting are rising. It may also seem harsh on the BBC at a time when the real income of the independent companies has been rising rapidly and is expected to continue doing so.

It is wrong, however, to consider the first proposal in isolation; it is part of a package designed to hold down television costs by bringing pressure to bear on both the BBC and ITV. The third proposal can be seen both as a means of holding down costs, by threatening the monopoly of the television unions, and as a way of expanding consumer choice, by providing greater access to the channels.

The main proposal intended to pave the way for the move to the full broadcasting market was the incorporation in all television sets sold or rented after 1 January 1988 (if not earlier) of the peritelevision socket and associated equipment to provide the means for subscription television. The BBC's move to subscription was scheduled to occur in the Committee's Stage 2, when there would be a 'proliferation of broadcasting systems, channels and payment methods'. In the interim period the most important proposal was the negative one that the BBC should not seek to finance its broadcasts by selling advertising time.

No Advertising on the BBC

The Committee's decision on advertising was based on its view that competitive selling of television time would reduce consumer welfare because advertisers are only interested in the size of audiences, not in how much the audiences are enjoying the programmes they watch. Thus, it was feared, a move to advertising-financed BBC television would crowd out programmes which a relatively small audience enjoys intensely.

The decision on advertising involved an interesting conflict between the Committee's two objectives of improving productive efficiency and enhancing consumer welfare. If productive efficiency is the primary objective, allowing the BBC to sell advertising time would have been a highly effective way of achieving it. The increased supply of advertising time would inevitably have lowered its price. If (as my calculations suggest) the price elasticity of demand is less than one, i.e., if an increase in supply causes total revenue to fall, the ITV companies would be left with a smaller share of a smaller total advertising revenue. Possibly the Committee felt that the loss of revenue, at least in the short term, would be too severe and also believed that the loss of consumer welfare would outweigh the potential gains from greater productive efficiency.

PUBLIC SERVICE TELEVISION

The Committee sees future development of television broadcasting as both a potential benefit and a threat. The benefit will derive from improvements in efficiency in production and consumption; the threat will be to PSB.

The potential benefits in productive efficiency are fairly readily understood, given the Committee's fears that the 'comfortable duopoly' raises costs unnecessarily. However, it seems rather less clear about the potential increase in consumer welfare. On balance the Committee seems slightly more concerned about the threat to PSB.

In para. 580 of the Report public service is defined as 'simply any major modification of purely commercial provision resulting from public policy'. According to this definition the scope of public service television is probably broader under the current system than it would be in the full broadcasting market. This is because, at present, the *laissez-faire* result has to be corrected in two ways: (a) to bring the pattern of programmes closer to the maximisation of consumer welfare; and (b) to adjust consumer preferences in the light of public policy.

It is necessary to maximise consumer welfare because half the system consists of two advertising-financed channels. For reasons already discussed, when there is only a limited number of channels profit-seeking contractors will be concerned with audience size rather than audience satisfaction. The adjustment of consumer preferences is necessary if there are public policy views about programme content. For the ITV companies, the IBA does not distinguish beween these two types of correction. One may add that both corrections are also helped by the ITV companies themselves which, bolstered by large profits, have their own combination of patronage and paternalism (and generally believe in high standards).

The Committee believes that the move to a full market in broadcasting will much reduce the need for consumer welfare adjustments. The new channels will, presumably, include ones financed by advertising so that the problems associated with a limited choice of channels will tend to disappear. A competitive environment may, however, reduce the scope for adjusting consumer preferences. The 'comfortable duopoly' allows the existence of programmes which are protected by scheduling arrangements or which are, in effect, subsidised by more popular programmes. Such programmes would disappear under competitive conditions – hence the Committee's proposal for a PSB Council which would subsidise them directly and overtly. (In a multi-channel system, it would presumably be impossible to protect such programmes through scheduling.)

It is not completely clear whether the Committee believes that the benefits outweigh the threats or vice-versa. Reasonably enough, it proposes changes to help ensure the potential benefits while proposing a new institution to reduce the threat.

THE FUTURE OF TELEVISION BROADCASTING

The proposal to index the licence fee is intended as an interim measure for the Committee's Stage 1. And the suggested installation of peritelevision sockets in all sets is viewed as a first step towards subscription finance for the BBC, which the Committee sees as an essential element of a true broadcasting market. As the Report states in para. 552:

> 'Viewers must be able to register their preferences directly and register the intensity of their preference. The only system which will fulfil these conditions is "pay per view".'

The Committee is, correctly, cautious about predicting future developments in broadcasting. It outlines the main sources of additional channels as cable, satellite and new terrestrial channels. Cable franchises are being granted and now cover about 2·5 million homes. (At the beginning of 1988 about 1·5 million homes were passed by cable, and franchises have been granted for areas covering a further million homes.)

BSB is scheduled to begin operating in 1989 with three channels; and Astra, which could have eight or more English-speaking channels, was launched in late 1988. Finally, two additional terrestrial channels could be available by 1992, and the UK has gained two additional UHF channels. Some re-arrangement of existing channels would allow about 70 per cent of households to receive a fifth channel and about half that proportion to receive a sixth channel.

The New Channels

The potential success of the new channels will depend on (a) broadcast material; (b) cost of programmes; and (c) cost of transmission/reception. We can include the costs associated with collecting revenue under the cost of programmes. The success of the new channels will also depend on the rules and charging systems imposed on the BBC and ITV. For the moment we can assume that they will continue to be financed by the licence fee and advertising respectively. We can also assume that the licence fee will have to be paid by all owners of television sets, regardless of which programmes they watch.

Viewers will not, of course, be prepared to pay for programmes which are no better than the programmes they are able to watch for nothing. Thus, to attract audiences, the new channels will have to offer better programmes. (A 'better' programme may simply be one that is shown at a more convenient time.) Since the existing channels already show a considerable variety of programmes it will not be an easy matter to introduce material that either increases total viewing or takes audiences away from the BBC and ITV. There may, however, be times of day during which, because of current schedules, it will be easy to do so. (Sunday mornings come to mind.)

It may also be possible for the new channels to bid certain events away from the existing channels (as appears to be the case with BSB and football) but the existing channels will presumably be free to bid them back and there will eventually be an auction process to share the rents. If the new channels can capture audiences because they face a different regulatory régime we can expect the BBC and ITV to argue fiercely for equal treatment. (It will not matter how high or low the playing field is, as long as it is flat.)

Although there must be some uncertainty about it we can accept that the new channels will be able to provide some programmes which generate new audiences or take audiences away from the BBC and ITV. It is, however, difficult to believe that the new channels will have an advantage in terms of programme costs. They will have no advantage in buying from third parties and if their own productions, or programmes bought from independent producers, are cheaper than those made by the BBC and ITV the result will, presumably, be to drive down the costs of the latter.

This may be highly desirable from the point of view of productive efficiency but it will not provide the newcomers with a permanent advantage. To give an analogy from newspaper production, Mr Rupert Murdoch (if one may describe him as a newcomer) is unlikely to gain a permanent advantage from his introduction of new technology.

As far as costs of transmission and reception are concerned, the new channels, particularly satellite and cable, would seem to be clear losers. Terrestrial television is extremely cheap to deliver. The National Economic Research Associates (NERA) Report includes the following Table.[2]

2 *1992 and Beyond ... Options for ITV: An Assessment for the ITV Association by National Economic Research Associates*, London: NERA, 1988, p. 40.

TABLE 1

ESTIMATED COST PER YEAR

(to reach 20 million households)

	£ million in total	£ million per channel
Terrestrial (four channels)	350	87·5
Satellite (up to 16 channels)	900	86·2
Cable (more than 20 channels)	1,000	50·0

It has been estimated that a fifth channel would involve capital costs of less than £20 million. As Table 1 shows, the average cost per channel is lowest for cable. (The marginal cost of extra channels on cable is close to zero.) But it is the cost per viewing household that matters and so far cable has achieved a penetration rate of only about 15 per cent. To be profitable the new channels must cover their costs. If take-up rates are low, a high proportion of total broadcasting costs will be taken up by transmission and reception. If, as seems likely, programme costs are similar for all channels, the newcomers will suffer a considerable disadvantage unless they can attract a high proportion of households. (It is most unlikely, incidentally, that they will be able to solve the problem by showing programmes which are cheap but popular. In general, cheap programmes attract small audiences, as the experience of BBC2 and Channel 4 clearly shows.)

The important point is that, because of the popularity of existing terrestrial channels and the high costs of non-terrestrial channels, it may be difficult for the new channels to offer effective competition. The result must partly depend on how inefficient, in terms of production and consumption, the existing channels are, and on the size of their monopoly profits. If the existing channels are failing to meet consumers' wishes, actual or potential competition will be extremely effective. We have seen the benefits of such competition in the past, as for example when commercial television was first introduced and when 'pirate radio' forced changes on BBC radio.

As mentioned in the previous section, 'Public Service Television', a fear implied in the Peacock Report is that the gains to consumer welfare may not be very significant (since the present arrangements successfully 'mimic the market'), but the loss of PSB (in the sense of interference with free market results) may be serious unless specific arrangements are made to preserve it. The relative seriousness of the loss will of course depend on whether one believes that broadcasting should include a public service element.

FINANCE AND EFFICIENCY

My main concern is that the Peacock Committee may be wrong in its assumption that we are moving towards a proliferation of channels which will make television broadcasting akin to publishing. But even if there are many extra channels one must ask whether the result will (or should) in any way reflect the model of perfect competition for conventional goods.

For example, Collins, Garnham and Lockley emphasise the special features of broadcasting production and consumption – the immateriality of the product, the role of novelty, its 'public good' aspect and its zero marginal cost of production.[3] Some of these features are common to all cultural goods and services, and they all present problems in welfare economics. Collins *et al.* argue that competition may reduce, rather than increase, programme diversity because of the risks associated with innovation. They also point to the tendency towards concentration of ownership in the cultural industries:

> 'Technology may provide an escape from spectrum scarcity, but economic forces will ensure that the ownership and control of channels will be concentrated in a relatively small number of enterprises'.[4]

The NERA Report gives a similar warning: 'programme standards could fall and the range of programmes offered could narrow'.[5]

Optimal Funding of Television

The question that concerns me more, however, relates to the possibility of television being dominated by the current four channels for longer than the Peacock Committee envisages. If that is the case, we are far removed from real atomistic competition in supply and direct expression of consumers' preferences in demand.

It therefore becomes relevant to ask the question: How much should be spent on television? We either have to answer the question directly or develop systems and institutions that produce a level and pattern of spending which corresponds to a satisfactory allocation of resources. We do not have to ask how much should be spent on boots and shoes, since we believe that market institutions will solve the problem satisfactorily; but we do have to ask the question in relation to television.

The Peacock Committee provides the following implicit answer. Spending on television should be equal to a proportion of revenue derived from a licence fee which is fixed in real terms at its 1986 level *plus* the revenue that can be earned from selling a limited amount of advertising on two channels.

It would be an extraordinary coincidence if the resulting revenue corresponded to an optimal allocation of resources to television broadcasting. Neither the licence fee nor the revenue derived from advertising provides any direct expression of consumer preferences. The licence fee buys the right to watch all channels, whereby the law-abiding viewer has a choice

---

[3] R. Collins, N. Garnham and G. Lockley, *The Economics of Television*, London: Sage Publications, 1988.

[4] Collins *et al.*, *ibid.*, p. 110.   [5] NERA Report, *op. cit.*, p. 7.

between buying the licence or going without television completely (at least in his own home). We can thus assume that, for those who pay it, television broadcasts from all four channels are worth at least as much as the licence fee. But we do not know, without further investigation, whether the consumer might be prepared to spend more on television, and get a better service from it.

Advertising-funded television must pay some regard to consumer preferences since advertisers are interested in audience size. But there is no reason at all to believe that the value placed on 53 minutes of television by viewers is equal to the value placed on seven minutes of television advertising by the advertiser. Suppose, for example, that the IBA raised the proportion of advertising to 10 minutes in every hour. My calculations suggest that advertising revenue would fall and so, presumably, would the expenditure on television programmes. Would that represent a Pareto improvement (in the sense that all benefit)? (All proposals that affect television advertising revenue will affect expenditure on television production to some extent. Under the present system the Government has to take these effects into account.)

We cannot even answer the question: Do we spend too much or too little on television? We cannot readily answer that question in relation to health expenditure, of course, but at least we know that we have to try to answer it, since we have ruled out the possibility of directly expressed consumer preferences. (An analogy with the health service might be a decision to limit spending on health to its index-linked value in 1988 plus whatever the hospitals could earn from selling advertising space on the walls of wards.)

The Peacock Committee's proposals for Stage 1, as previously mentioned, are concerned with efficiency in production rather than consumption. The most important exception was its decision to continue, at least for the time being, the use of the licence fee, rather than allowing the BBC to advertise. That decision did involve a particular view of consumer preferences and rested on the assumption that the competitive selling of advertising would reduce consumer satisfaction.

As the Committee admitted, the proposal to allow Channel 4 the option of selling its own airtime appeared to contradict that finding. Presumably the hope was that potential gains in productive efficiency (through cutting the revenue of the ITV companies) would outweigh possible losses in consumer welfare (through competitive selling of television advertising time).

The Funding Options

I have discussed the politics of the Channel 4 proposal in my report on the feasibility of self-finance.[6] In this report I suggested that the proposal

---

[6] A. Budd, *Channel Four – Post Peacock – The Financial Implications of Recommendation 14*, London: Channel Four, 1986.

TABLE 2

RESULTS OF PEACOCK PROPOSALS ON BBC AND CHANNEL 4
ADVERTISING FOR BBC, ITV AND ADVERTISERS

	Nice	Nasty	Nasty
BBC	No advertising on BBC	Index-linked licence fee	Move to subscription
ITV	No advertising on BBC	Channel 4 to sell its own advertising time	Franchises to be auctioned
Advertisers	Channel 4 to sell its own advertising time	No advertising on BBC	

could be seen as a way of appeasing the advertisers by reaching a balance in which the three interest groups have one nice outcome from the Peacock Report and one or two nasty ones. The results can be seen in Table 2.

It is ironic that the ITV companies so strongly disliked the idea of Channel 4 selling its own advertising time that they supported the introduction of a fifth (advertising-funded) channel instead. That option would almost certainly harm their interests far more severely.

Although the proposed move to subscription finance for the BBC was not intended to come into operation during Stage 1, one can ask whether it would be appropriate under current conditions, given the White Paper proposal that the BBC might use subscription to support its revenue. The Peacock Committee was not explicit on this point and it would be wrong to impute views where none were expressed. However, the Committee's general preference was clearly for subscription (and eventually for pay-per-view) because of its great concern for the direct expression of consumers' preferences and its belief that this can be achieved only through pay-per-view.

The Peacock Report recognises that the collection costs associated with subscription or with pay-per-view may be so large that they outweigh the potential benefits in consumption efficiency. It also recognises the 'public good' aspect of television with its zero marginal cost of consumption. But it does not seem to be unduly worried by these problems. For example, when discussing advertising funding with many channels the Report says (para. 556):

'Even if it were reasonable to postulate that the number of channels would increase, any advantages of no direct charging to consumers would be outweighed by the direct expression of consumer preferences which a charging system allows'.

This statement suggests that subscription finance is better than advertising finance. The Committee also believes that subscription finance will be better than the licence fee when Stage 2 is reached. But whenever it is introduced, subscription will involve charging for a service with a zero marginal cost. How serious a problem is this likely to present, particularly if subscription is introduced under current conditions?

The Peacock Committee reported, with some scepticism, estimates of willingness to pay directly for BBC services. For example, 45 per cent of respondents were prepared to pay up to £1.20 per week which was approximately equal to the licence fee. The Jonscher Report,[7] on the basis of a small sample, examined the question in rather more detail. Jonscher's results suggested that there was no level of subscription fee which would finance the current level of spending on BBC1 and BBC2. Jonscher deduced from this finding that subscription was inferior to the licence as a means of financing BBC television.

That conclusion may be correct (subject to the Peacock Committee's reservations about the licence and its non-responsiveness to consumer preferences), but there appears to be a far more startling implication, namely that the British public would not willingly finance BBC television in its present form.

If Jonscher's findings are correct, BBC television is viable only because viewers pay the licence fee in order to watch all four channels. If the licence fee were linked directly to BBC1 and BBC2, viewers would not support it. Does this mean that BBC1 and BBC2 should be closed down or at least reduced in scale? Obviously not, since it may be true – and Jonscher argues that it is true – that the current arrangement offers considerable consumers' surplus. In principle, if one person is prepared to pay the full cost of television programmes then they would be provided free to everyone else. But in practice it is most unlikely that the BBC will be able to exercise the kind of discriminating monopoly that would be required to cover its costs. (Jonscher further argues that the evidence suggests that consumer welfare would be increased if more money were spent on BBC2.)

If there cannot be discriminatory pricing there will be a case for some sort of subsidy or a continuation of the licence. Is that what the Peacock Committee means by PSB? And would such a case receive sympathy from the proposed PSB Council? If it is all too complicated and if the licence is insufficiently responsive to consumer preferences, might advertising finance be better after all? But that in turn poses a question raised earlier: If we rely on advertising, should we seek to ensure that revenue is maximised, which may mean leaving it with the ITV companies and further reducing its supply?

An alternative would be to rely on the research currently undertaken by

[7] Home Office, *Subscription Television*, London: HMSO, 1987.

the BBC (and mentioned so warmly by the Committee) on audience appreciation and ratings. If that research allows the BBC (or any other potential supplier of programmes) to mimic the market successfully, could it not be used as the basis for a licence fee, or for a subsidised subscription? If that were the case, one would expect the research to deal specifically with willingness to pay, to be conducted independently and to be widely published.

There are more questions than answers, and I could add to the list. For example, what is meant by universality and how is it linked to PSB? Does universality mean wide and free availability? Are Jonscher's results on subscription consistent with the observed willingness of some households to pay very large rates per hour to own and use VCRs? And if they are inconsistent, what does that imply for the possibility of a successful subscription-funded channel showing premium material? Finally, moving towards a more market-based television system might result in a reduction of the quality of programmes. Should a liberal economist be prepared to accept that outcome?

CONCLUSION

The Peacock Report looks to a future in which technical progress removes the special features (associated, for example, with spectrum scarcity) of television broadcasting. We all know how to cope with atomistic competition in which consumer preferences are directly expressed through payment. In such a case we leave it to the market. The Committee assumes that such conditions will obtain in the future and suggests ways of accelerating progress towards them. Let us hope it is right. But it may be wrong about the future and come perilously close to confirming the old joke about the economist faced with the unopened tin of meat and a missing tin opener: 'Let us assume the tin is open'.

PART II

FINANCING OF
TELEVISION

5

FINANCING FOR BROADCASTING

David Sawers

Baxter Eadie Limited

THE WHITE PAPER, *Broadcasting in the '90s*,[1] is a curious mixture of the libertarian and the paternalist. Its strengths are its recognition that change is inevitable because technology and the market have changed; that these changes can benefit the consumer by providing a wider choice of programmes; and that future government regulation of the industry should encourage competition. Its weaknesses are its desire to regulate the content of television programmes, but not the systems employed to bring television services into the home; its failure to treat the BBC as an equal to the commercial services; and its restriction of market forces to the frequencies allocated to television by government, not to the full range of frequencies available to the United Kingdom.

The developments which now permit the achievement of consumer sovereignty in television are the ability to charge viewers directly for the programmes they watch; the increase in expenditure on television advertising in the UK, which now far exceeds the revenue required to finance two television services; and the availability of satellite, cable and microwave transmission systems which can carry an almost unlimited number of services into the home. The space in the radio spectrum also permits at least one more terrestrially broadcast television channel.

The technological and market factors which appeared to limit the number of television services are thus fast disappearing, and so are the technological factors which seemed to make a licence fee or advertising

---

[1] Home Office, *Broadcasting in the '90s: Competition, Choice and Quality*, Cm. 517, London: HMSO, 1988.

the only practical sources of finance for the basic television services. The Conservative Government therefore feels free to lift the constraints which have helped to justify the present system, and to leave broadcasters – except the BBC – to make their own choice between advertising and subscription. The concept of public service broadcasting (PSB) has become obsolete because the technological monopoly which justified it has disappeared.

This choice of financial means remains constrained, however, by our inheritance from the past: the television sets which cannot receive satellite transmissions without new aerials and tuners, and lack the black boxes which permit broadcasters to obtain payment for their services; and the institutions (the BBC and the independent television (ITV) contractors) which have developed with the present system. The pace of change in the home will inevitably be slowed down by this need to replace or modify existing television sets, and the investment that is therefore required before viewers can enjoy more choice.

The White Paper's deficiencies result from its failure to apply market forces consistently throughout the industry; failure to recognise what is in practice required to maintain competition between suppliers of television services; and failure to accept that a democratic society is one in which broadcasts, like books and newspapers, are not subject to government control over content.

THE OBJECTIVES

The policies outlined in the White Paper should be judged by their likely success in maximising the welfare of the viewer. They would need to be designed to ensure that present (and potential future) developments in technology could be exploited to provide the viewer with the maximum choice of programmes, the widest possible diversity of political opinions, and the greatest possible influence over the nature of the programmes supplied.

These objectives are most effectively met if the state plays the smallest possible part in the financing of television and in the provision of programmes. Indeed, the criteria for government regulation of television services should be the same as those for the press, and designed to maximise the consumer's influence over the programmes supplied. The government should be concerned only with the number of suppliers and their method of supply, not with the content of the programmes they supply.

Governments in democratic societies should ensure that there is competition in the supply of television programmes, and that entry to the industry is as easy as possible, given the economics of the business. They should also make certain that political opinions can be freely expressed on television services; that no one political party can influence the programmes on television services as a whole; that no single organisation, such as a news service, can dominate any one element of programming; and that access to the radio spectrum is controlled by commercial and not governmental bodies and criteria.

Freedom of expression on television should be protected by maintaining diverse sources of television programmes: monopoly is as undesirable in the television industry as it is in the newspaper industry. Governments should not own or directly influence the suppliers of programmes. The present organisation of television services in Britain gives the government a degree of influence over television programmes that is a potential threat to freedom of expression, as the interventions of Mr Norman Tebbit, when Chairman of the Conservative Party, and Lord Wilson of Rielvaux, when Prime Minister, have demonstrated.

The degree of independence from governmental interference achieved by British television services has depended upon politicians usually exercising self-control rather than exploiting the influence they have over the BBC, in particular, as an organisation funded by taxation and run by government appointees. The strength of this self-control depends upon the personalities of the politicians in power, and has therefore varied over the years. The political independence of television producers is too important to be left to the chance that politicians will not want to interfere. It is surprising that the maintenance of the licence fee is so widely supported – and desired by the BBC – when the difficulty of combining this source of finance with political independence has been recently demonstrated. Power is where the money lies, and the BBC cannot be wholly independent of government when its funding depends upon the government.

The White Paper shows some good intentions, but the statutory powers of the Broadcasting Standards Council (established in 1988 by the Government to set standards for the portrayal of sex and violence, taste and decency on television), the powers of direction retained by the government, and the numerous obligations still placed on the ITV companies and the BBC are all essentially undemocratic. British viewers may yet find that they have to rely on television services broadcast from abroad for wholly uncensored programmes; even here, the White Paper expresses the Government's hopes of exercising some control.

THE DEFICIENCIES OF THE LICENCE FEE

The licence fee is a means of financing television that would only be adopted, in the circumstances which now prevail, if governmental influence over television programmes was desired. There is no more need to finance television services through a tax than there is to finance newspapers in such a way.

This desire for tax-financed television is sometimes expressed as a wish to protect the quality and range of television programmes from the influence of advertisers. Paternalism of this sort has influenced British broadcasting policy since the 1920s, reflecting a domestic version of the attitude of the colonial administrators who knew what was best for the natives. The British governing classes, while despising such imperialism, have shared this attitude in their desire to influence what is shown to the rest of the British population. They have sought to ensure that broadcasting was controlled by people who would present attitudes which they consider sound.

The Centre for Television Research at the University of Leeds, in a study for the Peacock Committee, argued, for example, that PSB should be

'a force for cultural integrity, helping society in all its parts to bind, reconnect and commune with itself amidst all the fragmenting distractions. This requires institutions that can provide strong national programming services in the fields of news and current affairs, drama (from soap to culture), sports, popular music, the arts and coverage of major events of national and symbolic importance'.[2]

Licence Fee Encourages Ratings Competition

The licence fee has been considered superior to advertising as a source of funds because it ensured freedom from commercial influence, in exchange for which the broadcasters were prepared to accept dependence on the government. They expected, somewhat naively, that this dependence would not be translated into influence.

Political influence has, indirectly, lessened the difference between the effects of advertising and the licence fee on programmes. The desire of the BBC to demonstrate that its programmes are popular, and that it therefore deserves a large licence fee, has put its programme-makers under similar pressure to ensure large and constant audiences as is experienced by ITV producers. The contrast between the effects of the licence fee and advertising on television programmes has therefore become a matter of shades of grey rather than black and white, as the BBC has overtaken the ITV companies' share of the audience.

The Case for Pay TV

Economists have argued that the licence fee is a suitable form of finance for television because it matches the cost structure of the television business. The costs of a television service are not related to the size of the audience (except that the investment in transmitters determines the number of viewers a service can reach) and an extra viewer will not affect the service received by other viewers. A charge that is fixed, like the

---

[2] Home Office, *Research on the Range and Quality of Broadcasting Services*, Report of the Committee on Financing the BBC, Appendix G, Part 17, 'Programme Range and Quality', London: HMSO, 1986.

licence fee, encourages viewers to watch more television and to maximise their benefits from the available supply of programmes.

This argument, like much of economic analysis, omits factors which weaken its relevance to real life. Viewers, as the Peacock Committee pointed out,[3] are interested in the amount that they are charged for watching television; and, as the debate over the BBC's licence fee showed, the amount cannot be settled by objective criteria. What is more, viewers are also keenly interested in what they are shown; and a licence-fee régime gives them no chance to express their opinions directly to the suppliers of programmes.

The fundamental error of this argument is its assumption that all programmes are equally attractive to viewers, so that their welfare is maximised by spending more time in front of their sets. But no viewer would agree that all programmes have the same appeal. If programmes can provide differing benefits to viewers, time spent in front of the set cannot measure the viewer's welfare and the simple economic measures of welfare cease to be relevant.

The main benefit from introducing payments for television programmes is expected to be greater influence over programmes by viewers; suppliers will have more knowledge of what viewers want to see and more incentive to supply it. Paying to view could therefore increase viewers' enjoyment from a given length of time in front of the set. The relevant question is: How much can payment for programmes improve the viewer's enjoyment per hour of viewing time?

Competition between suppliers of television services is also said to be impracticable if all costs are fixed, so that an established producer can drive out new competitors because its marginal costs are zero. This argument again falls down because it assumes that the competitors would each be offering the same programme. In practice, they would be offering different programmes, so that competition would be in the nature of the programmes supplied as much as, or more than, in the price charged. In the process of competing for the viewers' attention, programme suppliers would be more likely to provide what viewers wanted if they had to win their income directly from viewers than if they obtained their finance from a licence fee. Competition is therefore a mechanism by which the viewer's welfare could be increased, as is true for other consumer goods.

Dissatisfaction with Existing Programmes

Market research is the preferred method of obtaining viewers' opinions when either advertising or the licence fee are used to finance programmes. This method was also used in Russia to determine what consumer goods should be produced; and there is some evidence that it has not been much more successful as a substitute for the price system in the television

---

[3] *Report of the Committee on Financing the BBC*, Cmnd. 9824, London: HMSO, 1986.

industry than it was in Russia. Mr Jeremy Mitchell, former Director of the National Consumer Council, told the Peacock Committee that 'it would not be wise for broadcasters to assume consumers think that everything is wonderful in the world of British broadcasting', and pointed out that in a MORI poll the proportion of viewers who said they were satisfied with the quality of television had been only 46 per cent. He added:

> 'all our experience of measuring consumers' attitudes shows that you can normally expect about 75-80 per cent to say that they are satisfied with a service, whatever it is. Forty-six per cent satisfaction is a very low figure'.[4]

Another indication of viewers' dissatisfaction with British television services is the high British ownership of video recorders, which are used to watch alternative services in the form of films. In 1987, ownership in the UK was second only to Japan, with recorders in 60 per cent of the homes which contained television sets. More than £400 million was spent on the hire of video tapes in that year.

The licence fee therefore does not seem a particularly attractive method of financing television services. It provides the opportunity for governments but not viewers to influence the content of programmes. It is therefore politically dangerous and economically inefficient.

THE LIMITATIONS OF ADVERTISING

Advertising as a source of finance for television, like the licence fee, deprives the viewer of direct influence over the programmes supplied; but it also deprives the government of any direct influence over programmes. What it does introduce is the influence of the advertiser, who is interposed between the supplier and the viewer of programmes. The main influence on programming is therefore the advertiser who pays for it; the viewer has an indirect influence, in that the advertiser wants his message to reach as many viewers as possible. But the advertiser is not interested in the strength of a programme's appeal to viewers, so long as they watch it; and he is usually anxious to avoid programmes which might offend.

The Costs of Advertising

Advertising thus avoids one disadvantage of the licence fee but introduces another. The advertiser will take a closer interest in programming than the government does – although his interest will have fewer direct political connotations, it may still influence the opinions which a television service expresses, through the advertiser's desire to avoid offence. This desire may lead him to encourage broadcasters to provide programmes of a certain blandness and uniformity; services financed by advertising appear to provide less varied programmes than those financed by a licence fee.

---

[4] Cmnd. 9824, *ibid.*, p. 41.

The cost of advertising to the viewer is almost certainly less than that of the licence fee. Its costs represent any increase in the price of goods which can be attributed to advertising, plus any annoyance that may be caused when programmes are interrupted by advertisements, but less any entertainment or information which the viewer gains from these advertisements. The frequency of the commercial breaks appears to be the factor that determines whether the cost is significant. According to a survey of viewers conducted by CSP International in a study for the Home Office, the present frequency of commercials on British television does not seem to cause a significant cost. Advertisements annoyed more viewers than any other programmes – a third of a small sample – but a quarter of the sample found them amusing. It was their frequency and the extent to which they interrupted programmes which caused annoyance. More advertisements would therefore mean more annoyance.[5]

Advertising thus seems the closest thing to free finance for television. But it puts decisions about programmes into the hands of advertisers as well as television companies, without giving the viewer a direct influence over this choice. Programmes will not therefore reflect viewers' desires as much as they could, and the benefit that viewers gain from watching television will be correspondingly smaller. Advertising therefore seems marginally preferable to the licence fee, so long as the frequency of commercials is no higher than it is now in Britain.

The Growth of Advertising Revenue

The amount of advertising revenue that would be available in this country to finance services other than ITV depends upon the price and income elasticities of demand for television advertising, and future economic growth. Research for the Peacock Committee suggested that the price elasticity of demand for television advertising was less than one, while the income elasticity of demand was about two.[6] These estimates imply that an increase in the supply of advertising time would reduce prices, so that the growth in total advertising revenue would be reduced and the revenue of the existing ITV companies would fall for two or three years. They also imply that revenue would grow at 6 per cent a year if economic growth was 3 per cent a year and supply was unchanged.

Such estimates of elasticities should not be regarded as gospel. The behaviour of the television companies suggests they believe that price elasticity is higher than one, because they want to increase the supply of advertising time. French experience in 1987, when an increase of 20 per cent in the supply of television commercial time was accompanied by an

---

[5] *Subscription Television: A Study for the Home Office*, London: HMSO, 1987, pp. 144-45, and Annex, 'Consumer Views on Television', p. 24.

[6] M. Cave and P. Swann, *The Effects on Advertising Revenues of Allowing Advertising on BBC Television*, London: HMSO, 1985; G. Yarrow, C. G. Veljanovski *et al., The Effects on Other Media of the Introduction of Advertising on the BBC*, London: HMSO, 1985.

increase of 30 per cent in real advertising revenue, suggests that the price elasticity was more than one at that time.

A new type of service might in any case create new opportunities for advertising, and so stimulate demand; there is no relevant British experience from which to forecast the elasticities to be expected in such circumstances. The French experience in 1987, when new advertising-financed services were launched, may be more relevant to such conditions than British experience of increasing the hours of advertising on ITV or of introducing Channel 4 as an extension of the ITV system.

In 1985, the ITV companies' income from advertising was large enough for them to spend some 62 per cent (or £340 million) more than the BBC on programmes. The BBC's costs per hour of programming were already more than twice the European average in 1984,[7] and ITV costs must therefore have been more than three times the European average. (The hourly cost of programmes on Channel 4 is about 33 per cent of that on the main ITV system.)

The implication is that ITV costs have been inflated by the buoyant revenue from advertising, and that advertising could finance more programmes than the crude figures might suggest. The ITV companies could therefore get by on less than they have been spending, if their income were reduced. Some of their savings would come from reduced pay and increased productivity. If the supply of advertising time is not increased (by introducing new advertising-financed services), the costs and profits of the ITV companies will continue to rise. Charges for television advertisements are bound to go on rising if demand increases but supply does not.

British Satellite Broadcasting (BSB) and Sky Channel[8] should introduce their services in 1989, and may be followed soon after by Maxwell Communications. These satellite services will be partially financed by advertising, but they are likely to grow slowly because viewers will have to install special aerials to receive the signals.

The costs of the BBC seem a reasonable indication of what two national services would cost in the UK. ITV's advertising revenue in 1986 was already adequate, on this basis, to finance three services of BBC standard rather than two: the BBC provided two services for about £600 million, while ITV provided two services for £958 million.

In 1989, advertising revenue should be sufficient to finance two or three national services in addition to the ITV contractors. The amount by which advertising revenue exceeds the reasonable requirements of the ITV companies may reach £750 million a year in 1989, which is more than

---

[7] *Subscription Television: A Report for the Home Office*, London: HMSO, 1987, p. 118.

[8] BSB is the consortium awarded a franchise by the IBA to broadcast three satellite channels direct to viewers in the UK using a specially built high-powered satellite. Sky Channel is owned by News International.

the BBC spends on its two services, and this surplus would grow at between £100 million and £150 million a year for as long as the economy continued to expand at about 3 per cent a year.

The surplus advertising revenue should therefore be adequate to finance three new services with costs comparable to those of the BBC by 1990, if they could win viewers from ITV and the BBC. The ITV companies would then have to reduce their expenditure to match their reduced means. It is a mistake to assume that the existing expenditure of the ITV companies represents their God-given share of advertising revenue, and not a sum that is liable to erosion once competitors appear.

As we have seen, the BBC's costs are twice the European average, which suggests that advertising could support more than three new services by 1990; as does the possibility that the new services will be inherently cheaper than the present BBC and ITV services, because they will repeat programmes more often. If they follow the pattern of the specialised US channels, the new services will repeat each programme several times. Viewers will be offered a choice of channels rather than a choice of programmes on each channel, and each service will be broadcast on several channels.

Such a policy will clearly reduce the cost of each advertising-financed channel. The services proposed by BSB and by Sky Channel might each cost as much as one BBC or ITV channel, although they will provide three or four channels financed by advertising.

THE SCOPE FOR SUBSCRIPTION

Subscription is the only method of financing television that can allow the viewer to exercise a direct influence over the programmes supplied; but it can do so only if it takes the form of charging the viewer for each programme he watches. In this case, the viewer's likes and dislikes are translated into payment or non-payment for individual programmes, thus giving the supplier an immediate financial incentive to supply more of what is liked and less of what is disliked.

Because the price for each programme can be varied, the size of the audience is not the only criterion of success; the strength of the viewer's interest in a programme can also be reflected in the price charged. Television services can, under this system, be sold in the same way as other consumer goods and services; and the viewer can have as much influence over the supplier as he does over suppliers of magazines or motor cars.

Methods of Payment

The alternative form of subscription service (pay-per-channel), which charges the viewer a monthly subscription for the right to watch all of a service, has so far been more widely used than the pay-per-view system. In this case, the supplier of the service does not get a direct indication of the viewer's interest in individual programmes – it is the whole service that is being sold.

The supplier is interested in the number of subscribers he can attract, and for obvious commercial reasons will want to offer a service that is different from the 'free' services which are also available; but he will not have the same incentive to offer programmes which are strongly liked by a relatively small audience as would the supplier of a pay-per-view service. The effect of subscription finance on the programmes supplied may not be very different from that of advertising, although subscription services which compete with advertising-financed services can be expected to provide different programmes.

Both systems rely upon some form of scrambling or encryption of the television signal, which only becomes viewable if payment has been made. The signal can be sent out by broadcasting, or by cable. Technical progress in such systems has recently been rapid, and there is now no difference between the cost of systems which can charge for each programme or by subscription.

The cost of administering a pay-per-view system would, however, be higher. The capital cost of the decoding equipment needed for each television set might be between £50 and £100 when it was in large-scale production. If the service is provided from a satellite, like the one planned by BSB, an aerial and a tuner have to be added – costing another £150 to £350. These costs are likely to fall as the number of units produced increases and the technology progresses. They can also be reduced if some or all of the decoding equipment is incorporated in the television set when it is made. If integrated into a set, it could cost as little as £25.

Experience with Subscription Television

Subscription services have been operating in the USA since 1972; most are distributed over cable networks, and rely on monthly payments. Pay-per-view programmes started in 1985. By the end of 1986, there were 21.6 million subscribers to the ordinary subscription services, and 2.7 million subscribers to the pay-per-view services.[9]

The largest European service is Canal Plus in France, which charges a monthly subscription of 150 francs (£12.60 at the purchasing power parity exchange rate) and a deposit of 480 francs (£40.40) for a decoder. Its service is broadcast over the VHF wavebands which were left vacant when other television services were transferred to the UHF frequencies. It had 2.3 million subscribers by March 1988, 3.5 years after starting to broadcast, and its income from subscriptions was therefore approaching £350 million a year, and still rising.

Most subscription services are based on films and sporting events; they

---

[9] *Subscription Television* . . ., *op. cit.*, p. 19.

differentiate their product from that of 'free' services by providing programmes which could not otherwise be seen. Recent films and major sporting events are the most obvious programmes in this category, and therefore the type of material with which most services begin. They do not, however, limit themselves to such programmes. For instance, Canal Plus in France provides news and some documentary programmes; in the USA, Home Box Office and Cinemax show documentaries; the Discovery channel specialises in current affairs; the Disney channel specialises in children's programmes; and the Cable News Network finances one channel of its news service by subscription. These channels are examples of the tendency to specialise in one type of programme when there is a multiplicity of services, as there is in the USA. The viewer then changes channels to find the type of programme he wants, and can expect to find the same programme repeated several times at different times of day.

Deficient Analysis of Market for Subscription Television

This specialisation, which applies to cable services financed by advertising as well as by subscription, appears to have caused CSP International to conclude that subscription services would only provide entertainment and not information – a surprising conclusion, because there is some contradictory material in its own report to the Home Office.

Two of the largest American subscription services show documentary programmes. According to the CSP Home Office report, one news-only service is provided on subscription, and this is carried by several subscription services. Confusingly, the report states in another table that these services provide no 'informative' programmes, and relies on the latter table for the statements in the text.[10]

The US experience suggests that while the character of subscription services will naturally be influenced by the types of programming available from other services, they can be expected to provide an increasing variety of programmes as they become more numerous. But this variety will primarily be supplied by many services each showing different types of programme, not by each service showing a variety of programmes – as the few British television channels do. Comparing the programmes supplied by these few British services with the programmes shown by a few of the many US subscription services, as CSP International did,[11] is therefore misleading.

CSP also argued (from discussions with a sample of 84 British viewers) that viewers would pay little for 'informative' programmes such as news and documentaries. The programmes it expected viewers to pay most to see were new films, major sporting events, and light entertainment. This

---

[10] *Subscription Television . . .*, *op. cit.*, pp. 33, 34, 36 and 42.

[11] *Subscription Television . . .*, *op. cit.*, pp. 29 and 42.

conclusion is surprising, because news and documentary programmes attract large audiences and CSP's own research showed that news and some documentary programmes were among the programmes considered most interesting.

CSP judged, however, that the programmes which viewers were most likely to pay for were those considered both interesting and exciting by a substantial proportion of viewers, or which made them feel happy. Viewers considered that news programmes were the most interesting programmes, but they did not find them exciting. This judgement does not appear to provide conclusive evidence on viewers' willingness to pay. More market research on a larger sample and more analysis of what viewers actually pay to watch in other countries seem to be needed before anyone draws conclusions as to the pattern of demand for Pay-TV.

CSP's research was aimed at identifying the largest potential markets for Pay-TV programmes. However, if the market for pay-per-view programmes is being studied, this approach seems mistaken; the types of programmes which should be sought are those which viewers have a strong desire to see, but which they cannot see on the 'free' services. For the entrepreneur planning a Pay-TV service, the strength of the desire to see such programmes will be as important as the number of people wishing to see them. Clearly, the strength of this desire must be the major determinant of the amount that an individual is willing to pay.

Another omission from CSP's research was any investigation of willingness to pay for types of programmes that are not usually shown on television. If viewers were willing to pay for programmes which they could not otherwise see, such rarities might be among those which could profitably be provided. For example, if viewers were prepared to pay 25 per cent of the cost of a visit to Covent Garden, opera and ballet might well become profitable programmes.

CSP's market research suggested that viewers would like more choice of programmes than they now receive; the coincidence of similar and popular programmes on BBC and ITV irritated many viewers. The research also suggested that tastes varied within families, so that a wider choice of programmes would be most valuable to those with two or more television sets in their home. There thus appeared to be a substantial demand for more television programmes, which is, of course, now being partly satisfied by hiring video cassettes, at a cost of about £420 million a year. CSP concluded that viewers were most likely to subscribe to new channels if they offered a narrow range of programmes which matched viewers' tastes – which seems to be what subscription services provide in the USA and in France.

Summary of Evidence

Experience of subscription television suggests that it will provide viewers with programmes which are different from those already available. The pay-per-view services in the USA have found that subscribers will spend rather more on these services than they would spend on normal subscription services ($14.25 a month compared with $10.42 a month). French subscribers to Canal Plus pay substantially more (nearly $19 a month), perhaps because Canal Plus has less competition. Despite the cost of equipment and administration, both types of subscription service appear to be capable of making a profit. When compared with CSP's research, the experience of other countries (with samples of millions rather than tens) seems to provide firmer evidence for the prospects of subscription television.

THE SPACE IN THE SPECTRUM

More Channels Technically Possible

The number of television services provided in Britain has been limited to date by government policy rather than by the space available in the radio spectrum. The White Paper now accepts that there is space for a fifth service (reaching about 70 per cent of the population) in the UHF channels on which other television services are broadcast. There might also be space for a sixth service reaching 50 per cent of the population, if more frequencies were used for television. And there could also be more television services in the VHF channels, if government permitted the television companies to bid against the mobile radio services which are now allowed to use this part of the radio spectrum.[12]

Satellite Television

More services can be supplied, although at higher cost, from transmitters on satellites. There is space in the spectrum for numerous satellite transmissions, as long as they are low- or medium-powered. Most of these services are now distributed to homes along cable systems; several such services are already operating in Europe, and they are common in the USA.

A new group of medium-powered satellites is, however, currently being launched, which can be received in homes with aerials 2 or 3 feet in diameter; literally dozens of services can be provided by such satellites. Astra, to be used by Sky Channel, W. H. Smith and probably Maxwell Communications, is one example of such a satellite. It can broadcast on 16 channels, of which Sky Channel would use six – starting early in 1989. Sky Channel will be financed by advertising and subscription; W. H. Smith's service, on two channels, will be financed by subscription; and Maxwell's service, on another two channels, would probably be financed by both subscription and advertising.

High-powered direct broadcast satellites (DBS) require an aerial 1 foot

---

[12] *Subscription Television . . ., op. cit.,* pp. 165-66.

in diameter for reception, but can only broadcast on five channels. The one British DBS satellite will be used by BSB, which is due to start its service late in 1989. BSB will broadcast on three channels; and its services will be financed by advertising, except for an evening service of films on one channel that will be financed by subscription. Two more DBS channels have been allocated to the UK. The White Paper proposes that the franchise should be sold by June 1989.

The drawback to satellite services is that aerials have to point towards the satellite, so that different aerials – or adjustable aerials – are required to receive from two satellites, unless they are close together in space. The medium-powered Astra and high-powered BSB satellites are far apart. This means that receiving from both will be expensive; viewers are therefore likely to watch one or the other.

Cable – Unlimited Channels

An almost unlimited number of services can be provided over cable, but laying it is expensive; this high cost has limited the expansion of the cable network in Britain. There are only about 190,000 homes connected to a cable, of which an estimated 90,000 are connected to broadband cable which can carry many programmes and other services. The use of cable might be accelerated if telephone companies were permitted to distribute television services along their networks, as the Peacock Committee suggested; but the Government has postponed a decision on this for several years.

The Government has, however, proposed that suppliers of local television services should be free to choose between cable and a microwave relay, which can broadcast a television signal over an area within sight of the transmitter. Microwave relay can therefore serve much the same area as a cable system but requires much less investment.

The Commercialisation of Spectrum Management

If a truly free market were to be created for television, the radio spectrum would have to be thrown open to commercial pressures. The present system of administrative allocation of wavebands (by national governments and inter-governmental agreements) has left the UK with fewer services than France. British services were also removed from VHF wavebands (which used to carry BBC 1 and 2 and ITV services) faster than they were in other European countries, so that no sets in Britain can receive VHF signals any more, although many can still do so in Europe. The Government has decided that it will not permit television companies to use VHF bands, even if they are willing to pay more for them than the communications services to which they are now allocated: apparently faith in market forces does not rise to these heights.

Introducing a new service on VHF in Britain would in any case be much more expensive than the launch of Canal Plus in France, which uses the old VHF transmitters of Télédiffusion de France (TDF) and can be received by most television sets, although some households have needed a new aerial. In Britain, new tuners as well as new aerials would have to be added to television sets before a VHF signal could be received, and new transmitters would also be required, to replace the old VHF transmitters that have recently been dismantled. The cost of re-starting VHF services would, however, still be lower than that of starting a satellite service. If they had the chance to buy space in the VHF wavebands, television companies would probably therefore outbid the mobile radio users.

One effect of government regulation of the radio spectrum has been to force television companies to adopt the more expensive systems of transmission – cable and satellite. By the laws of the perverted economics which are so often believed by politicians, the extra investment required for these expensive systems was expected to stimulate economic growth. In practice, it simply meant that the growth of new services was stunted.

In the next few years, British viewers could receive the five new DBS channels from the BSB satellite and eight or more satellite channels from Astra. In addition, more channels will be available later on the Eutelsat satellite, cable services will continue to spread, and one extra service will start in 1993 on the UHF frequencies. In the longer term, more satellites may be launched, the government may relent over the use of the VHF frequencies or microwave relays may be introduced to provide yet more services around towns.

Sky Channel and Eutelsat would be received easily only in the southern half of England; the UHF service might not be transmitted near the east coast, and might need some new transmitter masts and new aerials, but would be cheaper than satellite services for both supplier and viewer. There could therefore be at least 13 new services by 1990, and possibly more thereafter. But the objective of national coverage for television services will perforce have been abandoned.

Commercial rather than technical factors will therefore determine how many new services are provided. There should be sufficient revenue from advertising alone to finance three more services of BBC standard by 1989-90. More services may be viable in practice, because costs may be lower than those of the BBC, and subscription will provide another source of income. Subscription revenues could quickly be built up to a significant amount – as the experience of Canal Plus demonstrates. Satellite services would take more time to develop than a service on UHF, so a new UHF service would be the most attractive opportunity, although it will be the last to start.

Competition is not likely to become intense enough to start eroding the revenues of ITV companies until after the next batch of ITV contractors have started broadcasting in 1993. How much their revenues and profits are eroded will depend on the state of the British economy, and thus on advertising revenue, as well as the popularity of the new services. But the 1990s seem bound to be a period of contraction rather than growth for ITV businesses. The Treasury's hopes of gaining more revenue from the new ITV contractors than it has obtained from the present contractors seem likely to be disappointed, because the franchises will no longer be a licence to print money.

The number of new services that appear will depend both on the advertising support they can obtain and the subscription revenue they can earn. Neither is predictable. But expenditure on video recorders and cassettes in this country, and expenditure on subscription television in other countries, suggest that the British public would spend much more than it now does on television if it were given the chance.

THE CONDITIONS FOR FREEDOM IN TELEVISION

Freedom of Expression

The prospect before the television viewer, if the White Paper is implemented, is one of multiplying services. But these services will remain subject to a degree of censorship by the new Independent Television Commission and the Broadcasting Standards Council (BSC), with government ministers still peering over their shoulders. The BBC and the ITV contractors will still be obliged to preserve political impartiality, and ITV companies will be barred from expressing their own opinions on politics or religion. The government would retain powers of direction over television companies, as were used recently to prohibit the broadcasting of direct statements by representatives of terrorist organisations.

Despite the prospective increase in the number of television services, which could lead to as many different opinions being expressed on television as in the Press, the Government therefore seems determined to strengthen the existing restrictions on freedom of expression. Although there is an element of farce in the proposed activities of the BSC and its preoccupation with sex, organisations with statutory powers have to be taken seriously and can pose a real threat to freedom.

This collection of political and moral regulators for television programmes would have been more appropriate to Franco's Spain than they are to a democratic society like the UK. It is to be hoped that the Government will think again about the desirability of giving the BSC any statutory powers over what is broadcast, and will relax the proposed restrictions on the freedom of ITV contractors, and the BBC, to express political opinions.

The Government ought to appreciate that the multiplication of television services, which it welcomes and encourages, renders obsolete the need for impartiality and the presentation of all points of view on each channel, however valid these requirements may have been when there were only one or two channels. It accepts that the multiplication of services ends the need to maintain the balance between different types of programme on each channel; it should therefore appreciate that the same argument applies to the balance between different points of view.

The disturbing aspect of the Government's attitude to the regulation of television is that it may show its desire to maintain a residual control over the opinions which are expressed on this influential medium. If Ministers could reflect on their likely reaction to the exercise of such influence by the Labour Party, perhaps they would appreciate more clearly the case for political independence for broadcasters.

Setting Technical Standards

The desire to regulate the content of television broadcasts goes with reluctance to set technical standards. Although the White Paper states that it is clearly in the interests of viewers that the subscription systems used by different broadcasters should be compatible, it also states that the Government does not plan to prescribe standards itself at present: it hopes that the industry will agree standards which provide adequate compatibility. The three companies which have so far announced plans for subscription services have said they will use three different systems, so that this hope is unlikely to be fulfilled. The Government's conclusion displays a degree of naivety that might not be expected from an institution that can draw on so much technical advice – a naivety which threatens its other objective of encouraging competition among the suppliers of television services.

These suppliers can compete effectively only if they are using the same standards, so that viewers are free to switch between the different services. If suppliers use different standards, they erect barriers against their competitors, which can be overcome only if the viewer buys some extra equipment. Broadcasters may therefore see a commercial advantage in being technically different, although a multiplication of technical standards will increase the costs to the consumer.

The present rate of technical progress in the television industry makes the setting of standards a more difficult process. Setting a standard implies stopping technical progress and deciding that what can be done now will be the basic system of broadcasting to be used for perhaps the next 25 years. This kind of decision is usually taken internationally, by consensus among broadcasters. But consensus is less easily reached when there are more broadcasters, when there is sometimes a degree of flexibility about the standards agreed, and when they do not have the force of law.

Recently, for example, European broadcasters agreed that a new system developed by the Independent Broadcasting Authority (IBA) called D-Mac should be used for broadcasting from satellites, because it provides a better picture than the present PAL system and is more suitable for encryption (i.e. for subscription television). Broadcasters then disagreed about the precise form of D-Mac that should be used; and when Sky Channel came to choose the system it would use to broadcast from the Astra satellite, it opted for the existing PAL system.

Now that Sky Channel, BSB and W. H. Smith all wish to broadcast subscription services, the three companies appear to have selected three different encryption systems. Viewers who wish to watch all three services will therefore have to invest in three decoders. The main motive for this proliferation of systems seems to be the desire of each broadcaster to separate its market from that of its competitors.

Television without Frontiers

There are practical difficulties about influencing decisions by companies which broadcast from outside the UK, as two of the subscription services will do. Standards should ideally be international; but a national government ought to be concerned about systems used to supply its citizens, because they affect both the degree of competition between suppliers and the welfare of its citizens. Standardisation is of course necessary if decoders are to be incorporated in television sets when they are made, which is much the cheapest way of providing them.

The White Paper shows that the Government is prepared to use much ingenuity to regulate the content of television services provided from abroad. If it were willing to use as much ingenuity to regulate the technical standards of these services, it would have much more effect on the welfare of the viewing public. If one standard was used instead of three, a viewer's investment in decoding equipment could be reduced by two-thirds, and more viewers would therefore be likely to subscribe to these services. It is unlikely that the difference in cost between any of the systems now available could match this saving; and still more could be saved if the three companies shared the administrative system required to charge viewers for the programmes they watch.

The case for standardisation seems overwhelming, if the welfare of the viewer is the yardstick; but it may well seem undesirable to each individual supplying company. Where there is such a conflict of interest, government cannot leave standards to be determined by the broadcasters alone. Intervention to establish standards is an inherent part of a regulatory process that is intended to maintain competition in the television industry.

No efforts to achieve standardisation of subscription systems can overcome the differentiation of the satellite market between Astra and BSB, caused by the very different orbits the two satellites employ and the consequent need to install different aerials to receive each service. There would still, however, be large benefits to the viewer if all services from Astra used the same subscription system. The Government ought to be trying to achieve this objective in the short term, and European standardisation thereafter.

Method of Financing

The White Paper has linked the future finance of the BBC to subscription, although the linkage is less precise than it was in the Peacock Committee report. The licence fee may be run down if income from subscription can be built up, but the White Paper does not say how the BBC is to start obtaining income from subscriptions. Is it expected to start making some of its programmes available only for payment, or to require some small payment for the right to watch any programme?

The details of the proposal need to be spelt out before its feasibility can be assessed. Money can clearly be raised from subscriptions, as foreign experience shows – Canal Plus in France raises more than enough to pay for BBC1 – but there will be many competitors for the potential income. The BBC may not be able to support itself on subscription alone.

The Future of the BBC

The missing element in the proposal for the BBC's future is freedom for the BBC to accept advertising. Without this freedom, it would be at a disadvantage in competing with other television services. They would be able to employ both sources of finance, while the BBC was supposed to be making itself independent of the licence fee on subscription finance alone. Such a policy seems unrealistic.

It is right that the future size of the BBC should depend on its ability to raise income commercially, in competition with other suppliers of television services. It has no inherent right to income from taxation; in a world where a multiplicity of services can be placed before the viewer, the former state monopolist becomes an anachronism. It should only survive if the viewers wish it to survive; and the viewers' wishes can be interpreted only by the BBC's ability to finance itself commercially. It should therefore be given full freedom to obtain finance from any commercial source, and the licence fee should then be gradually reduced.

Pricing Spectrum

The missing element in the White Paper is any provision for the sale of space in the radio spectrum. ITV franchises may be auctioned, but television companies will not be able to bid against other users of the radio spectrum for the right to use the airwaves. Such auctioning of airspace would be the logical conclusion of the Government's market-orientated approach to broadcasting, and would ensure the efficient use of the radio spectrum. Government allocation of space in the radio spectrum cannot ensure that this scarce resource is used efficiently; if it were auctioned, it might be found that television companies would pay more than telephone companies, for example, and that more terrestrial television services could therefore be provided – which would require less investment by the viewer in new aerials. If the Government had the courage of its convictions, consumer/viewers would be the beneficiaries.

97

CONCLUSIONS

The verdict on the White Paper must be that it is a great improvement on its predecessors, but could be made yet better. The improvements could come from

o   abandoning the illiberal provisions for control over the content of television programmes;

o   strengthening government regulation to maintain competition within the industry;

o   ensuring free and fair competition between the BBC and other television companies for commercial revenue; and

o   permitting television companies to compete against other users of the radio spectrum for the right to use this scarce resource.

The scope for improvement therefore lies in the scope for adopting essentially more liberal policies, which allow greater freedom of choice for the individual viewer and the supplier of television services. The less government seeks to influence the content of television programmes, the healthier will British democracy become; the more government limits its intervention in the television industry to maintaining competition between suppliers of services, the more will viewers gain.

6

THE ROLE OF ADVERTISING IN BROADCASTING POLICY

Cento Veljanovski

*Research & Editorial Director,
Institute of Economic Affairs*

THE BASIS for the reform of commercial broadcasting in the UK has been stated in the Conservative Party Manifesto, the Green Paper, *Radio: Choices and Opportunities,*[1] and the long-awaited and much-delayed broadcasting White Paper.[2] In the Conservative Party Manifesto of 1987 the Government pledged that it would:

'follow a policy of more competition, variety and innovation in our domestic networks . . . The development of the broadcasting industry will be allowed to occur, wherever possible, commercially'.

While this principle, repeated many times, appears to offer the prospect of radical reform, it could easily be side-tracked by an inflated concern for the preservation of existing broadcasting institutions as part of an effort to maintain programme standards. The reform of broadcasting involves considerably more than the preservation of the programming remits of the BBC and Channel 4, and extends well beyond the issue of viewer choice.

The purpose of this chapter is to consider the subtle interrelations between advertising, television and viewer welfare. It begins by outlining a conceptual framework for the analysis of advertiser-supported broadcasting and then identifies the problems that beset commercial television. It argues that the interests of advertisers should play a more important role in determining future television policy, and concludes with a positive set of proposals for the reform of television in the UK.

---

[1] Cm. 92, London: HMSO, 1987.

[2] *Broadcasting in the '90s: Choice, Competition and Quality*, Cm. 517, London: HMSO, 1988.

FRAMEWORK

Broadcast television is a complex industry because it simultaneously provides two services – programmes to viewers and audiences to advertisers. As an economic activity, television has, therefore, to cater for both these markets. A coherent policy must take into account the interests of both viewers and advertisers.

The interests of the advertising industry have been largely ignored in the structuring of the British television system. Indeed, the system is built on the overt monopolistic exploitation of advertising by ITV. Television policy has been determined by (changing) ideas of what is in the best interests of viewers. Even the Peacock Report[3] ignored advertisers when it developed its 'market for programmes' framework. The desirability of reform, according to Peacock, was to be determined exclusively in terms of the extent to which television maximised viewers' preferences for programme type, quality and diversity.

A more *general* economic objective for television would be to maximise the joint economic welfare derived from the two activities of advertising and programming. This approach would imply a trade-off between the welfare of viewers and the gains to be achieved by creating a more competitive and efficient television advertising industry. However, although the Peacock Report and this 'joint economic welfare' approach differ in content and their implications for policy, they spring from the same source – a concern for consumer welfare, consumer choice and the allocation of resources to their highest-valued uses. The interests of advertisers are not evaluated in terms of the profit position of those companies advertising but according to consumer gains from advertising – improved information, greater product innovation or enhanced competition.

Having said this, even the most committed free marketeer will agree that the television industry cannot be governed by *laissez-faire* principles. Unrestrained competition in a television sector principally financed by advertising will not necessarily maximise viewers' welfare or choice. This is because when broadcasters compete for audiences they usually find that the best way to maximise their audience share is to show similar mass-appeal programmes. As a result, competition between a small number of channels leads to insufficient diversity in programming and wasteful duplication of programme types. However, this proposition becomes weaker as the number of channels increases, since some channels will eventually be able to maximise their revenue by showing minority and special-interest programmes.

If the basis of funding television were changed from advertising to subscription there would be less of a tendency to duplicate programmes. Subscription would also take better account of viewer preferences because

---

[3] *Report of the Committee on Financing the BBC*, Cmnd. 9824, London: HMSO, 1986.

of the direct contractual and monetary link between viewers and broadcasters. But this discussion begs the question of whether terrestrial broadcast television is more likely to maximise its profits through advertising or subscription. In an ideal world we may still find that the most profitable use for most television frequencies is the joint provision of advertising and programmes. The choice of funding is itself determined by economic considerations – no one system is superior when the costs, effects on consumer welfare and technology are taken into account.

Broadcast television is an industry where some propositions concerning the efficiency of competitive markets do not hold. For example, there are no forces which will ensure that television advertising will become cheaper if the costs of making programmes are reduced. This is because the price of advertising is determined by the available airtime and audience size, not by programme costs. Thus, advertiser-supported television is an industry generating economic rents (profits in excess of a reasonable rate of return which are not eroded by competition).

KEY FEATURES OF BRITISH BROADCASTING

This section summarises the features of British commercial television which are critical to assessing its efficiency.

Monopoly

Independent television (ITV) is organised as a system of regional monopolies in the sale of advertising time. The principle that no two broadcasting organisations should compete for the same source of revenue has been preserved, although cable and satellite television can compete with ITV for advertising. Channel 4 is a national channel. It and Welsh Channel 4 (which provides a Welsh-language service) are financed by a levy on the ITV contractors broadly in proportion to their advertising revenue. In return the ITV contractors sell Channel 4 advertising time and keep the proceeds.

Duplication

British television has evolved into two broadcasting organisations each with two channels which compete for audiences. BBC1 and ITV are mass-audience channels and compete for ratings vigorously.

Complementary Programming

BBC2 and Channel 4 are minority channels and have schedules which complement the output of BBC1 and ITV respectively. Under the Broadcasting Act 1981, Channel 4 has a remit to show complementary programming to the ITV schedule which limits its audience share to around 8 per cent of the total audience. This ensures that Channel 4 does not pose a competitive threat to ITV's monopoly of advertising.

Government-Owned Channels

Television in the UK appears to have a large commercial component in comparison with other countries in Western Europe. Yet in reality it has three government-owned channels – BBC1, BBC2 and Channel 4. Channel 4 is a subsidiary of the Independent Broadcasting Authority (IBA) – the regulator of commercial television and radio.

Universality

A major objective of the British public service broadcasting (PSB) system is universal service. Each channel should show programmes that cater for all tastes and have wide appeal. And the whole nation should have access to the same number of channels. The goal of universality has seriously inhibited the introduction of greater competition in the television sector. The recent Department of Trade and Industry (DTI) study[4] concluded that if 20 per cent of the population were willing to receive fewer than four channels, 80 per cent of the population could receive more than eight terrestrial television channels.

The Independent Broadcasting Authority

The IBA is a nationalised industry. It is at once a regulator (through the extensive programme regulations it administers), a telecommunications company (it owns the transmitters which it leases to the ITV contractors), and a broadcaster (through its ownership of Channel 4).

THE EFFECTS OF THE PRESENT STRUCTURE

The present system of British television has been justified on a number of grounds – insufficient radio spectrum to allow more channels, paternalism, and the claim that more competition would lower programme standards and reduce the choice available to viewers. The debate has been focussed on these issues while the high costs and other restrictions on viewer choice and programme diversity that the present system imposes have been conveniently ignored.

What are the effects of the present structure? Again, this question must be analysed in terms of the welfare of viewers and advertisers.

Viewers

The observation that a *laissez-faire* television industry would reduce programme diversity and standards is obviously not the same as saying that the present PSB system maximises choice and diversity. Public service television clearly provides a different mix of programmes to that one would expect to see if all four channels were funded by advertising.

It is argued that if vigorous ratings competition were permitted there

---

[4] *Deregulation of the Radio Spectrum*, London: HMSO, 1987.

would be wasteful duplication of programming. This claim presupposes that there are a limited number of channels. However, when it is realised that 'channel scarcity' has been created by government regulation, *and* that many more than four channels could profitably co-exist in a free market, this argument is greatly weakened. As the number of channels increases, it becomes more likely that several will eventually be able to maximise their revenue by showing entirely different minority programmes (see Chapter 10).

Yet the British broadcasting system is based on competitive programme duplication, which arises because BBC1 engages in overt ratings competition with ITV. It is perhaps the only public television channel of its type in the world to do so. Thus, the same phenomenon used to justify blocking competitive commercial television channels forms the basis of PSB. One of the consequences of the BBC's decision to compete for ratings was described by Professor Steiner, a visiting American economist, several decades ago when only BBC1 and ITV existed:

'. . . at present the two existing channels fall far short of effectively utilizing the opportunities for choice. All signs point to the fact that the BBC is choosing to behave like a competitor (albeit a non-commercial one that is not insensitive to public service responsibility). It competes actively – even frantically – for *share* of the audience rather than trying to provide a total service that is as good as possible. It is much closer to an American network than to the imaginary [public broadcaster] ... Since ITV is also like an American network (although with some differences) the two are fairly close together: while there are real differences between BBC and ITV they can easily be exaggerated. If there is disquiet about programming it is not because of the absence of exceptional programmes on each channel, but because the overall programme fare seems thinner, more repetitious and more predictable than necessary'.[5]

This system of PSB has imposed large direct costs in the form of monopoly rates for television advertising (below), and a range of 'hidden' costs. Apart from squandering the opportunity to maximise choice, it has led to restrictions on other media. These restrictions are designed to protect the existing broadcasting institutions from damaging competition, thus further reducing the choice available to the British viewing public.[6] For 60 years the cable network industry was permitted to relay only BBC and ITV programmes, without being able to offer viewers alternative programmes. This has retarded the expansion of cable television which in other countries provides a wide and varied choice to the viewer.[7]

---

[5] P. Steiner, 'Monopoly and Competition in Television: Some Policy Issues', *Manchester School*, Vol. 24, 1961, pp. 107-137, extract quoted from p. 123.

[6] C. G. Veljanovski and W. D. Bishop, *Choice by Cable*, Hobart Paper 96, London: Institute of Economic Affairs, 1983.

[7] See R. B. Gallagher's contribution to this volume, Chapter 10: 'American Television: Fact and Fantasy', below, pp. 178-207.

In addition, the Government's protectionist policies have led to significant cost-inefficiencies in the commercial sector. As the Peacock Report concluded: 'both the ITV and the BBC sectors suffer from cost and efficiency problems arising from what we have called the comfortable duopoly'.

Advertisers

ITV is the sole seller of television advertising time and it possesses market power in the sense of being able to raise the price at which television airtime is sold to advertisers. Surprisingly, the claim that ITV contractors have monopoly power has been challenged even by economists.

ITV has market power, firstly, because television advertising differs in many important respects from other forms of advertising. This is supported by empirical studies and the findings of the Office of Fair Trading (OFT). In their investigation of share deals the OFT commented that 'the special characteristics of television are such that the Office considers it . . . as a separate market' because of 'television's combination of mass audience, audio-visual colour presentation and the general impact'.[8]

Secondly, ITV contractors can influence the price of airtime even though the amount of time which can be devoted to advertising is fixed by the IBA. It is frequently argued that the price of television advertising fluctuates in response to the demand for television advertising which in turn is pro-cyclical. On this basis, it is claimed that price is determined by demand and not by the actions of ITV contractors.

The inability of ITV contractors to influence price has been greatly under-estimated, largely because the above analysis focusses on the wrong variable. A monopolist can raise price by restricting the supply of his good or service. The effective supply of advertising is not the number of minutes devoted to advertising but the number of minutes multiplied by the number of people watching – the number of 'advertising messages', or its empirical counterpart, commercial home minutes (CHM). ITV is able to act monopolistically by reducing its audience share, thus decreasing CHM.

There are indications that some ITV contractors may have been flexing their market power more vigorously in the past few years. In 1987 the cost to advertisers of buying access to television audiences was 30 to 50 per cent higher in some months than in the same period of the previous year. Although this price increase was partly fuelled by the consumer boom and the growth of the economy, another cause was the unprecedented fall in ITV audiences. In 1987 ITV's audience share was the lowest since the inception of commercial television in the UK.

The question arises: Why should ITV decide to exercise its monopoly

---

[8] *Thames Television Limited*, London: Office of Fair Trading, 1984, para. 3.4.

position (which it has had for decades) more aggressively in recent years? One possible reason is that many more ITV contractors are now publicly listed companies which must satisfy their shareholders with favourable profit increases. Another may be the adoption of a deliberate strategy on the part of some ITV contractors, generated by the fear of future competition, to 'milk' their monopoly positions and leave the industry when franchises come up for renewal.

THE ECONOMIC VALUE OF ADVERTISING

In order to establish the case for a more comprehensive inclusion of advertising into broadcasting policy it is necessary to show that advertising *per se* improves consumer choice, industrial efficiency and the competitiveness of the economy. If this is established then the continued monopoly of ITV imposes major costs on consumers.

Some Relevant Statistics

Advertising is a significant economic activity. In the UK in 1986 over £5.1 billion, or 1.4 per cent of Gross Domestic Product (GDP), was spent on advertising of all forms. About £1.7 billion of this total was spent on television advertising (for recent trends see Table 1). The 25 firms with the largest advertising budgets collectively employed nearly 1 million people and produced output valued at £55,537 million, or 14.9 per cent of GDP.

Advertising also provides the average television viewer in Britain, 'free' of charge, with:

o   Two national channels, one breakfast-time channel and a channel for Welsh-speaking people.

o   A choice of nearly 10,800 hours of television programmes per year and about three hours of programmes per day which the viewer actually watches.

Advertising: Cost or Benefit?

In the past advertising has attracted a bad press – it was alleged to create wants in consumers, to be the outcome of wasteful rivalry between large firms, and generally to create barriers to competition. An objective evaluation of the evidence simply does not support these claims which, for the most part, were based on *a priori* theorising rather than careful empirical analysis. More recent studies of the impact of advertising generally do not establish that there are major disadvantages arising from advertising and many demonstrate that there are positive benefits.

The rest of this section deals briefly with some of the most frequent criticisms of advertising.

TABLE 1

COMMERCIAL TELEVISION ADVERTISING REVENUE, 1983-87

	Net advertising revenue[1]		Total television advertising expenditure[2]		Television expenditure		Commercial home minutes (CHM)		Cost per thousand CHM	
	£m	% growth	£m	% growth	% of Total	% of Total display[3]	Millions	% Growth	£	% Growth
1983	824	18.3	1,109	19.5	31.0	39.9	134,209	10.8	6.18	7.5
1984	911	10.5	1,249	12.6	30.8	40.0	146,553	9.2	6.31	2.1
1985	983	7.8	1,376	10.2	31.0	40.4	150,406	2.6	6.72	6.5
1986	1,183	20.4	1,675	21.7	32.7	42.7	151,013	0.4	8.11	20.7
1987	1,326	12.1	1,872	11.8	32.4	43.0	146,498	-3.0	9.42	16.2

(1) Excludes TV-am. (2) Includes advertisement production. (3) Excludes classified press advertising.

Source: Broadcast Financial Review.

Advertising is Anti-Competitive

It is frequently claimed that advertising creates barriers to entry, entrenches monopoly and inhibits the competitive process. This boils down to the empirical proposition that large firms can increase profits simply by spending more on advertising.

Despite four decades of intensive research by economists it has not been possible to find robust evidence to support this claim. Professor Richard Schmalensee of the Massachusetts Institute of Technology (MIT), in perhaps one of the most comprehensive statistical and theoretical investigations of the impact of advertising, states: 'We thus reach negative conclusions. There is no evidence to suggest that advertising outlays have permitted firms to create barriers to entry'.[9] Subsequent surveys of the evidence have come to the same conclusion.[10]

A random sample of the more recent empirical research published in scholarly economic journals does not support the proposition that advertising is anti-competitive.[11] Most of these authors have found that it is profits which lead to higher advertising expenditure, and not the other way around (that is, the more profitable and efficient firms advertise most). One recent study of particular interest is by Dr Lynk who examined the impact of the introduction and growth of television advertising in the USA. On the basis of extensive statistical analysis of three separate and independent sources of data, Lynk concludes

> 'that a relatively larger shift of an industry's advertising into television advertising results in a reduction in the size disparity among its sellers. The central implication is that increases in the level of information transmission (resulting from the expansion of television advertising) cause small sellers to grow relative to large'.[12]

Increased competition in television advertising, according to this study, benefits smaller firms.

Advertising Increases Prices

It is often simplistically argued that because advertising costs money this must be reflected in a mark-up on those goods which are advertised. Therefore, logically, advertising raises prices. However, again the evidence points in the opposite direction – advertising reduces prices. It is well documented that in markets where advertising is banned, prices are higher

---

[9] *The Economics of Advertising*, Amsterdam: North Holland, 1972, p. 244.

[10] For example, M. C. Sawyer, *The Economics of Industries and Firms*, London: Croom Helm, 1981, p. 121.

[11] A. Ayanian, 'The Advertising Capital Controversy', *Journal of Business*, 1983; A. J. Ardnt and J. L. Simon, 'Advertising and Economies of Scale: Critical Comments and Evidence', *Journal of Industrial Economics*, Vol. 22, 1983, pp. 229-242; L. J. Gomes, 'The Competitive and Anti-Competitive Theories of Advertising: An Empirical Analysis', *Applied Economics*, Vol. 18, 1968, pp. 599-613.

[12] W. J. Lynk, 'Information, Advertising, and the Structure of the Market', *Journal of Business*, Vol. 54, 1981, pp. 271-303.

than they would otherwise be. These bans have been shown to lead to excessive variation in the prices of goods and services, and empirical studies generally conclude that when advertising is permitted prices fall substantially without any deterioration in the quality of the service provided.[13]

In an analysis of branded products Duncan Reekie has shown[14] that advertising is a marketing device that reduces other marketing and production costs (the latter due to larger volume production). Reekie shows that for those products which are intensively advertised the costs of advertising are more than offset by lower retail margins for producers.

THE COST AND VALUE OF ADVERTISER TELEVISION

The desirability of television advertising as a method of financing television can now be assessed. It provides 'free' television. Television financed by advertising is the by-product of a device that is necessary for competition and efficiency and as such does not impose a direct cost on the viewer or consumer *per se*. For the same reasons that consumers as a class do not pay for the price mechanism when it works properly, so they do not pay for broadcasting when it is used as an advertising device.

The value of this 'free' television to viewers is extremely difficult to measure. In a recent report by the Home Office it was claimed[15] that viewers in the USA valued television programmes at seven times the revenue spent on television advertising. If this multiple were applied to British television it would suggest that the consumers' surplus generated by ITV and Channel 4 is around £11.2 billion per year. If the benefits of television advertising to the rest of the economy were half this amount, say, £6 billion, then the total welfare benefits generated by advertiser-supported television in the UK would be around £17 billion per year.

THE NEW MEDIA DO NOT INCREASE
GENUINE COMPETITION

The final point is that the growth of the new media, principally cable and satellite television, is unlikely to make significant inroads into ITV's monopoly of advertising in the next decade. Indeed, paradoxically, it may serve to entrench ITV's monopoly position in the medium term.

The new media will definitely give the viewer more choice. By 1990 there could be as many as 14 new satellite television channels in addition to the 17 satellite television channels which are currently available. Cable

---

[13] See the evidence in the OFT's report, *Opticians and Competition*, London: OFT, 1982.

[14] Duncan Reekie, *Advertising and Price*, London: Advertising Association, 1979.

[15] Home Office, *Subscription Television*, London: HMSO, 1987.

television will increase programme choice significantly, although its geographic coverage will be more restricted than satellite television.

The impact of the new media on advertising costs will depend on their share of the audience and the way they are funded. Cable and satellite television are, however, unlikely to increase the competitive pressures in the television advertising market because many channels will be funded by subscription, with only a small proportion of time devoted to advertising. To the extent that cable television is successful in diverting audiences away from ITV, it will reduce the supply of advertising time and drive up its price. Satellite television is more likely to be funded by advertising. But nearly one-third of the proposed satellite channels are likely to be subscription channels. Of the remaining ones, a proportion of their audiences will come from the BBC. Thus, the net effect of satellite television on ITV's dominance is unlikely to be significant within the next decade.

POSITIVE PROGRAMME FOR TELEVISION

We can conclude that the new media will not significantly erode ITV's monopoly position for some time. It is therefore important that competition be introduced in terrestrial television. The White Paper moves much too cautiously and, through a combination of programme regulation and other restraints on competition, ensures that effective competition will not be felt in the UK for some considerable time. The Government has a number of options available to increase the degree of competition without seriously impairing the level of programming.

Privatise Channel Four

The first step is to privatise Channel 4. As I have argued elsewhere,[16] if Channel 4 obtains 14 per cent of net advertising revenue it can be financially independent of ITV and a free-standing entity. (In fact, sale of Channel 4's airtime represented 15.6 per cent of ITV's net advertising revenue up to the end of March 1988.)

The formation of a separate sales force would also generate additional revenue as Channel 4's airtime currently sells at 10-20 per cent below the price of ITV time. This discount probably arises because ITV is insufficiently vigorous in selling Channel 4 time – there is an obvious conflict of interest in one sales staff selling airtime on two potentially competing channels. The proposal that Channel 4 should sell its own airtime has now been accepted by the Government.

Reshuffle Programming Remits

The privatisation of Channel 4 would not be sufficient to foster competition in the sale of television advertising. It should also be freed

---

[16] C. G. Veljanovski, '£90 Million: Channel Four's Price Tag', *Televisual*, September 1987, pp. 37-42.

from its current remit and be permitted to compete outright with ITV. This would allow Channel 4 to increase its audience share, taking some viewers from ITV and some from the BBC.

What would be the effects of this reform? Clearly there would be a significant change in the output of Channel 4 from small-audience programmes to more 'light entertainment'. Within the commercial sector this would decrease programme diversity; it is unlikely that the addition of one or more commercial channels would alter this conclusion. But this does not mean that the choice available to the viewer would be reduced. The BBC would still have two channels devoted to public service broadcasting. The range of choice available to the viewer could be preserved and even increased by reshuffling 'remits' between the four existing channels: transfer BBC1's remit to Channel 4 and give Channel 4's remit to BBC1. There is no reason why Channel 4 should retain its minority audience status when there is another PSB channel which is behaving as a commercial channel in attempting to attract the mass audience. BBC1 should be restrained from competing for audiences and told to give the viewer a genuine alternative channel.

This reform would, in one move, increase competition and genuine choice for the viewer, and would do it swiftly. It has the advantage of keeping the PSB system intact and does not make the mistake, made hitherto, of confusing objectives with broadcasting institutions. One may support a Channel 4-type channel but not the preservation of the existing Channel 4! Unfortunately, the White Paper rejects this proposal (below, p. 113).

More Channels

The privatisation and widening of Channel 4's audience should be accompanied by the franchising of additional commercial channels, in the form of either national, regional and/or local television. It is now clear that sufficient spectrum can be made available for more television channels. The DTI report on deregulation of the radio spectrum[17] indicated that there was sufficient spectrum within the present arrangements for a fifth channel and possibly some urban channels in the major conurbations. If required, more spectrum could be made available.

Impact of the Proposals

The introduction of more competition would achieve substantial reductions in advertising costs and put pressure on ITV production and operating costs which are relatively high due to a combination of cost-padding and feather-bedding arising from its protected monopoly position. And there is another attraction. The increase in supply of advertising time

---

[17] *Deregulation of the Radio Spectrum in the UK*, London: HMSO, 1987.

through the ITV system and additional commercial channels would have less of an immediate impact on ITV finances than the equivalent amount of time on the BBC, because Channel 4 and other, new channels would take audiences away from both ITV and the BBC. Moreover, the proposals would strengthen the relative financial position of the BBC by reducing the growing 'income gap' between the BBC (which has its licence fee tied to the retail price index) and ITV (whose revenues would probably continue to grow at a real rate of over 5 per cent per annum).

ANTICIPATING THE CRITICS

This section anticipates some of the criticisms of the above set of proposals.

Cultural Ghettos

First, it will be argued that these proposals would turn the BBC into a 'cultural ghetto'. The BBC's strength, it is frequently contended, arises from the fact that it is large and diverse, and competes with ITV. Its size and diversity allow it to attract talent and enable it to experiment and be innovative. That Channel 4 is also able to do this without a large budget is perhaps sufficient to indicate that the claim is greatly overstated.

The major point, however, is that, while the present structure may allow the BBC to pursue its own public service objectives, it has effectively inhibited others from experimenting in providing viewers with the type and variety of programmes they actually want (e.g. the cable television industry; and the pent-up demand for films, as indicated by the dramatic growth of ownership and rental of video recorders in the UK).

In addition, it does not address the question of why a public channel, which has a guaranteed income, acts as if it were a commercial broadcaster. The role of a public service broadcaster should be along the lines of the 'arts council' approach suggested by Peacock, and be more in tune with official statements about the purpose of PSB. To suggest that the BBC can be a significant and innovative force in British television only by pursuing ratings is really to give the game away! The BBC should offer its viewers programmes which the commercial sector does not, for the structural reasons identified above. It has to be recognised that the BBC, with two national channels and a guaranteed income, is in a very protected and privileged position.

Undermining the Financial Base of PSB

Another criticism of these proposals is that they would damage the ability of commercial television to finance programming and to comply with any PSB obligations that government continued to impose on the commercial sector. This claim is based on a rather simplistic financial projection of the impact of greater competition. Competition fragments audiences and therefore reduces revenue. If costs escalate and revenue falls, programme expenditure will also fall, with a corresponding decrease in the quality of British television. But competition will also make these organisations leaner and more efficient. There is growing evidence that the labour and production costs of many ITV contractors are excessive and that they are already being reduced.

Although competition will reduce the revenue of individual advertiser-supported channels, it will expand the scope for industry to use television. There is evidence that competition expands the use of television advertising and also revenues. In the UK, expenditure on television advertising has been growing at an average annual rate of 5.6 per cent in real terms since 1970, and has taken an increasing share of total advertising expenditure.

In the USA television advertising is far more developed and more competitive. Expressed as a proportion of GDP, US television advertising expenditure is 0.54 per cent – three times the average expenditure in Europe and 40 per cent more than in the UK. The most dramatic expansion in television advertising expenditure in America took place at a time when the average number of channels increased from seven in 1975 to 10-11 by 1985. Thus competition is likely to expand advertising revenue in the long run.

CONCLUSION

There is an urgent need to introduce more competition in commercial television. The reason for this urgency is that the high costs of television advertising are damaging the competitiveness of the economy; and the expansion of the new media, cable and satellite television, is likely to entrench ITV's monopoly of television advertising.

By improving the competitiveness of the television advertising industry the Government could ensure that programme standards do not fall. It simply has to privatise Channel 4 and allow it to compete with ITV. Programme standards could be maintained at their current levels, if not higher, if the BBC did not engage in ratings competition and took over Channel 4's distinctive programme remit. In this way viewers would have a genuine choice of programmes and the advertisers would have genuine competition in the purchase of airtime. The Government has one of those rare opportunities whereby it could achieve two objectives with the same policy change.

The White Paper rejects this approach. It is adamant that Channel 4 must keep its remit (as a small-audience channel), but there will be changes. It will sell its own advertising time, and it may have to change its structure. Yet the whole plan collapses when one draws out the implications.

First, the only conceivable reason for independent selling of airtime is to increase the competitive pressures on ITV. However, if Channel 4 continues with its present remit, the competitive pressure will be minimal. Indeed, advertising rates on Channel 4 are likely to *increase* since most ITV companies have been less than vigorous in selling Channel 4 airtime to advertisers. The trade-off looks a poor one – greater financial instability for Channel 4 *without* increased competitive pressures to bring down advertising rates.

The weakest aspect of the White Paper proposals for Channel 4 is the menu of proposed changes to its structure, or what the White Paper calls, in a rare lapse into the old Home Office jargon, 'constitutional models'. The White Paper seriously suggests that Channel 4 should remain a nationalised industry owned by the new regulatory body, the Independent Television Commission, that is, maintaining the *status quo*. The other 'models' are a private-sector company (with significant financial guarantees) or some link with the proposed new Channel 5.

The authors of the White Paper have got it wrong. If the object of the exercise is to increase competition, choice and efficiency, then upholding the remit of Channel 4 cannot, as the White Paper argues, be 'an essential part of the new pattern of television broadcasting'. Public service broadcasting must be defined and financed in a coherent way, not side-stepped by the wholesale preservation of institutions from our existing uncompetitive broadcasting sector in the new world of greater choice and commercial freedom.

7

ADVERTISING REVENUE AND BROADCASTING

Brian Sturgess

Barclays de Zoete Wedd Research Limited

FOR YEARS the ITV companies could have been considered an investor's dream – steady profits squeezed only by excess costs, levy payments and subscription payments to support Channel 4. Since 1970, apart from a very few years, real growth in ITV revenue has been greater than the real growth of GDP. The source of this income was, of course, the establishment of a network of regional monopolies for the sale of commercial airtime over the airwaves granted by a statutory body in 1955, the Independent Television Authority, now the Independent Broadcasting Authority (IBA).

ITV – THREATS TO THE MONOPOLIES

ITV's monopoly of television advertising is now threatened. Cable television does not yet constitute a significant competitive challenge. By the early 1990s, however, the benefits of interactive cable services, which allow viewers to communicate with the cable operator, may have been introduced thus permitting advertisers to gain an immediate response to local and regional promotional activity. Satellite television services provide the greater challenge to the ITV companies. The costs of transmission by satellite will fall as total availability of satellite channels increases. It is estimated that by 1995 there will be up to 375 transponders (channels) available for low-power satellite services into Europe and up to 30 Direct Broadcasting by Satellite (DBS) transponders.

Within this future environment, the ITV companies, released only in 1986 from the fear that the Peacock Committee would recommend limited advertising on the BBC, are facing the prospect of a fifth and even a sixth channel by 1993, according to the Government's White Paper. The Government also proposes a new system of competitive bidding for franchises. All these factors are of great relevance for the financial prospects of the ITV companies. Unless the total market for television advertising expands proportionally, ITV's revenues will come under severe pressure.

In this chapter the television advertising market will be examined in some detail to isolate the distortive effects of monopoly.

THE IMPORTANCE OF ADVERTISING REVENUE

Advertising is a crucial source of revenue for the media. In the USA, a vast and diverse system of radio and television broadcasting has been built up financed solely from advertising. For some media, such as the cinema or mass circulation newspapers, a direct payment by the consumer is the primary source of revenue as it has been with cable television in its recent phase of development in the USA. But the final decision to launch a newspaper or a magazine, whether or not it is to be funded by sub-scription or advertising, remains a private one based upon assessments of commercial viability.

In the early years of television, spectrum scarcity and the difficulty of excluding non-payers made it feasible to finance the medium only through general taxation, a poll tax or by selling airtime (i.e., audiences) to advertisers. A mature, less regulated industry might encompass a variety or a mixture of funding mechanisms, but the actual choice would depend upon market-related rather than legal or technological issues. Television has for some time achieved that phase of maturity. Cable, satellite, the prevalence of video recorders, the possibilities of addressability using conventional terrestrial techniques, and availability of more spectrum for broadcasting, and for Microwave Video Distribution Systems (MVDS), offer a rich range of distribution systems for supplying audio-visual images to household television screens. This contrasts with the poverty of options allowed the regulators of the UK's television sector.

All of these competitive possibilities, with the addition of a fifth channel and direct broadcast satellite television from Astra (the 16-channel medium-powered satellite) and BSB (the UK direct broadcast satellite with three to five channels), will eventually help to reduce advertising airtime prices in the UK. However, relief for advertisers will be reached quickly enough only when the ITV contractors move from acting as regional monopolies to competitive suppliers of airtime.

Many recent discussions of television advertising in the UK treat it as if it were based on markedly different principles from those experienced in other markets. The advocates of the special interest groups argue, of course, in favour of special treatment. In practice, television advertising in the UK is essentially in the hands of a collection of 14 state-allocated monopolies (the regional ITV contractors).

The UK television advertising market is rife with distortions arising mainly from the regulatory system that has protected the regional ITV contractors.

The Determinants of Television Advertising Expenditure

Most macro-economic studies of the determinants of television advertising expenditure have found significant relationships between television advertising, company profits and consumer expenditure. There is further evidence that the amount of total advertising devoted to television is also positively related to the level of import penetration in consumer markets and to the deregulation of service industries which create new categories of advertisers. For less mature markets than the USA and the UK, an increase in the supply of commercial airtime devoted to advertising has also led to an increase in the total expenditure on television advertising.

Advertising expenditure devoted to television in the UK grew rapidly from the introduction of commercial television in 1955 and had reached 22.3 per cent of total advertising expenditure by 1960. It then continued to increase its share of total advertising expenditure to 25.6 per cent in 1963, 29.7 per cent in 1982, reaching 32.7 per cent by 1986. In 1987, the ITV contractors, excluding TV-am (the commercial breakfast franchise), received a total income of £1,326 million from selling advertising airtime. Despite this increase in its relative importance, television advertising has exhibited a strong pro-cyclical pattern and its growth has varied over the period 1970-87 by less than company profits, but by more than consumer expenditure.

This has been reflected in the pattern of inflation in advertising rates over the period. The real cost per thousand (CPT) adults fell from the late 1960s, apart from a cyclical upturn over the period 1971-73, to reach a disastrously low point in the recession of 1975. Only since that year has there been a continual rise in rates. This inflation is the most important factor explaining rising television revenues in the UK. For example, from March 1986 to March 1988, the (average) network CPT adults rose by 36.6 per cent from £4.62 to £6.31, whereas ITV network revenue rose by 29.5 per cent to £117.4 million.

The evidence suggests that the income elasticity of television airtime in the UK has a value in excess of unity. This implies that as real GDP increases, the demand for television airtime expands more than proportionally. Much attention has been focussed on attempts to estimate the size of the price or rate elasticity of demand for television airtime. The consensus derived from econometric studies and advertiser surveys seems to be that the elasticity is approximately one. This means that a 1 per cent increase in the price of advertising messages leads to a 1 per cent decrease in the quantity demanded.

This is not good news for the existing ITV contractors because it implies that an increase in the supply of airtime sufficient to cause a sizeable decrease in rates would leave total advertising revenue unchanged. If extra airtime resulted from an increase in the number of competitive channels, then the same total revenue would have to be shared among a larger number of channels and the existing television contractors would lose market share. This, in turn, would place extra pressure upon the ITV companies to reduce their labour costs. In the longer term, extra channels would have to be accommodated by the additional demand for airtime arising from the general growth of demand in the economy.

THE UK MARKET FOR TELEVISION AIRTIME

National or Regional?

Most studies of the advertisers' demand for television airtime have based their research on the artificial and false assumption that there is a national market in television airtime. The regional television markets have, in these studies, been aggregated into one national market and the network average airtime cost calculated as the weighted (by revenue share) average of each contractor's airtime costs. Apart from TV-am, however, no such national market exists in the sense that airtime is bought and sold in it. As a result, the commissioned research on this subject during the last three years has been a waste of the sponsors' money.[1]

The price of television advertising time is usually measured in terms of the cost per thousand (CPT) viewers. The network average CPT is not equivalent to a 'price' that would prevail if there were a national market for television airtime. It is known in the advertising industry as the 'all station average' and is used solely as a reference point to assist agency media buyers in their negotiations with individual ITV contractors. It is therefore not possible to use it to determine the impact upon advertising rates of an increase in the supply of advertising messages (i.e., those watching advertisements multiplied by the number of viewers, a formula called commercial home minutes (CHM)). The reason is that the dispersion of CPT away from the network average CPT is not based upon

---

[1] M. Cave & P. Swann, *The Effects on Advertising Revenues of Allowing Advertising on BBC Television – A Report for the Committee on Financing the BBC*, London: Home Office, 1985; G. K. Yarrow, C. G. Veljanovski *et al.*, *The Effects on Other Media of the Introduction of Advertising on the BBC – A Report for the Committee on Financing the BBC*, London: Home Office, 1985; A. Budd, *Channel Four – Post-Peacock: The Financial Implications of Recommendation 14*, London: Channel Four, 1986; NERA, *1992 and Beyond . . . The Options for ITV*, London: ITV Association, 1988; Booz, Allen & Hamilton, *The Economics of Television Advertising in the UK*, London: Economists Publications, Special Report No. 113, 1988; C. G. Veljanovski, *Television, Advertising and the Economy*, London: Incorporated Society of British Advertisers, 1987.

TABLE 1

TELEVISION AIRTIME INFLATION, 1986-88

	Housewife Cost Per Thousand			Airtime Inflation	
	March 1986	March 1987	March 1988	1987/86 %	1988/87 %
Thames	6.11	7.50	9.13	22.7	21.7
LWT	8.23	9.95	11.27	20.9	13.3
TVS	6.34	8.11	9.41	27.9	16.0
Anglia	4.00	4.82	5.96	20.5	23.7
Central	4.20	4.81	5.97	14.5	24.1
Granada	3.89	3.88	4.75	–0.3	22.4
Yorkshire	4.18	4.36	5.16	4.3	18.4
HTV	3.87	4.36	5.10	12.7	17.0
STV	4.03	4.27	4.90	5.9	14.8
Tyne Tees	3.04	3.22	4.14	5.9	28.6
TSW	4.22	4.62	6.44	9.5	39.4
Ulster	3.16	3.94	4.48	24.7	13.7
Grampian	3.22	3.57	3.81	10.9	6.7
Border	2.64	2.81	3.52	6.4	25.3
Network avge.	4.62	5.26	6.31	13.9	20.0

the size of regions, nor upon the socio-economic make-up of the audience, but upon each contractor's share of the total audience.

Regional Variations in CPT

The cost to advertisers of television airtime varies widely across the country (Table 1). In March 1988, the CPT for housewife audiences was a low of £3.52 in the Border transmission area and as much as £11.27 on LWT, which has the weekend franchise in the Greater London area. The network average for that month was £6.31. It would be difficult for any marketing manager to argue that a housewife watching the same advertisement in London at the weekend is over three times as valuable as one watching Border TV.

Does Audience Composition Explain Cost Differences?

One argument that is often advanced to explain differences in the CPT between the ITV contractors is variations in the affluence of the regions. Television contractors in London and the prosperous South-East deliver audiences which have higher disposable incomes and more desirable purchasing patterns which are more attractive to advertisers. While this is certainly true, this factor alone is not sufficient to explain the deviations of individual contractors' share of total network revenue from their share of net audience.[2]

If differences in CPT are caused by the wealth of the audiences in each area, this is easily tested. The market in that case would price each audience category at the same price. The explanation of regional variations in CPT would then be solely attributable to the fact that one region had more affluent people than another. However, airtime costs per thousand ABC1 adults (i.e., those classified by the Central Statistical Office as professional and managerial) show wide regional dispersion. The network average in March 1988 was £12.72, but the cost ranged from £16.46 on LWT to £7.19 on Border – a multiple of 2.3 times. This explanation is therefore not very strong.

The Absence of Targeting

The value of an advertising slot is defined largely by the number of adults or housewives watching. In the industry jargon, one person watching an advert or substantial part of it is registered as an 'impact' or message. This crude definition of the audience does not mean that targeting of groups of individuals (such as businessmen, sportsmen, the young, and so on) does not exist. It is simply that for most buyers of television advertising airtime under current measurement systems the dominant audience is housewives.

Targeting using television can be an expensive business, particularly if the advertiser is searching for audiences which are desirable but do not watch much television, such as ABC1 males and young adults. It is therefore often much more cost-effective to buy adult or housewife audiences. In March 1988, the CPT on Thames Television ranged from £5.80 per thousand adults to £71.88 for young adults in the age group 16-24. In many cases, targeting using television consists of the blunt instrument of buying adult or housewife impacts and inspecting the composition of the audience afterwards to determine required complementary media support.

The supply of housewife impacts depends upon a number of factors, only one of which can be marginally influenced by contractors:

Total TV Viewing	—	Socio-economic factors/leisure patterns
Commercial Audience Share	—	BBC Share *vs.* Network Share in each region
Airtime Minutage	—	Regulated by the IBA

In each television franchise area, the effective supply of housewife impacts is determined by all three of these factors. Only the ITV

---

2 Because ITV regional broadcasts overlap – so that about 10 per cent of the population can receive more than one ITV service – audiences must be allocated arbitrarily to one or other of the ITV companies to calculate their net audience.

TABLE 2

ITV CONTRACTORS' SHARE OF REVENUE
AND AUDIENCE, MARCH 1988

	Share of Network Revenue %	Share of Housewife Messages %	Share of ABC1 Adult Messages %	Share of Net ITV Households %
Thames	15.90	10.9	12.3	—
LWT	11.20	6.3	8.7	—
London	27.10	17.2	21.0	19.9
TVS	11.30	7.6	9.1	9.0
Anglia	6.13	6.5	6.5	6.4
Central	14.50	15.4	14.4	15.2
Granada	10.51	14.1	12.0	11.9
Yorkshire	9.23	11.1	9.8	10.3
HTV	6.33	7.9	7.3	7.6
STV	5.32	7.1	7.2	6.1
Tyne Tees	3.70	5.6	4.3	5.2
TSW	2.41	2.4	2.7	2.9
Ulster	1.40	2.1	2.4	2.3
Grampian	1.30	2.2	2.1	2.0
Border	0.69	1.2	1.2	1.2
	100	100	100	100

contractor's audience share can be affected slightly by programme choices. The relevant CPT for each segment of the total audience is then determined by the revenue of the contractor divided by the number of messages.

AIRTIME AS A COMMODITY MARKET

The 'commodity market' nature of television airtime buying in the UK is quite easily demonstrated. Airtime is sold in an auction system where each 30-second slot is allocated to the highest bidder. In an ideal world, with a uniform socio-economic structure across the country and with no differences in viewing patterns by region, the revenue share of each contractor should approximate to its share of net households. It is illustrated in Table 2 that this model does not approximate to reality. Net households are calculated after taking account of overlap areas on regional boundaries caused by variations in transmitter strength and the topology of a TV region. Table 3 takes the percentage deviation of a contractor's market share from net households and compares it with similar percentage deviations for its share of housewife messages and of adult

TABLE 3

INDICES OF REVENUE AND AUDIENCE CATEGORY PENETRATION,
MARCH 1988

	Market Share Index[1]	Housewife Impact Index[2]	Adult ABC1[3] Impact Index[4]
London	136	87	105
TVS	126	84	101
Anglia	96	102	102
Central	95	101	95
Granada	88	118	101
Yorkshire	90	108	95
HTV	83	104	96
STV	87	116	118
Tyne Tees	71	108	83
TSW	83	83	93
Ulster	61	91	104
Grampian	65	110	105
Border	58	100	100

Notes:

(1) (Share of Network Revenue – Share of net ITV Households ÷ Share of net ITV Households x 100.
(2) (Share of Housewife Impacts – Share of net ITV Households ÷ Share of net ITV Households x 100.
(3) Defined as professional and managerial socio-economic categories.
(4) (Share of ABC1 Impacts – Share of net ITV Households ÷ Share of net ITV Households x 100.

ABC1 messages. There is a negative correlation between the market share deviation and the housewife audience deviation over twice as strong in absolute value as the positive relationship between market share deviation and the deviation of adult ABC1 messages.

Empirical research as part of consultancy work on behalf of some ITV contractors, carried out by the author covering a longer time-period, has shown that on average 85 per cent of the variation of the network share from the share of ITV households can be explained by differences in the housewife cost per thousand across regions. This leaves only 15 per cent to be explained by differences in the contractor's sales and research teams, by differences in the socio-economic profiles of the TV regions, and by random factors.

In the USA, the market shares of total advertising revenue of competitive stations are usually proportional to their audience share. In the UK the situation is the opposite. Deviations of the market shares by region from the contractor's share of net households are inversely proportional to the contractor's share of the housewife or adult audience.

Each contractor then is a monopolistic supplier of a relatively homogeneous commodity within its region. It has little control over the quantity of this commodity that is placed upon the market at frequent intervals, but the market resembles an auction market in that whatever quantity is available must be sold. The price of airtime is always demand determined and the CPT in Table 1 relate to differences in the supply of audiences by contractor.

Although for most ITV contractors, the supply of audiences is effectively fixed, giving it little control over its CPTs, in recent years some contractors have attempted to reduce the number of minutes of advertising and others have placed local advertisements on air during peak time.

Impact on the Elasticity of Demand for Advertising

The above analysis implies that the elasticity of advertising demand for ITV airtime will vary widely across contractors. In ITV regions where the housewife CPT is greater than the network average, where the contractor is delivering a supply of audiences generally less than its share of total net television households, the elasticity of demand for commercial airtime would be higher than one. This means that an expansion in advertising messages would lead to a more than proportionate decrease in CPT. This applies to ITV contractors in the South of England (Thames, LWT and TVS). For those contractors where the relevant CPT figure is less than the network average – mainly, but not exclusively, the contractors in the North of England and Scotland – the elasticity of demand for airtime is less than unity. Hence contractors in the South would seek to increase advertising time and/or audiences while those in the North would not want to expand either. These regional variations also exist for Channel 4, and go a long way to explain why all the ITV contractors do not sell Channel 4 airtime with the same degree of enthusiasm.

Regulation of Advertising Distorts the Market

The above analysis points to one of the distortions introduced by the regulation of television advertising which imposes the same minutage requirements on all contractors.

ITV contractors act as revenue maximisers. Television broadcasting supported by the sale of advertising time is a business with a high degree of operating leverage. In the short run, most of the costs of a television channel are fixed so that after the break-even has been reached, a small percentage change in advertising revenue leads to a more than proportionate change in net operating surplus (profits). It therefore follows that unrestrained ITV contractors would seek to maximise revenue. Thus an ITV contractor experiencing an elasticity of demand in excess of unity would have an incentive to expand the supply of audiences through extra minutage. Even if the extra minutage caused a marginal reduction in its effective audiences, they would have a beneficial impact upon revenues. In contrast, contractors with an elasticity of demand of less than unity would not want extra airtime that expanded the supply of audiences.

The distortions of the regional monopoly system have been exacerbated by the 1980s trend towards the flotation of ITV contractors on the stock market. Access to the capital market has meant that the ITV contractors have been able to raise funds for diversification outside their core business areas. Furthermore, those contractors that have performed worst in their obligation to provide a television service attractive to the households in their franchise area, have performed best in terms of revenue gains on the back of buoyant demand for television airtime.

Deregulate Advertising Minutage

The number of minutes devoted to advertising is decided by the IBA on a national basis and is uniform for all the ITV contractors. Under the present regulations an ITV contractor can broadcast advertisements for 7 minutes in peak time and an average of 6.5 minutes throughout the day. The IBA also seeks to ensure that all advertising time is sold so that the maximum becomes the actual average minutes of airtime per hour available to advertisers.

This obviously distorts the television advertising market. It follows that these distortions could be removed by allowing each contractor to adjust its own airtime minutage per hour within certain minimum and maximum limits ranging, for example, from 3 to 12 minutes. This would introduce a certain measure of control for contractors over the supply of audiences actually offered region by region. It would remove the problems that occur from the existing regulation that all minutage be sold. This regulation also has the effect of inflating airtime costs in economic boom conditions and leads to a rapid fall-off of rates in a recession.

THE US EXPERIENCE

It is instructive to consider the experience of the USA in the television advertising market. Until the early 1980s US television broadcasting was dominated by the three national network broadcasters, ABC, NBC and CBS. Network advertising revenue as a proportion of total television advertising was 35.8 per cent in 1987.

From 1976, rising television advertising rates had increased the real cost of advertising in the economy as the demand for airtime outstripped supply. From 1976 to 1985, as new product categories began using television advertising, an index measuring US network television rates rose from 100 to 250, some 70 points greater than the rise in the cost of consumable goods and services supplied by advertisers.

The attraction of each network's commercial airtime supply and the rate per minute depend upon its share of the total network audience. Yet taking all three networks as a group, with a near monopoly over television airtime, as total network audiences fell airtime rates rose for a commodity in increasingly scarce supply to advertisers. However, the availability of alternative television outlets, such as local television, barter syndication (where networks offer programmes to independent television channels in return for the right to sell advertising time on the channel) and cable, has eventually led to a substitution of spending away from the networks.

In 1985, the rise in network rates levelled off and prices have not increased significantly throughout 1986 and 1987. In 1985, broadcasting revenue, including television and radio, increased by only 3.7 per cent, compared with a rate of increase of 20.5 per cent in 1984. The networks earned revenue of $8,280 million in 1984. Non-network television and radio revenue rose by 8.5 per cent in that year, but as the networks still accounted for 67 per cent of the total their poor performance depressed the industry's growth rate.

Local television advertising has risen from 19.6 per cent of all television expenditure in 1970 to 28.8 per cent by 1986. Cable television increased from 13.2 per cent of US households in 1975, following deregulation, to 43.7 per cent in 1984 and it passed 50 per cent in November 1987. According to Nielsen, 45.5 million US households were cabled, i.e., 51.1 per cent of total households, by February 1988. Cable advertising was small during the late 1970s, but it rose from 1.9 per cent in 1983 to an estimated 5.1 per cent of all television advertising by 1988.

Furthermore, ratings on basic cable channels have consistently increased as the networks have faced decline. Basic cable viewing in the last quarter of 1987 increased by 14 per cent over a 24-hour sample while total television viewing fell by 3 per cent, again because of the disproportionate share of the network's audience loss. This increase in audience and advertising revenue allows cable to invest in higher quality programming which should further enhance its strategic position *vis-à-vis* the networks.

THE FUTURE

Time has run out for the UK's distorted system of television. BSB will launch its three- (and possibly five-) channel service in December 1989. Rupert Murdoch has recently introduced Sky Television using the Astra satellite (launched in December 1988). The crucial question from US experience is the audience that these competitive media will gain. A major impact cannot be expected on current advertising rate inflation until the new media penetrate 30-50 per cent of UK households. On most assumptions about the take-up of dishes, this is unlikely to be achieved before the mid-1990s.

The distortions identified in the UK television market exist because of imbalances in the regional supply of audiences created by monopoly franchises. The ideal regulatory régime must create a system where suppliers of the highest level of audiences in any region are rewarded rather than punished by advertisers. Several conditions must be met if this is to occur.

o   *Competition*: In each regional market, there must be more channels selling airtime to advertisers at the same time of day and during the same days.

o   *Independent Channels*: In order to prevent the relatively fixed commercial audience being sold collusively, these suppliers must be independent. Separating the selling of Channel 4 airtime from the ITV companies, as proposed in the White Paper, would help achieve this condition and could be implemented relatively quickly.

o   *Commercial Flexibility*: In order to allow the television channels to act competitively, they must have flexible control over their supply of audiences. This could be attained by allowing contractors to vary the number of minutes allocated to the advertisements in relation to demand according to a maximum and minimum formula.

o   *Efficient Allocation*: Priority for the allocation of fifth and sixth channel franchises must be accorded to those areas in which the television audience is proportionally lower and the CPT proportionally higher than average.

PART III

DEREGULATION
AND COMPETITION

8

RADIO SPECTRUM MANAGEMENT:

An Economic Critique of the Trustee Model

John Fountain

Department of Economics and Operations Research,
University of Canterbury, New Zealand

INTRODUCTION

SOPHISTICATED TECHNICAL CHANGES in radiocommunications, like satellites and cellular radio, tend to receive a disproportionate share of attention in discussions of the role played by the radio spectrum in the 'communications revolution'. However, the increasing benefits society obtains from developments in radiocommunications depend at least as much on the property rights institutions regulating spectrum use as they do on technical developments. These property rights institutions are changing at a much slower pace than radiocommunications technology.

In all major Western democracies, property rights in the radio spectrum have developed under the influence of centralised planning institutions rather than through market processes. The nation state (and coalitions of states through international treaty and agreement) has played a dominant and active role in the basic decisions as to how much of which types of spectrum should be allocated to specific individual users for particular uses. Although it is well recognised that spectrum is a commercially valuable resource, like state-owned land, capital equipment, minerals or forests, the state has not managed the spectrum as an owner. Rather, it has assumed the role of a trustee of a common property resource, regulating access to, and use of, the spectrum through licensing and direct regulatory controls.

This chapter provides an analysis and critique of the trusteeship approach to allocating spectrum. The first section gives a brief description of the physical properties of spectrum. The next section explains what is

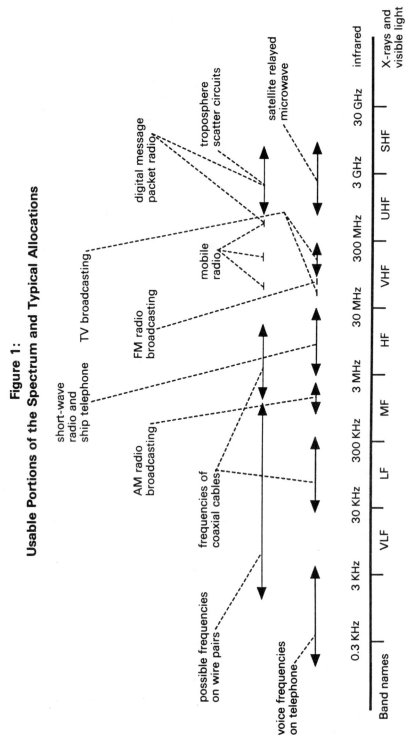

Figure 1:
Usable Portions of the Spectrum and Typical Allocations

meant by a property right institution and describes four alternative property rights institutions for spectrum. This explanation is followed by a case study focussing on the relevant features of the current common property and trusteeship institutions for radio spectrum management in New Zealand. While there are differences in detail between the functions of Radio Spectrum Trustees in New Zealand and those in the rest of the world, the general features are similar enough to make this economic analysis relevant for other countries.[1] The last section summarises the economic implications of the trusteeship approach.

WHAT IS THE RADIO SPECTRUM AND HOW IS IT USED?

Electromagnetic energy travels in the form of oscillating electric and magnetic fields. The frequency of oscillation of the energy can vary from several thousand to billions of hertz (cycles per second), as shown in Figure 1. The entire range of frequencies is known as the radio spectrum. To most of us, the most familiar part of the spectrum is the visible light portion, since our eyes are sensitive to electromagnetic energy travelling at these frequencies.

Energy Inputs

Figure 2 illustrates the various inputs used in radiocommunications. Energy is produced at a specific frequency in a transmitter, and an electronically coded message is loaded on to the carrier frequency by carefully controlling (modulating) the physical characteristics of the energy. The message-bearing energy is then launched by an antenna, the desired energy is intercepted and selected with a receiving system, and the electronic information signal is extracted.

During the radiocommunications process the electromagnetic energy which has been generated is distributed over a range of other frequencies, usually centred around the carrier frequency. The bandwidth of the travelling electromagnetic energy is the *widest* range of frequencies with significant amounts of energy. (Energy is typically higher near the carrier frequency and lower at frequencies further away from the carrier frequency.) For example, a frequency modulated (FM) radio station broadcasting typical programme material will have an average bandwidth of about 240 kilohertz (KHz − 240,000 cycles per second), a telephone quality voice message will be delivered over a bandwidth less than 12.5 KHz using mobile radio equipment, 25 KHz using Citizens' Band (CB) equipment, and 36 KHz using typical FM modulation of a satellite carrier.[2] A local broadcast television programme uses from 5,000 to 7,000

---

[1] Moreover, policy-makers in New Zealand are currently investigating alternative spectrum allocation systems with a view to facilitating the pro-competitive policies established recently for the formerly monopolised telecommunications and broadcasting industries.

[2] J. Martin, *Telecommunications and the Computer*, New Jersey: Prentice Hall, 2nd edition, 1976, p. 221.

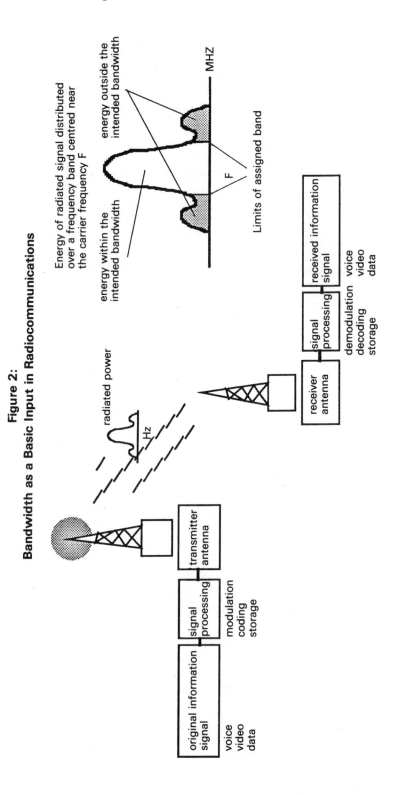

Figure 2:
Bandwidth as a Basic Input in Radiocommunications

KHz of bandwidth and almost 10 times as much bandwidth when broadcast from a satellite.

Since radio spectrum inputs can be measured, decisions about how much spectrum to use can be analysed just like decisions about the amounts of other measurable inputs (land, labour, capital goods, energy, etc.). However, radio spectrum inputs also have special physical properties that bear on the question of how to design institutions that will promote economic efficiency in spectrum use.

First, radio spectrum inputs *attenuate in area*. This means that the strength of the electromagnetic energy decreases the further the energy is from its point of origin. Signal strength decreases at a faster rate for energy at higher frequencies and for energy that follows the curvature of the earth.

Secondly, spectrum inputs *spillover into other frequency bands*. Because of practical limitations (e.g. cost and technology) on transmitters, receivers, signal processing circuits, etc., radiation intended for a restricted band of frequencies can extend into other bands (Figure 3).

Thirdly, the behaviour of spectrum inputs *cannot be perfectly predicted or controlled*. The duration of radiated energy, how far it travels, and how much bandwidth is being used at any given location, is influenced by many factors, some man-made (buildings, machinery, heat sources, etc.) and others environmental (atmospheric conditions, irregularities of the terrain, sunspot activity, etc.). Although scientific advancements are continually being made, there is uncertainty in the prediction and control of electromagnetic radiation.

Fourthly, *relative signal strengths matter* for communications. As a general rule, a desired signal in a given time, place and frequency band can be received and effectively processed to recover information if the strength of the *desired* signal at the receiving unit is sufficiently greater than all other undesired signals. That is, effective communication is *not* precluded by radiation from other sources unless the undesired radiation is too strong.

Since electromagnetic energy travels in both spatial and frequency dimensions it is convenient to describe the energy not only by range of frequencies over which it oscillates – bandwidth – but also in terms of the geographic area through which the energy travels and the time during which it travels. The three relevant dimensions of energy – time, area and spectrum – can be used to define a unit of spectrum resource, a TAS[3] package.

The geographic area over which magnetic energy travels is frequency-dependent. That is, energy travelling at different frequencies moves through the atmosphere in different ways. Generally, higher frequencies,

---

[3] This acronym originates with A. S. De Vany, R. D. Eckert, C. J. Myers, D. J. O'Hara and R. C. Scott, 'A Property System for Market Allocation of the Electromagnetic Spectrum: A Legal Economic-Engineering Study', *Stanford Law Review*, Vol. 21, 1969, pp. 1,499-1,561.

Figure 3:
Pollution Interference

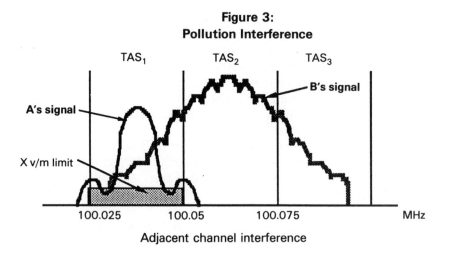

Adjacent channel interference

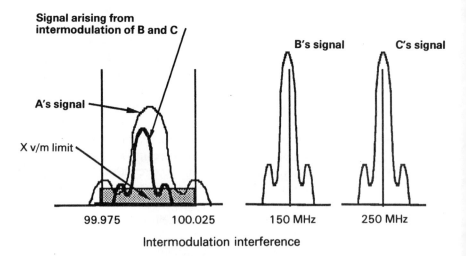

Intermodulation interference

such as those used for ordinary very high frequency (VHF) television broadcasts, travel in a line of sight direction, growing weaker with increasing distance from the source of transmission (an exact analogy is light from a lamp-post). Energy travelling at lower frequencies (below 30 megahertz (MHz) – 30,000,000 cycles per second), as in the amplitude modulation (AM) radio band, tends to follow the curvature of the earth and, under night-time conditions when energy from the sun is not exciting the ionosphere, it can be reflected and end up travelling many thousands of miles. Some of these effects can be predicted and controlled at lower frequencies, albeit imperfectly. It is possible, however, to exercise better control over the characteristics of energy in the spectrum above 30 MHz.

Interference

If two potential users or uses of a given TAS package originate energy on the same bandwidth at the same time in the same area, then one use may interfere with the other, degrading one or both communications. This potential for interference between uses of the same TAS package is not due to peculiar physical properties of electromagnetic radiation (although the spectrum's physical properties do influence the cost of preventing such interference). Rather, it reflects the fundamental economic problem of scarcity of spectrum: all those who wish to use a unit of resource (when it is provided at no cost – or at zero price) cannot be accommodated.

Interference created by simultaneous use of the same unit of spectrum resource by two or more users is no different from interference between competing, simultaneous uses of any other scarce resource. A piece of land cannot be used as a wheatfield and a playground at the same time without one use interfering with the other. A bus cannot transport freight from A to B and passengers from A to C at the same time. The same five minutes of secretarial time cannot be used for word-processing as well as answering a switchboard, without some degradation of either function. The potential for interference in the simultaneous use of land, capital, labour or spectrum resources are all examples of a similar type of scarcity.

The physical features of spectrum do create the possibilities for pollution-type interference. Figure 3 illustrates two cases: adjacent channel interference and intermodulation interference. The top panel shows adjacent channel interference, and the height of the curves representing A or B's signal at any given frequency indicates the strength of the energy from the signals at that frequency. The energy in A's signal is concentrated in TAS_1 between 100.025 MHz and 100.05 MHz. B's signal, in TAS_2, is centred in the adjacent band, 100.05 to 100.075 MHz, but a significant part of the energy from B's signal is spilling over into A's TAS package. This spillover has the potential to interfere with A's radiocommunications, either lowering the quality of received messages in A's production process or making the messages unintelligible.

The lower panel of Figure 3 illustrates intermodulation interference. A, B and C's TAS packages are not adjacent in the spectrum, yet B and C's signals at 150 MHz and 250 MHz respectively can intermodulate (combine) to generate energy in A's TAS package between 99.975 and 100.025 MHz. This spillover of energy from the intermodulation of B and C's signals may degrade A's messages.

Co-channel interference (not shown in Figure 3) is similar to adjacent channel interference. If two TAS packages are adjacent in the area dimension and originate energy on the same bandwidth, the signals of one operator may be strong enough to spill over into the TAS package of the other.

Figure 4:
Excludability

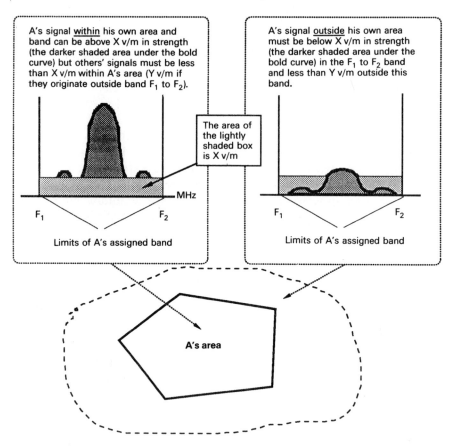

A's signal <u>within</u> his own area and band can be above X v/m in strength (the darker shaded area under the bold curve) but others' signals must be less than X v/m within A's area (Y v/m if they originate outside band F_1 to F_2).

A's signal <u>outside</u> his own area must be below X v/m in strength (the darker shaded area under the bold curve) in the F_1 to F_2 band and less than Y v/m outside this band.

The area of the lightly shaded box is X v/m

MHz

F_1 F_2

Limits of A's assigned band

F_1 F_2

Limits of A's assigned band

A's area

Excludability

Productive use of the spectrum for radiocommunications requires a predictable degree of excludability. One user originating energy in a TAS package must be able (legally and technically) to exclude other users from originating energy in that TAS package. Technically it is impossible (because it would cost far too much) for excludability to be absolute – electromagnetic radiation tends to spill over to some extent in all three TAS dimensions. For communications purposes, however, excludability does not have to be absolute.

Figure 4 illustrates the basic point. A is an operator wishing to exclude others from frequencies in the band F_1 to F_2 within the polygon-shaped area. Any other operator originating energy in the band F_1 to F_2 from a different area may be (practically and legally) prevented from radiating energy greater than some amount, say X volts per metre (v/m), within the band F_1 to F_2 and within A's area. Similarly, any operator radiating energy in any other band of frequencies may be prevented from radiating energy above another limit, say Y v/m, within the band F_1 to F_2 and within A's area.

Likewise, A himself will be excluded from generating radiation in other areas and frequency bands. Being assured[4] of a degree of excludability, A can raise the strength of his own signal sufficiently above the permitted signals of others to achieve his preferred quality of received messages.

Divisibility

Productive use of the spectrum also requires divisibility. TAS packages may be subdivided and combined along all three of the basic dimensions: time, area and spectrum. Frequency division multiple access (FDMA) is a technique used to divide a given bandwidth into a number of discrete bands that can be made available on an exclusive basis for different uses or users, either indefinitely (e.g. as leased circuits) or for as long as they are needed.

Alternatively, the time dimension can be broken up into discrete slots and the entire bandwidth made available on an exclusive basis to a user. This method is known as time division multiple access (TDMA) and is used increasingly wherever messages can be put in suitable digital form.

Space division techniques divide up a given geographic area into smaller cells or sectors and permit exclusive use of frequencies or time slots within those cells or sectors. All three subdivision methods can be used together, as illustrated by modern mobile cellular radio services.

Economic Properties of Inputs and Spectrum

From an economic standpoint, electromagnetic radiation that carries information is a scarce commodity, in the sense that demand exceeds supply at a zero price. Individuals are willing to give up valuable goods and services in order to obtain more spectrum (larger TAS dimensions) – largely for communications uses and for disposing of waste radiation by-products generated by the machinery and electrical apparatus used in other sectors of the economy.

Spectrum has the basic properties of any private good: use of a given TAS package by one person limits and in most cases precludes the simultaneous use of that same TAS package by others, particularly for communication purposes. Uncertainty in being able to predict and control electromagnetic radiation in the area and frequency dimensions means that interference can arise: the use of package TAS_1 by one agent has the

---

[4] For a more precise discussion of the degree of certainty radiocommunications operators have about excludability, see John Fountain, *The Economics of Radio Spectrum Management: A Survey of the Literature*, Wellington, NZ: New Zealand Department of Trade and Industry, 1988, pp. 24-25.

potential to affect adversely the use of package TAS_2 by another agent, especially if TAS_2 is close to TAS_1 in an area or frequency band. In short, spectrum is a scarce, private good, a factor of production with the potential for pollution-type interference.

PROPERTY RIGHTS IN RADIO SPECTRUM

The potential for interference in radiocommunications is often used to justify the necessity for centralised management. Otherwise, it is argued, chaos would ensue. But is the alternative really 'chaos'? The alternative to centralised management of land, labour or capital resources is not usually imagined to be chaos. Yet, as we have seen, there is the same potential for interference between two uses of the same unit of these resources at the same time and in the same area as long as those resources are scarce. Why should units of radio spectrum be different?

Contrary to conventional wisdom, the answer to this question is not that spectrum resources have peculiar physical properties, giving rise to interference. In most regions of the spectrum, interference problems – actual or potential – are primarily due to poorly defined and inadequately enforced property rights.

There are four broad, alternative systems of property rights in the spectrum that must be considered:

o   Communal property.

o   Communal property under exclusive trusteeship by a government department.

o   Private property under sole management by an owner.

o   Private property under decentralised and dispersed ownership.

Communal property rights in a resource mean that everyone has a right to use the resource, no one has a right to exclude anyone from using the resource, and these rights are enforceable at reasonable cost. Communal property rights in a resource held under exclusive trusteeship by a government department make all communal property rights subject to limitations imposed by the government department acting as a trustee, rather than an owner, of the resource. The constituency of the trust and the limitations on the discretion and decision-making processes of the trustees are analysed later in this chapter.

Private property rights under sole ownership give exclusive use of all units of a resource to one agent – the owner of the resource – with whom every other user must negotiate in order to use the resource. Private property under decentralised ownership divides the resource in some way between many agents and assigns to the owners the right to exclude other users or uses. Private property rights in units of goods mean:

o   The right to control uses of that unit.

o   The right to transfer (subdivide, share and combine) to others in exchange for a payment.

o   The right to bear risks of changes (i.e. lose or gain from such changes) in physical features or market value of the unit.

Spectrum Property Rights in the USA

Communal property rights institutions are not likely to persist in the face of significant increases in the potential economic value of the resource.[5] This proposition is well illustrated by the introduction of commercially valuable broadcasting activities during the 1920s in the USA.

The rapid development of broadcast stations in the USA from 1922 to 1925 (increasing from 60 to 564 stations over this period) and the interference problems that developed (notably in the MF band where radio broadcasts were situated) are often referred to as a period of 'chaos' in broadcasting. There was a rush for bandwidth in populated areas to exploit the potential commercial value associated with broadcasting. Claim-staking occurred and, not unnaturally, disputes over squatters' rights emerged. When sufficient commercial value was at stake such disputes were brought to the courts. The courts, in turn, began to define and delimit the individual's rights in spectrum use. For example, Coase cites a case in 1926 where squatters' rights were upheld: it was decided that the operator of an existing station had a right to prevent a newcomer from using a frequency so as to cause any material interference.[6]

Politicians recognised that something had to be done rapidly in order to prevent the establishment of private property rights in the spectrum through private litigation in the courts. Their objective was pecuniary: the spectrum was viewed as a very lucrative continent being explored and appropriated by private interests without making any payment to the state!

Clearly, a choice had to be made between a system of private property rights in spectrum developed through squatters' rights validated in the courts, and a system of common property under state trusteeship.[7] In 1927 legislation was passed cutting off the development of private property rights in spectrum and establishing a system based on centralised management under the trusteeship of a government agency, now known as the Federal Communications Commission (FCC).

Demands for exclusive use of spectrum simply became too valuable to ignore, either for the state or for business enterprises. The competition for

---

[5] Harold Demsetz, 'Towards a Theory of Property Rights', *American Economic Review*, Vol. 57, May 1967.

[6] Ronald Coase, 'The Federal Communications Commission', *Journal of Law and Economics*, Vol. 2, 1959, pp. 1-40.

[7] Ronald Coase, *ibid.*, pp. 31-32. A proper economic history of the early development of property rights in the spectrum has yet to be written.

potential future wealth from the resource during the historical transition period from communal property to centralised management under state trusteeship created 'chaos' for some. This transitional 'chaos' has been wrongly attributed to the inherent physical properties of the radio spectrum. In fact, it reflects the competitive striving for wealth by business and political agencies triggered off by sudden increases in the value of a resource.

The disputes arising between gold rush miners, as they try to establish exclusive claims and prevent or control claim-jumping, illustrate the same economic forces as the 'chaos' in broadcasting in the USA during the 1920s. This chaos was simply 'gold rush fever' operating in relation to spectrum inputs. But the final outcome, in terms of establishing a system for defining, enforcing and allocating property rights, took radically different directions in gold and in spectrum. Private property rights emerged for minerals like gold, while centrally regulated rights under government trusteeship emerged for spectrum.

RADIO SPECTRUM TRUSTEESHIP: A CASE STUDY

Property rights systems can be assessed on their ability to generate *information on alternative use-values (static and dynamic) of resources* and to provide *incentives for people to take account of information on alternative use-values* in their activities of production, exchange, consumption and investment. This section assesses radio spectrum trusteeship under a government department from this economic perspective.

The scope of radio spectrum trusteeship in New Zealand is broad. It is an offence under New Zealand legislation[8] to erect, construct, establish, maintain or use any apparatus for the purpose of. effecting radio-communications without a licence from the Postmaster General (the Radio Spectrum Trustee).[9] Radiocommunication activities are defined broadly to include any transmission, emission, or reception of signs, signals, impulses, writing, images, sounds or intelligence of any nature by the free radiation in space of electromagnetic waves of frequencies between 10 KHz and 3,000 gigahertz (GHz – one billion cycles per second).

There are several types of licences and each type has a set of restrictions governing permissible and prohibited activities relating to radio communications, some of which are specified in the Radio Regulations 1970, and related legislation. For example, sound radio and television broadcasting activities in New Zealand require a 'warrant' issued

---

[8] The Post Office Act 1959 (para. 164) and the associated Radio Regulations 1970 (para. 9). The regulations governing radio spectrum allocation in New Zealand were carried over into the Telecommunications Bill when the former New Zealand Post Office was dissolved and broken into three separate state-owned corporations in 1987. These regulations are currently under review.

[9] In order to facilitate cross-country comparisons, the Postmaster General in New Zealand and his delegates administering the Radio Regulations will be referred to as Radio Spectrum Trustees.

according to the Broadcasting Act (administered by a judicially independent regulatory agency, the Broadcasting Tribunal) as well as a broadcasting station transmitting licence.

There are, however, a number of important regulations governing *all* licences that are particularly relevant to the specification of common property and trusteeship property rights in the radio spectrum. Paragraph 27 of the Radio Regulations ensures that every limitation and restriction in the Radio Regulations is a term and condition of a licence.

The rest of this section deals with the following characteristics of the system in New Zealand:

o   Exclusive ministerial discretion over construction and operation of radiocommunications systems.

o   Restrictive licensing of spectrum users.

o   Restrictive licensing of spectrum uses.

o   Protection of the State Telecom monopoly.

o   Restrictions on technical input modifications.

o   Prohibitions on harmful interference to other users.

Exclusive Ministerial Discretion Over Construction and Operation of Radiocommunications Systems

The Radio Spectrum Trustee is the only agent with unlimited discretion in the building or operating of radiocommunication systems in New Zealand. The Radio Spectrum Trustee also has unlimited discretion to alter the terms and conditions of licences as 'he thinks fit'. His decision in these matters is final.[10]

These are real powers. They have been used to alter radio-communications services and costs, and to retard productivity-improving developments in spectrum use. For example, before the 1980s the Radio Spectrum Trustee's powers were used to prevent the development of FM sound radio broadcasting in New Zealand. A change of sound broad-casting policy in the 1980s required the clearing of all land mobile operators from the 94 to 100 MHz band, to which was added a requirement that land mobile licensees in the 81 to 88 MHz and 100 to 108 MHz bands change their equipment, at considerable expense and without compensation, to smaller channel spacings. In addition, innovative applications such as FM subcarrier technology (whereby additional data is 'piggy-backed' onto an ordinary FM radio broadcast signal), or the use of terrestrial or satellite radiocommunications links developed in the private sector, have simply been refused.

Political expediency restricts the use of ministerial discretion, par-

---

[10] New Zealand Radio Regulations, paras. 6, 8, and 13.

ticularly in the alteration of terms and conditions of licences. But this same political expediency creates uncertainty from the standpoint of a radiocommunications system operator about the terms, conditions and tenure of a licence.

It is possible to balance ministerial discretion and property rights within the overall trusteeship approach by establishing an independent regulatory agency. For example, any alteration in the terms and conditions of a broadcasting warrant in New Zealand is subject to the judicial processes of the Broadcasting Tribunal, which considers criteria such as public interest, avoidance of certain kinds of monopoly and efficiency in spectrum use, when exercising discretion.

Leonard Waverman's comparative study of regulation by government department and by independent tribunal in telecommunications in Canada[11] revealed considerable differences in:

o   The type of information about user needs reaching the ultimate regulator.

o   The size and distribution of negotiation costs borne by users (including costs of monitoring the regulatory agency).

o   Incentives to act in an economically efficient manner.

Given a choice between placing trusteeship in the hands of a government department or in the hands of an independent regulatory agency, Waverman's analysis suggests the latter is likely to be more economically efficient. But the choice need not be limited to these two methods.

If a private property rights system were adopted for TAS packages, uncertainty about the state unilaterally altering terms and conditions of property rights according to the dictates of political expediency would be effectively removed, or at least put on a par with uncertainty in other resources. The discretion of the state would be limited by normal laws of contracting with private property holders. This is not to say that private owners might not themselves introduce other forms of uncertainty absent under trusteeship (such as harmful interference, discussed below), but it would at least reduce uncertainty about political expediency affecting spectrum property rights.

Restrictive Licensing of Spectrum Users

As we have seen, radiocommunications resources (TAS packages) can be shared. The efficiency gains from so doing are potentially very large. Yet New Zealand's Radio Regulations prohibit mutually advantageous sharing arrangements by making every licence personal to the licensee in the sense that

---

[11] L. Waverman, 'The Process of Telecommunications Regulation in Canada', Working Paper No. 28, Ottawa: Economic Council of Canada, 1982.

'no licence or the holder of any permit, certificate, or authorization, shall *assign, sublet, transfer*, or otherwise dispose of, or for the purpose of *profit* admit any other person or body to participate in the benefit of any such licence, permit, certificate, or authorization'.[12]

Although this is a general regulation applicable to all classes of licences, it is only applied at the Radio Spectrum Trustee's discretion. CB and paging stations[13] are explicitly prohibited from sharing spectrum for purposes of providing commercial messaging services. These classes of licence are required to share a band of 325 KHz spectrum[14] – about 5 per cent of the spectrum bandwidth of a television channel – on a non-exclusive, communal property basis.

On the other hand, the New Zealand Post Office's (State Telecom monopoly supplier) point-to-point microwave circuits can be used to supply commercial messaging services, with exclusivity arranged by the radiocommunications supplier as part of its telecommunications business. Yet licences to operate similar microwave distribution facilities given to other agencies (e.g. the Broadcasting Corporation of New Zealand (BCNZ), the Ministry of Energy, Railways, etc.) continue to prohibit them from sharing TAS units on a commercial basis. Paradoxically, some third party messages must be carried as a condition of holding a licence. For example, television and sound radio broadcasting stations are required to handle third party messages originating from government departments free of charge.[15]

The use of FM subcarrier technology allowing data and/or voice messages to be delivered simultaneously with ordinary VHF-FM sound radio broadcasts has been prohibited, while a similar technology in television broadcasting – teletext – has been permitted. (Both types of services – teletext and FM subcarriers – are ways of sharing existing radiocommunications resources, including spectrum, with other users.)

Many of these inconsistencies in the application of prohibitions on sharing exist simply to protect revenue sources for select government trading enterprises in telecommunications and broadcasting. Yet this protection is carried out in ignorance of opportunity costs (i.e. the cost in terms of income that could have been earned from other uses). The common property trusteeship specification of property rights generates neither information nor incentives to make rational decisions on the basis of opportunity costs.

Why doesn't the trusteeship approach generate relevant economic information? By specifying as a matter of law that resource sharing will not be permitted without ministerial discretion, the potential benefits from

---

[12] NZ Radio Regulations, para. 20 (my emphasis).

[13] NZ Radio Regulations, paras. 127, 143.

[14] New Zealand Post Office specification RT3, 1983, p. 4.

[15] NZ Radio Regulations, para. 150.

innovative spectrum sharing will have to be very large indeed for an individual user even to attempt to negotiate sharing possibilities. The Radio Spectrum Trustee will generally enforce the State Telecom's monopoly as telecommunications supplier.

Alternatively, the wider 'public interest' (i.e. bringing everyone in as a potential communal right holder) will be raised. Many users who could potentially benefit from spectrum resource sharing will find the costs of trying to influence ministerial discretion (including the cost of uncertainty about likely effectiveness) too high.

The cost of organising a collection of individual users to act together to alter legislation or ministerial discretion will be larger still. However, as the potential benefits of redefining property rights in spectrum increase, it is likely that significant numbers of user-group lobbies will arise.

It does not take much sophisticated theorising to predict the bureaucratic chaos that the electronic data processing and information services industry would be in if ministerial discretion had to be consulted and/or altered for sharing programmers, software, processing power, storage, databases, etc., because of communally defined property rights and government trusteeship in these resources. In all likelihood, the bureaucratic chaos would be avoided as businesses and government agency managers sought more flexible, if less effective, ways of meeting their information processing needs. Fortunately, there are private property rights in all significant electronic data processing (EDP) resources so bureaucratic chaos is not only avoided but replaced by dynamically efficient competition.

However, the technologies of the telecommunications and computer industries are converging. One of the great uncertainties in future computer network design is where to locate network and processing intelligence – in user terminal equipment or in the operator's network. These developments challenge the belief that computer technology prevails inside the boundaries of a building and telecommunication technology prevails between user premises.

The efficient and economical sharing of computing and managerial resources both within and between business and government enterprises no longer respects spatial boundaries. If radio spectrum-based technology is going to play a useful productivity-raising, cost-reducing, performance-enhancing role in future business and government activities, restrictions on sharing spectrum will have to be abandoned.

Even if information on opportunity costs were generated, there is little incentive for the Radio Spectrum Trustee to use such information. The Trustees (or regulators) do not own the spectrum so they do not personally gain by leasing or selling rights to share in its use; nor do they own the other activities related to radiocommunications and therefore have no financial incentive to tie in their activities with the new resource-sharing proposals.

TABLE 1

CATEGORIES OF LICENCES

Type of Station	Type of Service
Aircraft station	Telecontrol and telemetry
Ship station	Paging
Land mobile station	Experimental
Land (base) station	Amateur
Fixed station	Broadcasting
Citizen station	Amateur

Regulators are trustees, under a system of property rights that generally outlaws profitable use of resource-sharing in valuable spectrum inputs, and insulates the Trustees from any of the usual constraints put on trusteeship of private property – namely competition from management by other Trustees. If the Trustees are motivated at all by commercial considerations it is motivation to protect the revenue of the state-owned telecommunications and broadcasting enterprises.

Restrictive Licensing of Spectrum Uses

Related to the restriction on non-transferability of radiocommunication resources between users is an explicit regulation prohibiting transferability of radiocommunications resources between uses:

'a licence issued under these regulations shall not authorize the licensee to take part in any radiocommunication service [other than the services indicated in the licence]'.[16]

The broad categories of licences outlined above are used to define particular types of communication outputs and to restrict licence-holders to providing only those limited types of services. There are further restrictions on types of messages that can be sent, types of stations that can be communicated with, and fixed points between which communication can occur.

Stations of one class are generally permitted to communicate only with stations of the same class, e.g. ship stations to ship stations, citizen stations to citizen stations, but not citizen to ship stations. Common carrier-type public correspondence or using mobile, citizen, amateur, telemetry or paging stations is prohibited, as is the transmission of news, entertainment or pre-recorded material likely to be of interest to any segment of the general public.[17]

---

[16] NZ Radio Regulations, para. 30.

[17] NZ Radio Regulations, paras. 89, 92, 106, 127A, 128, 130, 142-146.

These restrictions are analogous to the commodity and route restrictions imposed upon transport operators in New Zealand before the reform of the Land Transportation Regulations in the early 1980s, and they have similar implications for the inefficiency of radiocommunication resource utilisation. This type of regulation seriously inhibits the transfer of spectrum between different classes of users that is essential for economic efficiency in a growing, innovative, competitive economy.

In dramatic contrast to the inefficiencies of trusteeship concerning shared use and transfers for profit are the quasi-private property rights allocated in the USA to satellite users and to local digital transmission users. These operators have *de facto* exclusive rights to blocks of spectrum but do not have restrictions on shared use or transfer between uses. They have become exceedingly adept at flexibly subdividing the TAS packages they control in either the time or frequency dimension to allow users exclusive use of TAS packages on demand. As previously discussed, the two basic methods of TAS subdivision either make available a pool of carrier frequencies and assign them on demand to individual users for as long as they are required (FDMA); or the entire bandwidth is used to make available a stream of time slots that can be assigned on demand to different users (TDMA).

Consequences of Exclusive Rights

If a radiocommunications supplier has exclusive rights over TAS packages using, say, 100 MHz of spectrum, and uses technology for dynamically assigning exclusive channels to users, any growth in demand for a new service (say, local distribution of data) will (a) be signalled to the spectrum supplier through the fact that users in this class are willing to make higher bids than some of the other users, e.g. for mobile and broadcast uses; and (b) permit the shareholders in his company to increase their personal wealth by relocating some spectrum from the lower-valued uses to the higher-valued uses.

Employing technology that makes it possible to re-allocate spectrum between users and uses, and property rights permitting the spectrum supplier to do so on an exclusive, divisible, transferable (in part) basis, has two important consequences. First, *information* is created about alternative use-values of radio spectrum, and secondly, there are strong *incentives* (based on people's desires to improve their personal standard of living) to act on this information. In contrast, the regulatory apparatus imposed by trusteeship simply ignores such information and incentives and legislates against such transfers.

How much is given up by restricting the transfer of spectrum between users and uses? The answer varies from case to case but US experience indicates that gains in terms of productivity improvements, reduction of lengthy installation delays for local telephone circuits and expansion of the digital carrying capacity of local services can be very significant.

One example concerns the use of digital radio electronic messaging services using spectrum for urban regional communications rather than cable circuits provided by conventional telephone companies. In the USA in the early 1980s, the average time for obtaining a leased line was six months, with variability from two to 12 months. And the demand for high-capacity switched services in many areas either exceeded local loop capacity on landline circuits or would exceed that capacity in the near future.[18]

Users of these wideband services, or others who need leased lines quickly for security services, credit card verification, automated banking, financial information and management services, etc., find it exceedingly costly in terms of lost business opportunities to wait six months or more for the necessary landline installations.

The radio spectrum-based services currently under development in the USA use cleverly designed subdivision of TAS packages in the area, time and spectrum dimensions, and the proprietary (exclusive ownership) access arrangements to eliminate these long delays in installation time (now reduced to days), speed up the rate at which cost-reducing digital technology is introduced, and generally put competitive pressure on suppliers to pass cost-reducing gains on to customers. Such innovative applications cannot possibly occur in New Zealand if the property rights defined in the Radio Regulations (paras. 20 and 30) continue in force.

Protection of the State Telecom Monopoly

Regulation 31 explicitly prohibits radiocommunication activities that might encroach on the State Telecom monopoly in telecommunications:

> 'Except with the authority of the Minister, a radio station shall not be used in any way to compete with Government communication services, and shall not transmit or receive radiocommunications the transmission or reception of which is calculated, in the judgement of the Minister to cause loss of revenue to the Post Office [*State Telecom Monopoly*]. Provided that, in an emergency, communications having for their object the preservation of human life, the protection of property or the detection of crime, may be transmitted or received without reference to the Minister.'

Whether many new forms of radiocommunications would cause a loss of revenue to the State Telecom monopoly in the rapidly growing markets for telecommunication services is a debatable question. At least the Broadcasting Tribunal has to debate the question in as far as it affects the revenue of incumbent broadcasters,[19] but regulation 31 puts the matter on the agenda of the Radio Spectrum Trustee.

---

18 L. M. Nirenberg, 'Tymnet's Use of Digital Radio for the Delivery of Value Added Services', reprinted in *A Collection of Tymnet Technical Papers*, McDonnell Douglas Network Systems Company, 1983, pp. 146-152.

19 New Zealand Broadcasting Act, Section 80.

In practice, this regulation has had its exemptions, such as the BCNZ, Railways, Ministry of Energy, Air New Zealand, the Police, and local body mobile systems which have developed their own networks, often with radiocommunications where appropriate (as judged by the network operators). Notable omissions from this list of exemptions are large or small private sector businesses, either singly or in joint ventures. Radiocommunication-based networks for private sector business have been systematically and effectively pre-empted from obtaining the right to construct, use and maintain their own networks.

Policy-makers in many countries, notably Japan, the UK, the USA, Canada, and more recently New Zealand, are increasingly responsive to viewing telecommunications markets as workably competitive. They see them as having conditions of entry and exit sufficiently free to keep suppliers – even ones with a dominant market share – pricing competitively, cutting costs, adopting and developing new technology and services at more efficient rates, and providing an extensive array of valuable customer services.

New developments in radiocommunications using either satellite or microwave terrestrial facilities (like cellular radio systems or local digital message services) have played a major role in establishing a competitive telecommunications environment, and bringing electronic communications users the sort of benefits that have been characteristic of the fierce competition in the electronic data processing/computer industry. Radio spectrum transmission methods substantially reduce the sunk costs of telecommunications operations, thereby significantly lowering barriers to entry and exit in telecommunications.

To translate the vision into reality, however, a new definition of property rights in radio spectrum is necessary. Private property rights giving exclusive use of TAS packages to one or many agents on an outright ownership basis or long-term lease from the state, unencumbered by restrictions on transferring or sharing use of the spectrum, must be formulated in New Zealand – as is already occurring in other countries (albeit in a limited fashion). Needless to say, there is no place for regulations protecting an established carrier in such a definition of spectrum property rights.

Restrictions on Technical Modifications

Radio Spectrum Trustees place severe constraints on technical innovation in radiocommunications:

> 'Any proposed alteration affecting the technical characteristics or the location or the functioning of the transmitting apparatus at any radio station shall be notified in writing to the Radio Inspector'.[20]

The 'technical' specifications cover many aspects, from relatively

---

[20] NZ Radio Regulations, para. 39.

minimal restrictions for telecontrol and telemetry stations that monitor machinery and equipment to the extensive list shown below for FM radio broadcasting stations:

o   The frequency of operation and limits on frequency deviation.

o   The permissible bandwidth of transmission.

o   Maximum levels of out-of-band emissions.

o   The authorised emission type.

o   The maximum effective radiated power in relation to coverage area.

o   The antenna directivity polarisation of the radiated field.

o   The maximum hours of operation.

o   The call sign.

o   The location of the transmitting site.

o   The modulation technique.

If the Radio Spectrum Trustees were simply performing a registration function for radiocommunications operators (rather like a land registry), these specifications would be, at worst, an annoyance and, at best, a useful source of information to facilitate negotiation between network operators and equipment manufacturers proposing to alter their spectrum-using operations. However, many of these technical parameters are actually set by the Trustees, not the operators, and they cannot be changed without consulting the Trustees.

In assessing any proposed changes, the Radio Spectrum Trustees will be guided by the Radio Regulations which, as we have seen, are heavily biased against using the radio spectrum to reduce communication costs or to improve communication performance by spectrum-sharing methods that generate profit for their organisers, especially for private sector businesses and consumers.

In fact, many of the specifications set by the Radio Spectrum Trustees are not technical but economic in character – dealing with the allocation of resources to different users. For example, CB operators, paging operations, mobile operations and telecontrol operations all have to operate in assigned bands on a communal property rights basis. Where the costs of negotiating joint agreements between users on exclusive use of TAS packages (e.g. time-sharing digital message traffic or spectrum-sharing cellular radio systems) are low in relation to the value users place on their own communications, one would expect joint user associations to develop quasi-private property rights – effectively sharing scarce bandwidth allocated to them. Such co-ordination is forbidden: bandwidth must be shared in the manner prescribed by the Radio Spectrum Trustee.

User associations are recognised by the Radio Spectrum Trustee, but their scope of activities and the actual rules of their association are severely restricted. To illustrate, in cases where the State Telecom monopoly cannot establish service rapidly enough, land mobile user associations will be recognised. However, policy on land mobile associations:

o   Prevents any tie in an association with an equipment manufacturer.

o   Prohibits charges for message handling.

o   Restricts contestability of user associations by recognising one at most.

o   Requires associations to allow all interested parties to participate.

o   Gives the Radio Spectrum Trustees pre-emptive rights/eminent domain over the user association if the State Telecom monopoly enters to establish services.[21]

That so-called 'technical' specifications are deeply interwoven with the economic allocation problem is evident in the following Radio Regulatory Trustee's policy statement on co-ordinating spectrum for land mobile spectrum users:

'As the basic concept of this policy [spectrum allocation for land mobile services] is one of co-ordination it is necessary to understand that by this is meant co-ordination of frequencies, services, sites, power supplies, base stations, control facilities, etc., to ensure that the advantages of mobile radio telephone service are available to all who need it, as economically and efficiently as possible and without fear or favour.'[22]

Prohibitions on Harmful Interference to Other Users

The final dimension to spectrum property rights in New Zealand is often taken to be the *raison d'être* for centralised management: the control of harmful interference. The full regulation in para. 40 reads:

'The licensee of any radio station shall operate the station in such manner as not to cause harmful interference and shall comply with all such directions and conditions as may be given or made by the Director General from time to time for that purpose.'

Harmful interference is interpreted as

'any emission, radiation, or induction which endangers the functioning of a radio navigation service or other safety services or seriously degrades, obstructs, or repeatedly interrupts a radiocommunications service operating in accordance with the provisions of these regulations'.

---

21 Radio Regulations (1970), Pamphlet RT1, Radio Division, Wellington, NZ: New Zealand Post Office, 1976.

22 *Ibid.*, p. 5.

This regulation imposes a duty upon anyone using the spectrum, whether for communication purposes or not, to avoid uses of the spectrum that interfere with incumbent licence-holders. Enforcement of the regulation depends on whether the Radio Spectrum Trustee deems exclusive use desirable or not. In the case of sound radio and television broadcasting, navigational and safety uses, and certain fixed services, the Radio Spectrum Trustees will try to position other spectrum users in such a way that interference will be minimal, at least as far as policy is concerned. The Radio Spectrum Trustee does not, however, accept any responsibility, or liability, for maintaining interference-free conditions.

What Is Interference?

Many types of medical and scientific equipment, virtually all machinery that generates either heat or electricity, such as automobiles, household appliances (including radios, videos and television sets), industrial equipment, and electric lighting and transmission cables emit electro-magnetic radiation in a random fashion over a wide variety of frequencies. This energy is known as 'man-made noise'. Although it is a by-product of some other activity, man-made noise is a use of spectrum as a dumping ground for wasted energy.

As previously discussed, radiocommunications users attempting to keep their energy emissions within their allotted bandwidth may, period-ically or systematically, generate energy at frequencies outside their particular bandwidth or area. This energy is known as 'spurious emissions'. These two types of interference, man-made noise and spurious emissions, may be called 'pollution-interference' in order to distinguish them from the 'scarcity-interference' that arises when two users compete to use a specific band of frequencies in the spectrum.

Interference and Property Rights

Scarcity-interference, as we have seen, applies to any type of resource for which private property rights are not well defined. All other things being equal, the most efficient solution to scarcity-interference problems is to define decentralised private property rights in the resource and then to have institutions which encourage competitive market interactions between resource-holders. Communal property rights under government trusteeship and private property rights with monopoly ownership are alternative solutions to scarcity-interference. However, both are inadequate when compared with encouraging the efficient allocation of resources, as is the case in competitive market institutions based on decentralised resource ownership.

Communal property rights under government trusteeship, in particular, are woefully deficient (from an economic efficiency standpoint) in dealing with scarcity-interference. This type of property rights régime is not used as a basis for allocating the majority of goods and services (including

151

labour skills, capital goods, technological innovations, land, consumer goods, etc.) in most Western democracies.

On the other hand, competitive markets, based on well-defined decentralised private property rights in resources, do an efficient job of dealing with scarcity when property rights are well-defined and enforceable at reasonable cost relative to the value of the resources. Information about alternative use-values of resources is generated in the form of bids and offers; and buyers and suppliers have incentives to act on the basis of this information in ways that improve economic efficiency.

The Role of Prices

Prices negotiated between buyers and sellers play a crucial role in establishing the efficiency of competitive market allocations. (The term 'prices' refers here to the average levels and the dispersion of bids, offers and settlements, not necessarily a single unique price.) Prices act as an information signal. A high price for commodity A, due to a shift in demand from product B to product A, signals that at least some users of A find it more valuable than before, and relatively more valuable than B, whose price will tend to drop.

Prices also act as an incentive. Personal wealth can be increased by searching out price information, discovering that demand for A has increased, and transferring some resources away from supplying B, or C, to supplying more of A. This incentive tends to increase the aggregate value (the total benefit to users) of resources in the economy.

In aggregate, consumers and producers are better off, although some will be worse off. Suppliers, in particular, face strong pressures to satisfy the market, or lose business (and wealth). Resource owners can gain or lose, depending on how specialised their resources are, and how adaptable they are to new and innovative uses.

Risk-Bearing in Competitive Markets

Private property rights in competitive markets also help to allocate risks. It is risky to invest in resources that are highly specialised to the production of one commodity (e.g. copper wire pairs underground-engineered for low-quality telephone calls).

In making risky investments, some managers have more foresight than others, and some are just lucky. To protect specific suppliers from such risks, the risks may be shifted to users. Protecting a specific supplier against a loss often means protecting a customer against a gain.

Private property leads to a pattern of risk-bearing that tends to be efficient for a broad range of commodities: investments at high risk of being made obsolete by changes in demand or technology will have to compete for resources (finance, labour or capital goods) in the same markets as investments less prone to these risks. Usually there is a great diversity of opinion amongst owners as to whether any particular investment is indeed a high or low risk. Investment decisions (and the continuous monitoring they demand) are not left up to one agent, unless that agent happens to have a monopoly of the critical resources.

Implications for Regulation of Spectrum

Generating information about risks, and incentives to bear and share risks, is vitally important to radiocommunications, simply because it is an integral part of the very rapidly changing and growing electronics communications industry. Specifications of property rights in spectrum can make risks of failure appear too high. Or the chances of success in other areas of communication may appear to be higher. In either case the flow of resources into, or out of, radiocommunications is different from that required for economic efficiency.

This discussion of the role of individual negotiations, prices and the significance of risk-bearing for economic efficiency is critical for a proper appreciation of regulations against harmful interference. No one is denying that a TAS package is worthless if the chances are high that anyone can, through intended or unintended means, dump energy on to a carefully controlled (modulated) energy pattern. But regulations intended to reduce uncertainty may also have undesirable, unintended effects.

There is a certainty/flexibility trade-off in the definition of property rights in radio spectrum. Increased certainty that others will be prevented from influencing the energy patterns in the TAS packages of some incumbent licensed users is obtained at a cost of reduced flexibility in input choices for all users.

However, the certainty allegedly created by centralised rights restrictions has to be viewed in the context of the overall uncertainty faced by firms (and by policy-makers). This is the uncertainty as to the present and future expected probability distribution of wealth (net social benefits) from radiocommunications activities.

When technical change and growth in consumer demand are rapid and uncertain, centralised monitoring and enforcing of regulations designed to limit technical flexibility can increase, not decrease, the overall risks facing society. This is because any short-term gains in certainty from being able to predict the technical effects of one producer's radiation (by knowing that the inputs of other licensed transmitters are constrained) have to be traded off against longer-term increases in uncertainty about the outcome of the regulation game, wherein entry conditions, technological options and service offerings in the future are decided or foreclosed.

Net benefits from resource use (whether as increased income to a firm or increased income and user benefits to society) involve a complex chain of inter-relations between various quantities and prices of inputs at different stages of production and marketing. A reduction in uncertainty in one link of this chain does not reduce uncertainty about net benefits if it creates increased risks in other links of the chain. If the Radio Regulatory

Trustees were able accurately to detect and monitor the licence-holders, technologies and services most likely to generate the greatest economic benefits, and *then* adopt a policy of carefully controlling inputs and technology, economic uncertainty could be reduced by centralised input control.

In practice, the Radio Spectrum Trustees are in a worse position than direct market participants in gaining the relevant information to be able to judge the future benefits of the diverse technologies and service offerings in radiocommunications. Yet the Trustees' decisions have a direct impact on these dynamic technical choices as well as on the immediate question of pollution-interference.

Radio Spectrum Trustees also have much weaker incentives to discover and/or act on relevant economic information than direct market participants since their individual wealth is by and large unaffected by the risks they take when protecting incumbent users. A system of private property rights in TAS packages removes both of these problems (information and incentives), although it does require investments, both private and public, in monitoring and enforcement resources to ensure that significant property rights violations will be detected, reduced and stopped.

Also, riskiness from different sources aside, the mean of the probability distribution of wealth (net benefits) may in fact be decreased if demands and technology are changing rapidly and centralised regulation with restrictive licensing is used as a method of allocating scarce spectrum resources. Even if there is a reduction in overall risk (a point that need not be conceded), the cost in terms of reduced average wealth may not be worth it.

When Should Interference Be Reduced?

In general the Radio Spectrum Trustees' goal of minimising pollution-interference is uneconomic. Less pollution-interference is desirable (other things being equal). But in order to reduce pollution-interference, valuable resources have to be spent on detecting, continuously monitoring, and actually controlling pollution. These activities require resources, labour skills, equipment, organisation, finance, etc., that have valuable alternative uses. In other words, it *costs* to reduce pollution. This is just as true of radio spectrum pollution as it is of water and air pollution. A trade-off has to be made in terms of a little bit less pollution and a little bit more of other goods and services (the ones that could be produced by the resources used for pollution control).

As a rule, in problems of pollution control, the efficient level of pollution is positive (not zero), and it occurs at a point where the marginal benefits from further pollution reduction just equal the marginal costs of pollution reduction. Therefore, simply because mobile radio users and television broadcasters, for example, cause one another interference, interference should not necessarily be eliminated, or even reduced.

Moreover, if a new service (say, local digital radio transmission) were to be introduced and were to create interference for some incumbent broadcast users, it would not generally be economically efficient to minimise interference by denying the local digital radio operator a licence to operate. Whether pollution-interference should be tolerated or reduced, who should be responsible for reducing it, and what means should be taken to change its levels are all questions that depend on the relative benefits of services of different types compared with the costs of achieving those different levels of services.

Sometimes interference can be reduced by one or the other agent altering timing of transmitter power, transmitter station or repeater locations, direction of antennae, transmitter frequency control, spurious emission levels, antenna systems, the ability of the receiver to filter unwanted signals, signal polarisation, modulation type, message coding, moving to a different frequency band, and so on.

Each of these actions has costs, either directly in terms of resources expended or indirectly in terms of opportunities foregone. And each of these methods may be more or less effective in reducing interference. The relative efficacy and costs of different methods of coping with interference will vary from case to case, as will the value of interference reduction to the different types of radiocommunications users.

To discover the best way of dealing with pollution-interference, and even the extent to which it is worthwhile, requires information on the costs and benefits of alternative pollution-reducing actions. This sort of information does not simply consist of skilled engineering measurements that compare the effects on interference levels for different classes of uses, using all the different methods available. It also requires information on the benefits of interference reduction (i.e., the users' valuations of improvements in the message quality), as well as the opportunity costs of the resources involved in reducing interference.

Most of the resources involved in interference reduction – better receivers, better transmitters, new locations, skilled technicians, and so on – have prices attached which can be used (more or less imperfectly) to indicate how much their owners have to be paid for their use. And most of the alternative outputs which can be produced from these resources are managed on a private property basis, and have prices which can be used as a guide to the relative value of benefits to users.

One of these options, however – changing frequencies or altering bandwidth usage – has no explicit price attached to it. Moreover, radio spectrum trusteeship precludes anyone from owning frequencies and bandwidth in the radio spectrum. This differs markedly from the way in which agents own receivers, transmitters, software, labour skills, locations, messages, and so on.

Private property rights in TAS packages enable information about costs and benefits of pollution reduction to be generated and, at the same time, create wealth incentives for that information to be harnessed. Only if negotiation costs based on private property rights are prohibitively high is sympathetic centralised control likely to be superior to negotiations between affected parties. Even in those cases, price incentives (e.g. pollution taxes) may be better controlling influences than direct controls over inputs. The problem of pollution control in radio spectrum management is not just a technical one; at this stage it is primarily an economic one.

The Frequency Denial Method

The restriction against harmful interference forms the basis for the frequency denial method of spectrum allocation employed in New Zealand. The general features of this spectrum allocation technique are common in Western countries. Essentially the technique has two stages. The first stage lists all frequencies in a proposed block of frequencies and checks to see if there is a possibility of pollution-interference occurring, given existing radiocommunication assignments. If there is potential for interference, the frequency is denied as a possible allocation. The second stage examines the required spacing between potential new broadcast stations so that no mutual interference occurs.

How does this technique work in practice? In a decision involving the 88 to 108 MHz band the Radio Spectrum Trustees in New Zealand accepted this allocation method and indicated that, at most, two wide-area coverage and three local-area coverage FM broadcast stations would be 'technically' available in major urban areas in a spectrum package 11 MHz wide between 89 and 100 MHz. An expert submission by a radio engineer pointed out that in Sydney there were seven FM stations actually operating in a band only 9 MHz wide.

The submission explored four interference mechanisms accounting for frequency denials and found that 93 of the 140 channels which had been denied (representing about 4 MHz of spectrum) could be readily accommodated by a variety of methods. These could be achieved by, for example, a few people tolerating a little occasional interference, by installing cheap filters on some television sets, by recognising that some possible interference mechanisms were highly improbable given high television transmitter powers, and that terrain features (like mountain ranges) permitted frequency re-use in different areas of the country.

The submission concluded that the information fed to the computer programme implementing the frequency denial method was very conservative and therefore seriously underestimated the number of 'technically' available frequency assignments for FM broadcasting.

To put these comments in perspective, we should consider the more sophisticated frequency-allocation planning done by Haakinson at the

Institute for Telecommunication Sciences in the United States.[23] Haakinson estimated that by relaxing FCC rules on frequency assignments to take into account changes in transmitter and receiver technology, as well as terrain characteristics, the number of technically available FM stations in major US broadcasting markets could in most cases be doubled. Dallas, for example, could average about two stations per MHz (44 stations in total in 20 MHz rather than the current 21). This is significantly better than the approximate 0.5 stations per MHz in the worst-case frequency-denial approach (their best-case approach was about one station per MHz).

While Haakinson's research concludes by advocating that the FCC seriously consider changing its procedures in order to approve new broadcast stations, his research is also relevant to a licensing régime based on transferable emission and admission rights (or TAS packages). Suppose, for example, that Haakinson's study had been commissioned by a potential new entrant to the industry, assuming transferable rights (licences) in spectrum. The only 'approval' the new entrant needs to gain is from the owners of the spectrum rights that the incumbent broadcasters are using (these owners may or may not be the incumbent broadcasters themselves).

Information from spectrum consultants can be used to predict the effect a particular transaction in rights can have both on the relevant physical characteristics for redefining rights (signal strengths in areas and frequency bands) and also on relevant economic characteristics. If the new entrant wishes to have a large population coverage with an omni-directional antenna and is willing to pay accordingly for spectrum rights (and other resources), it may be possible to convince holders of the relevant spectrum rights to relax restrictions on the permissible levels of interference within their boundaries.

These rights holders are likely to agree to such a redefinition of their rights only if the new entrant is willing to pay more for exclusive use than the incumbent broadcasters. (Their calculation must also allow for a reduction in the price that the incumbent broadcasters are likely to pay for a smaller region of non-exclusive use.)

Alternatively, the new entrant can agree to modify the pattern of his radiation with directional antenna so as to confine interference to a smaller area (and population). Owners of the relevant spectrum rights would agree to negotiate such changes if the lost benefit was less than the amount the new entrant was willing to pay for those spectrum rights.

These insights raise fundamental questions about the information used in centralised methods of spectrum planning, particularly economically

---

[23] E. J. Haakinson, 'Proposed Techniques for Adding FM Broadcast Stations in a Major Market', *NTIA Report*, Boulder, Colorado: National Telecommunications and Information Administration, 1980, p. 30.

TABLE 2

PROTECTION RATIOS

	0 KHz db	200 KHz db	400 KHz db
CCIR Recommendation 412-1	45	7	–20
FCC	20	6	–20
Haakinson	2	0	–50

relevant information. Out of the myriad ways of reducing interference, which is cheapest in relation to the benefits created? Should interference be reduced in some areas and increased in others? If so, which areas? What basis in either equity or efficiency is there for protecting incumbent operators and consumers?

Protection Ratios

The frequency denial method of spectrum allocation used in New Zealand is even more conservative in its approach than the FCC approach criticised by Haakinson, since it is based on Comité Consultatif International de Radiocommunication (CCIR) standards. Table 2 compares the protection ratios recommended by the CCIR, FCC and Haakinson.

The first column of Table 2 shows how much stronger the desired signal has to be than an undesired signal broadcasting on the same frequency in order to receive the desired signal correctly (the unit 'db' is simply a logarithmic measure of signal strength). The higher the protection ratio, the smaller the number of sound radio stations that will be permitted in any block of spectrum. Using information available from FM radio manufacturers, Haakinson found that only about 2 db protection was needed (i.e. the unwanted signal had to be 2 db units lower in strength than the wanted signal for accurate reception). For medium-priced receiving sets (of the sort manufactured in the late 1970s) a protection figure much lower than either the FCC or CCIR standards was identified. These required protection ratios are very much a product of receiver designs – designs which are in a continual state of change. The protection ratio of 20 db chosen by the FCC was based on receiver technology of the late 1950s with a built-in safety factor of 12 db.

The second column of Table 2 shows that, according to Haakinson, FM stations broadcasting on frequencies 200 KHz away can be as powerful as the desired station without creating interference – no protection is required. The FCC and CCIR recommendations suggest, however, that the desired station should be 6 to 7 db units more powerful than an unwanted station broadcasting on a frequency 200 KHz away in order to avoid interference with the desired signal. Haakinson's analysis indicates that no extra protection is necessary if modern, low to moderately priced receivers are used.

Moreover, when an unwanted signal is broadcast at a frequency 400 KHz away from the frequency of the desired signal (third column of Table 2), the desired signal can actually be weaker than the undesired signal – 20 db units weaker using FCC and CCIR standards or 50 db weaker using Haakinson's standards.

FCC standards for protection against interference from these 400 KHz removed signals are too stringent because they are based on outdated receiving technology. By 1977, in a similar situation, high-priced FM receivers could discriminate against unwanted signals 85 db units stronger than the wanted signal. Furthermore, in 1975 low-priced receivers could still receive well in the presence of an unwanted signal 50 db stronger (on a frequency 400 KHz away). Only receivers of a 1950s vintage would have been unable to discriminate against an unwanted signal more than 20 db units stronger than the desired signal.

If the FCC's standards appear to lag behind technology, the CCIR recommendations are even worse. Yet the CCIR recommendation was adopted by Radio Spectrum Trustees in New Zealand. Moreover, in New Zealand the spectrum planning subcommittees giving 'technical' advice to Radio Spectrum Trustees claimed that receiver performance required more signal protection than CCIR recommendations would provide. Their suggested minimum spacing between FM broadcast stations covering the same area is 800 KHz.[24] In some cases they recommend even 1,600 KHz separations to economise on the costs of expensive antennae hardware used for transmitting signals from a common transmission site.

Protection ratio standards and the alternative methods (input choices) of dealing with interference are clearly crucial in centralised, trusteeship approaches to spectrum allocation. They effectively determine how many FM stations can be positioned in the spectrum and what the likely quality of signal reception will be in any given geographic area. It is clear, however, that receiver performance has been in a state of continual change in a wide range of price brackets.

Similar remarks apply to developments in transmission technologies and their prices. In the face of continuous changes in technology and prices, should there not be a continuous monitoring of 'technically available' frequency allocations? Information is also needed from the listeners' standpoint about the trade-offs they are willing to make for extra FM receiver quality and potentially more channels to receive. Information is needed from suppliers about the trade-offs they are willing to make between extra expense on transmission sites and technology, and the extra revenues available from additional channels, compared with profit opportunities elsewhere.

---

[24] Broadcasting Tribunal, *VHF-FM Report*, Wellington, NZ: Justice Department, 1978, p. 79.

Both these types of information are notably absent from the engineering critiques of spectrum planning in New Zealand and Haakinson's critique of FCC spectrum planning in the USA. Haakinson's study has many refinements that make it superior (from a spectrum planning standpoint) to New Zealand's, yet both are really implementations of the same philosophy – the one in New Zealand based on centrally managed property rights in TAS packages under the trusteeship of an administrative arm of government.

Reasons for Inefficiency in Spectrum Usage

It is also worth noting that Haakinson's research has been around for five years or more, with no one acting on it. The reason is, of course, as we have seen, that the trusteeship approach to managing spectrum creates no individual incentives to capitalise on the spectrum savings available by redefining and assigning property rights in spectrum. The problem is not merely 'conservatism' in the types of information fed to the computer programme but, more fundamentally, how to motivate people to act efficiently on the basis of available information.

If no one can reasonably foresee a chance of appropriating some of the benefits from improved spectrum productivity, why do it? Indeed, if incentives are not there, the only information about spectrum productivity will come from academics and other 'disinterested' researchers – not from teams of skilled operators, managers, financiers, and entrepreneurs who will ultimately be delivering the services.

Joint ventures between network operators and equipment manufacturers (with an opportunity to profit from their efforts) are behind the very costly and time-consuming research on productivity-improving technology in radiocommunications, as with NEC's research into bandwidth compression techniques for satellite television,[25] Tymnet's research into cellular radio systems,[26] and Dataradio's research into VHF/UHF improvements for mobile services.[27]

When spectrum is available at no cost it makes sense for individual radiocommunications users to use as much of it as possible, since it can be a substitute for other inputs such as superior reception and transmission hardware. Because it has a zero price, however, the agents obtaining spectrum from the Radio Spectrum Trustee substitute spectrum for hardware without taking into account the opportunity cost of their spectrum usage.

These substitutions are the prime reason for increasing channel spacing

---

[25] H. Kaneko and T. Ishiguio, 'Digital Television Transmissions Using Bandwidth Compression Techniques', *IEEE Communications Magazine*, July 1980, pp. 14-22.

[26] W. G. Swinton, 'Caravan: Experiment in Wideband Local Digital Data Distribution', reprinted in *A Collection of Tymnet Technical Papers*, McDonnell Douglas Network Systems Company, 1983, pp. 95-100.

[27] Data Radio Inc., *Dataradio System 4800*, Montreal, Quebec, 1986.

from 200 KHz to 800 MHz in New Zealand. An immediate opportunity cost of conceding to these demands for excessive spectrum usage is the programme variety that listeners give up by having fewer channels to choose from. Unfortunately, under a trusteeship system, the spectrum planners do not have to incorporate these opportunity costs into their decision-making framework.

In a régime of private property rights, spectrum planners would have to negotiate with TAS package owners to make sure that the spectrum in between broadcast stations spaced 800 KHz apart remained idle. But enterprising spectrum owners would discover, and increase their wealth by the discovery, that broadcasters (either through subscriptions or through advertising revenues) were willing to pay more for extra programmes, or perhaps that VHF mobile systems or digital distribution systems were willing to pay to use that spectrum rather than have it remain idle.

These wealth-seeking incentives of TAS owners mean that potential spectrum users would have to weigh up whether the extra costs of better transmission or reception hardware were more or less than the prices TAS owners were charging for use (or non-use) of the spectrum they owned. In short, the negotiations required to obtain use of TAS packages from their owners and the prices generated in that process would lead to allocations of spectrum (and spacing of FM broadcast stations) and other radio-communications resources that would tend to increase the value of spectrum-based communications. In the absence of negotiations, or explicit prices associated with 'denying' the use of frequencies in the frequency-denial method of spectrum allocation, spectrum will inevitably be wasted.

This is confirmed by the wasteful use of the VHF spectrum by broadcasting television in New Zealand. In the Wellington area alone, nine channels (each one 7 MHz in bandwidth – 63 MHz altogether) are used to deliver two different television signals. It is even alleged that a third television channel will be 'required' to use UHF channels (very few sets in New Zealand are equipped to receive UHF signals), since the 11 VHF channels (77 MHz in all) 'cannot' support three television channels. Such excessive use of spectrum arises because Radio Spectrum Trustees have neither information on opportunity costs of spectrum use, nor incentives to act on such information.

If, for whatever reasons, the government is reluctant to distribute property rights to individuals, a state-owned enterprise with private property rights in spectrum, charged with the task of getting a commercial return on spectrum, would at least signal to the BCNZ in the price it charged that such excessive uses are not worthwhile because they are too costly in terms of foregone income from leasing the spectrum elsewhere.

Radiocommunications users like the BCNZ, who use 'excessive' spectrum, are not the only ones who need to face up to prices for spectrum use. Radio Spectrum Trustees themselves tend to stockpile frequencies for future uses – that is, they hold these bandwidths idle so that in the future new uses will have a chance of getting access to spectrum. Since spectrum is a resource that does not deplete, this is extremely inefficient – valuable UHF frequencies, in particular, are held for possible future broadcasting uses with no thought for their opportunity costs in non-broadcasting uses.

In a private property régime, regulators would have to pay owners for such stockpiling. Of course, with private property rights, future broadcasting users would be able to obtain access to spectrum inputs in the same way as they buy access to programmes, capital, buildings, and so on – through markets. The only reason stockpiling is required now is because the current property rights system makes it prohibitively expensive to dislodge incumbent licence-holders.

ECONOMIC IMPLICATIONS OF THE TRUSTEESHIP APPROACH

Radio Spectrum Trustees are performing five different tasks in relation to the radio spectrum:

(i)   The protection of revenue sources and investments of state departments and enterprises, particularly the telecommunications division of the State Telecom monopoly.

(ii) The allocation of a specific scarce resource (bandwidth in the radio spectrum) amongst competing users and uses, both current and future.

(iii) The monitoring, control and co-ordination of pollution-interference problems between different users and uses of the radio spectrum.

(iv) The allocation of risk-bearing in relation to current and future developments in radiocommunications, telecommunications, computers and electronic data generation and processing.

(v)   The allocation of resource flows to, and the relative growth rate of, the information sector of the economy.

The evidence from this case study is that the system of property rights in radio spectrum inputs developed under trusteeship is performing the last four tasks inefficiently, and probably even the first one. This evidence is consistent with economic theory on the performance of state regulatory bodies in the face of rapidly changing demand and supply situations. Information about opportunity costs is not generated and incentives to use relevant information about opportunity costs in decision-making are non-existent.

There are alternative ways of handling scarcity of spectrum inputs, the allocation of risks in radiocommunications, and pollution-interference.

Assume for the moment that travelling electromagnetic energy can be sufficiently controlled or 'fenced in', in all three dimensions of a TAS package, so that pollution-interference is not a problem. Then the allocation problem is one of dividing up plots of TAS units amongst competing users and uses.

If private property rights were defined in TAS units and assigned unambiguously to owners, giving rights to exclusive use, rights to transfer between users and uses (by subdivision or combination, free of restrictions on other inputs), and rights to bear risks (of gains or losses from changes in physical and market conditions), then spectrum markets would emerge, yielding prices for TAS units. These prices would act as effective information signals, indicating the value of units of radio spectrum to different users or uses. They would also provide wealth incentives to transfer inputs to more valuable uses quickly (in response to changing market conditions), as well as to undertake risky investments in developing new radiocommunications technology or services.

For this favourable outcome of the allocation problem to occur, it must be possible to enforce the private property rights in TAS units at reasonable cost. In particular, owners must be able to identify trespassers and enforce their rights through normal legal and contractual processes. In the spectrum bands above 30 MHz, modern technology and engineering skills, low prices of electronic components and general respect for private property rights suggest that excludability could probably be enforced at reasonable cost in relation to the value of the resource. The impossibility of identifying and stopping *some* trespassers at reasonable cost is no more of a case against private property rights in spectrum than it is against any other form of private property (e.g. land, vehicles, houses or equipment).

The fact is that it is too costly to eliminate *every* form of trespass and theft, no matter what type of resource we are dealing with. Moreover, it is not the absolute level of costs involved in enforcing property rights that is critical. As long as the costs of enforcing private property rights are less than the value of the net benefits produced, efficiency will be increased. Enforcement costs may be high in radiocommunications, but the rapid growth and convergence of computing and telecommunications technologies imply that the value of the benefits created will be correspondingly high.

Radio spectrum trusteeship must give way to new property rights institutions and competitive markets in radio spectrum inputs. Instead of treating spectrum as communal property managed under the trusteeship of a government department, spectrum inputs ought to be treated as private property – even if that private property is 'owned' by the state.

Many economists[28] advocate the development of a system of freely

---

[28] John Fountain, *The Economics of Radio Spectrum Management: A Survey of the Literature*, Wellington, NZ: Department of Trade and Industry, 1988.

transferable ownership rights in TAS packages. A viable alternative to such an institution, possibly serving as a transition to a later, decentralised scheme of freely transferable licences in spectrum inputs, is the development of a state-owned radio spectrum management corporation, charged with the following tasks:

o   Developing a set of legally enforceable, clearly defined, privately negotiable TAS emission rights and responsibilities for licence-holders.

o   Treating the spectrum as a new frontier of development, leasing out TAS tracts to new sub-developers and users, as well as to incumbent licensees, on a long-term, non-discriminatory basis, at fees determined through public auctions (of the sort used by government for tendering access to import licences and offshore fishing licences).

o   Abandoning the current restrictions on sharing spectrum inputs or other radiocommunications resources and technology by licence-holders, apart from the initial restrictions or registered caveats concerning liability for spurious emissions in any of the three TAS dimensions.

o   Providing (on a cost recovery basis) a public spectrum registration and transfer function, and interference-monitoring and enforcement services.

The alternative – continued trusteeship – will perpetuate economic inefficiency in spectrum utilisation and development.

9

RADIO DEREGULATION IN THE UK

Mark Oliver

Deloitte, Haskins and Sells

BROADCASTING DEREGULATION and liberalisation in the UK is likely to begin with the radio industry. The Government published a Green Paper on radio deregulation in February 1987[1] which set out plans for the radio industry into the 1990s and beyond, and they have reaffirmed this in the broadcasting White Paper.[2] The approach in both these documents, whilst liberalising entry into the market, stops short of a totally free market and the establishment of true consumer sovereignty.

This chapter examines in some detail the proposed changes and the current UK broadcasting regulations and structure. It then presents an economic framework for radio broadcasting in the UK within which to judge the performance of the current system and the proposed changes. Finally, it suggests reforms which will extend consumer choice and sovereignty.

THE PROPOSED CHANGES

The Green Paper and the more recent White Paper have given a clear picture of how the Thatcher Government will deregulate UK radio.

The Government plans to establish three new national networks in 1990 using frequencies which have recently become available. These frequencies were previously used by the police and emergency services,

---

[1] Home Office, *Radio: Choices and Opportunities*, Cm. 92, London: HMSO, 1987.

[2] Home Office, *Broadcasting in the '90s: Competition, Choice and Quality*, Cm. 517, London: HMSO, 1988.

and also by the BBC before it moved its radio stations to frequency modulation (FM) and reduced simulcasting – that is, broadcasting the same programme on two channels. These new national channels are to be commercial and each station will have to produce a variety of programmes.

The Government also intends to establish a new Radio Authority to replace the Independent Broadcasting Authority as regulator. It will adopt a lighter regulatory approach to programme content, advertising and sponsorship for the existing independent local radio (ILR) stations, new national stations and community radio. Alongside this development, there are plans to facilitate the introduction of community radio stations operating low-powered transmitters within a 10-kilometre radius. These will be aimed at local and ethnic communities and will be allowed to operate on slim budgets and facilities, subject to regulations governing political bias and obscenity.

Finally, the Green Paper made it quite clear that the Government had no intention of telling the BBC how to use its radio frequencies; more precisely:

> 'it should remain for the BBC, not the Government, to decide how these public service broadcasting obligations should be met, subject to the resources and frequency spectrum assigned to the BBC'.

THE CURRENT SITUATION

Industry Structure

Radio in the UK generated revenue of £320 million in 1986. It accounted for 25 per cent of BBC expenditure and about 2.9 per cent of the total non-classified advertising revenue. In an average week in 1987, about 75 per cent of the British population listened to some radio and 44 per cent of those able to receive ILR listened for some part of the week. Research has shown that the average adult spends about 8.5 hours a week listening to radio.

The commercial radio sector consists of local radio stations financed by the sale of advertising airtime. To date, 57 ILR franchises have been awarded, although there are now fewer companies operating, due to a recent spate of mergers. There are 30 BBC local radio stations and four BBC national radio services.

There are two types of competition in the system: first, competition between commercial radio stations for the franchises; and secondly, between commercial radio and BBC radio stations for audiences. The commercial radio system and the BBC system do not compete directly for finance.

In the wider field of entertainment, information and leisure activities, radio competes with television and with home entertainment products

TABLE 1

BBC NATIONAL RADIO STATIONS' PERFORMANCE IN 1988

	Direct costs £ million	Hours	Costs per hour £s	Audience share %
Radio 1	21.7	6,714	3,232	27
Radio 2	42.2	9,012	4,683	19
Radio 3	42.7	6,811	6,269	2
Radio 4	54.0	7,625	7,082	12
Total	160.6	30,162	5,325†	60

Source: *BBC Annual Report and Accounts*, 1987.

†Average for all stations.

(such as records, tapes and books) for audience time and finance. Developments in these home entertainment areas can affect radio considerably. For instance, the increasing cost of television advertising time helped push up radio advertising revenue by 27 per cent in 1987, whilst the superior sound quality available on compact disc has led to an increase in the audio quality of radio broadcasts.

The BBC

The BBC dominates radio in the UK. It accounts for about 70 per cent of audience listening and has total costs of £245 million. Like BBC television, it is financed by the annual licence fee.

The BBC's four national stations each cater for clearly defined categories of taste: chart music (Radio 1); middle of the road music, chat shows and sport (Radio 2); classical music (Radio 3); and news and drama (Radio 4).

Between them, in 1987/88, the four national stations produced about 30,000 hours of output at a direct cost of £160.6 million, which is just over £5,300 per hour. As shown in Table 1, together they had a 60 per cent share of the audience (with BBC regional and local radio providing another 12 per cent).

Commercial Radio

Commercial radio in the UK primarily consists of the ILR network. In addition, there are a number of pirate radio stations and Radio Luxembourg which is soon to be joined by Radio Tara, broadcasting from Ireland.

The ILR system has about 30 per cent of the national audience, and its share has been increasing in recent years at the expense of Radio 1. Some of the ILR stations, such as Clyde, achieve almost 40 per cent of the local

167

TABLE 2

INDEPENDENT LOCAL RADIO PERFORMANCE MEASURES, 1986-87
(Ranked by Turnover Per Potential Listener)

Station	Population in total survey area 000s	Turnover 1986 £000s	Turnover per potential listener 1986 £s	Local market listening share %	Profit before tax: latest available year £000s
Northsound	310	851	2.75	39	172
Moray Firth	220	495	2.25	37	34
2CR (Two Counties Radio)	580	1,211	2.09	29	*119
Radio Clyde	2,400	4,457	1.86	37	916
Mercury	550	948	1.72	26	296
West Sound	360	578	1.61	39	*81
Plymouth Sound	370	591	1.60	38	*(15)
Red Rose[1]	1,270	2,003	1.58	22	435
Devon Air	500	731	1.46	22	†*(81)
Saxon Sound	220	317	1.44	13	*(50)
County Sound	750	1,060	1.41	19	*(71)
Essex	1,220	1,697	1.39	21	143
Capital[2]	11,740	16,043	1.37	16	3,943
Swansea Sound	540	730	1.35	37	114
Downtown	1,520	1,999	1.32	33	272
Orwell	540	705	1.31	13	*(43)
GWR (Great Western Radio)	1,560	2,031	1.30	20	*119
Hereward	830	1,069	1.29	21	*(70)
Radio 210	850	1,085	1.28	22	139
Southern Sound	730	918	1.26	16	*49
Broadland	620	757	1.22	31	173
Severn	460	559	1.22	24	48
Piccadilly	3,690	4,440	1.20	23	765

Note: Some franchises have turnover attributable to non-franchise activities; however, only in the case of London Broadcasting Company (IRN) were these a significant part of revenue.

[1] Turnover and population figures have been adjusted to eliminate the contributions of Red Dragon and Radio Aire from the Group.

[2] Capital and London Broadcasting Company are part of a dual franchise so direct comparisons with other stations may be inappropriate.

audience and are the dominant radio stations in their area. Table 2 gives details of audience share.

Table 2 shows that the smallest stations, such as Northsound and Moray Firth, produce the highest revenue per potential listener. (Potential listeners are the total population in the station's Total Survey Area as agreed with the Independent Broadcasting Authority (IBA).) Some of the large urban stations perform less well in terms of revenue per potential listener.

TABLE 2 (Continued)

Station	Population in total survey area 000s	Turnover 1986 £000s	Turnover per potential listener 1986 £s	Local market listening share %	Profit before tax: latest available year £000s
Mercia Sound	780	937	1.20	27	*119
Metro	1,770	2,107	1.19	33	541
Hallam	1,340	1,544	1.15	24	140
Forth	1,320	1,495	1.13	26	305
Tay	520	569	1.09	25	*(100)
Chiltern	1,450	1,495	1.03	13	200
Red Dragon	880	876	1.00	17	217
Marcher	570	564	0.99	20	38
BRMB	2,550	2,495	0.98	18	*159
Invicta	1,380	1,350	0.98	19	†*(63)
Signal	790	768	0.97	29	*46
Viking	790	736	0.93	29	†*(23)
Wyvern	520	484	0.93	22	*16
Radio City	2,630	2,385	0.91	27	356
Tees	1,190	982	0.83	19	92
Aire	1,300	990	0.76	19	152
Beacon	1,800	1,332	0.74	23	137
Pennine	1,090	784	0.72	16	*24
LBC (London Broadcasting Company)[2,3]	11,740	7,019	0.60	10	*202
Trent	2,600	1,428	0.55	25	*113
Ocean	1,270	n/a	n/a	25	335

[3] Includes income from Independent Radio News.

* 1986 figures.

† Company since taken over.

Sources: JICRAR, *Annual Report and Accounts,* IBA.

Until 1987 only a handful of ILR stations made a profit. These were mostly the large urban ones. With the 27 per cent increase in revenue in 1987, every station that has reported for that period has shown a profit, as shown in Table 2.

LESSONS FROM PAST PERFORMANCE

Big May Not Be Beautiful

An analysis of the ILR statistics on audience share, size of potential listening population and average household income levels in their franchise area suggests that both the average revenue and the audience share in a franchise are reflected in the turnover per potential listener. There is a clear negative correlation between size of potential listener population and turnover per potential listener. This initial analysis implies that a series of local radio stations in a given region or nation is of greater value to advertisers than a single national or regional station.

Although many of the smallest stations have the highest turnover per potential listener, the fact that costs are not significantly reduced in smaller franchises means that many have made losses in the past. Industry analysts have suggested that a region with at least 400,000 potential listeners is needed to make a profit.

The minimum franchise size is of course based on the current level of costs which is in turn related to the IBA's requirements imposed on ILR stations. Losses made by many small ILR stations have led to mergers and extensions of regions in order to share some costs even though the evidence suggests that this results in a lower turnover per potential listener.

Commercial News and Features Stations Can Survive

The figures for BBC's national radio suggest that radio stations devoted entirely to news and features programmes can gain a respectable audience share – about 20 per cent of the national audience. Even though costs per hour are about twice that of the chart music station (Radio 1), the evidence would suggest that commercially orientated channels might find it more profitable to establish a news and features channel than yet another music station.

This is confirmed by LBC (the London news station) which attracts 10 per cent of the London audience as opposed to the 16 per cent gained by Capital Radio (the entertainment station).

FUNDING AND EFFICIENCY

An efficient economic system provides goods until the marginal cost of supplying them exceeds the marginal benefit which consumers receive. Such a system should also provide incentives for the least-cost method of production, in order to maximise economic welfare. Systems which enable consumers' preferences to be directly registered with suppliers, and allow free competition between suppliers, generally achieve this aim.

Radio broadcasting, however, is a public good. Consumption by one person does not restrict consumption by another, so the effective marginal cost of supplying an extra consumer is zero. Thus programmes would be supplied until the marginal value gained was zero. And when the marginal value of a service is zero, then its price will be zero. An efficient system would seem to imply one that charged nothing and had no income.

Traditional Solutions and Consequent Problems

Traditionally the answer to this problem has been to create a situation where the marginal cost to the consumer was zero, but where income was raised either from a licence fee paid by all consumers, or from advertisers who valued the system because it gave them access to consumers.

Unfortunately, this has left us with radio broadcasting systems where the consumer has no direct way of registering his or her programme preferences. In the case of BBC radio, which is financed by the licence fee, programme choice is likely to be dominated by the preferences of radio producers or by government, and only very indirectly by the listener. With advertising-financed channels, programme selection is likely to be largely dictated by the advertisers' desire to maximise the target audience exposed to their messages.

Rather inadequately (and how can second guessing the wishes of 40 million people be anything but inadequate?), the regulatory authorities have tried to substitute their own responses for listeners' preferences. In doing this they have constrained the wishes of advertisers, programme producers and governments. And all they have achieved is the imposition of their own values which are only very indirectly linked to those of radio listeners.

In addition, in their desire to control the broadcasting system, the regulators have restricted the entry of new suppliers (either by take-over of existing radio stations or the establishment of new operations), and taxed existing suppliers' profits, both of which have discouraged least-cost production.

Three Points of Analysis

Before considering the costs imposed by the current regulatory system, three matters have to be considered carefully.

1. *Any change to direct payment from an advertising- or licence fee-funded system, where costs are independent of output, involves some loss of welfare to radio listeners as well as a gain.*

The demand for a given mix of programmes is shown by the line labelled DD in Figure 1. This shows the willingness to pay for the output of the radio station. Figure 1 shows that a movement from a licence fee- or advertising-funded radio broadcasting system to a direct payment system, reduces viewer welfare by the triangle XDL for a given level of funding (i.e. areas $P_1 0YD$ and $PX0L$ are equal). This 'welfare loss' arises since a number of households no longer listen to radio because they do not

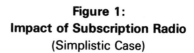

Figure 1:
Impact of Subscription Radio
(Simplistic Case)

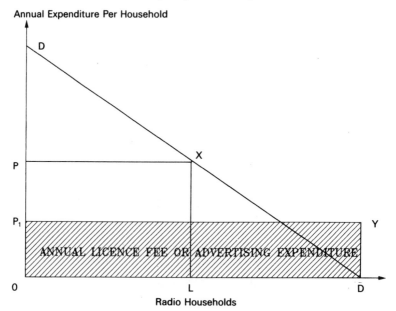

value the output sufficiently to pay the price charged. P_1 is the licence fee or the average advertising revenue per household and P is the subscription charge per household.

The imposition of a direct payment system is, however, likely to change the output of the station to one that is more in line with consumer preferences. This should move the demand curve to the right, as in Figure 2, indicating a greater willingness to pay on the part of each household. If $XX_1 DD_1$ in Figure 2 is greater than XDL, then subscription will have led to a net welfare gain.

In addition, if more competition were introduced on the supply side, either through a number of direct payment channels being introduced or by allowing the take-over of existing radio channels, then the expenditure necessary to produce any given output might be reduced. Thus a constant expenditure could produce more output of a given quality and again move the demand curve outwards.

Lastly, the introduction of a direct payment system for radio can be achieved only through the use of special consumer equipment which will block programmes from those who have not paid for them. This equipment will impose an extra cost on consumers. Obviously, the increase in household demand must outweigh the loss of welfare and the cost of consumer equipment if there is to be an improvement in consumer welfare.

Figure 2:
Impact of Subscription Radio
(Complex Case)

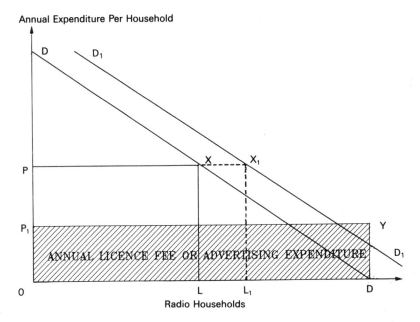

2. *The aims of advertisers may not be directly opposed to those of the broadcasting consumer.*

First, as the number of channels increases it will pay an individual broadcaster selling advertising airtime to target a specific audience which has value to advertisers rather than going for a small share of the mass market. A system with a large number of targeted channels is likely to reflect consumer value more accurately than one with a few mass-market channels.

Second, advertising does benefit consumers indirectly. It enables suppliers to provide consumers with information, thus cutting down the time spent by consumers finding the best products at the best prices, and it provides a forum for competition.

3. *Radio broadcasting uses up only small quantities of spectrum and costs much less than television broadcasting.*

Stereo radio channels take up about 0.5 megahertz (MHz) of capacity each. Compared with television, which requires 36 MHz of capacity, they are extremely light users of the radio spectrum. Radio channels can be on amplitude modulation (AM) or FM. FM provides a high-quality signal 24 hours a day and can be used for stereo transmission. AM radio is mono and has poor reception after dark.

The costs of radio broadcasting are far lower than for television. For instance, the BBC runs four national radio stations, 30 local stations and four regional services for about one-third of the cost of its two national television services.

THE ECONOMIC COSTS OF CURRENT REGULATION

Spectrum Usage

In the UK, broadcasting policy has sought to provide a service for all or nearly all the population. Achieving universality leads to decreasing returns as frequency usage increases. To reach the last 20 per cent of the population uses as much spectrum as the first 80 per cent. By using up so much spectrum, universality *reduces* the average number of channels available to listeners.

In addition, both commercial radio and the BBC have previously been allocated two frequencies. This has allowed them to simulcast, which has been extremely wasteful. Universality therefore restricts choice in some areas, thus imposing a cost upon these groups of radio listeners.

Programme Content and Quality

The IBA, which has regulated the commercial radio industry, is required to provide 'a public service disseminating information, education and entertainment'. According to the Broadcasting Act 1981, broadcasts by stations in each local area are expected to

> 'maintain a high general standard in all respects and in particular in respect to their content and quality, and a proper balance and a wide range in their subject matter, having regard to the programmes as a whole and also to the days of the week on which, and the times of day at which, the programmes are broadcast'.[3]

In addition, the Broadcasting Act asks for 'proper proportions' of domestic material and allows the IBA to request prior notification of programming schedules. The IBA can also require a minimum level of locally produced and oriented programming.

These regulations ensure that the IBA, through the franchising process and after, has a large say in the form and structure of a radio station's output. Whilst the desires of the IBA may reflect listeners' wishes, there is no certainty of this outcome. These programming restrictions are likely to impose high costs on the local radio company.

Copyright

Radio stations pay copyright royalties to two bodies: the Phonographic Performance Limited (PPL) and the Performing Rights Society (PRS).

---

[3] Broadcasting Act 1981, Section 2(2).

The PPL collects revenues for the record and tape industry whilst the PRS collects revenues for artists and performers.

PPL rates are currently being re-negotiated but at the time of writing stand at 2 per cent of Net Advertising Revenue (NAR) for the first year of operation, 3 per cent in the second full year and thereafter 4 per cent on the first £1,255,395 of NAR and 7 per cent on any extra NAR. PPL also restricts 'needletime' (playing of PPL records) to nine hours a day.

The PRS rates for stations with 25 to 75 per cent of their output covered by PRS are 5 per cent for NAR up to £1 million, 5.5 per cent for NAR of £1 million to £2 million, 6 per cent for NAR from £2 million to £3 million and 6.5 per cent for NAR from £3 million to £6 million.

The present near-monopoly position of these two bodies means that the radio stations have no choice but to pay their fees and impose an arbitrary limitation on the amount of music that can be supplied by a radio station.[4]

Transmission

The IBA has its own technical requirements and currently builds the transmitter system. Commercial companies such as Marconi have suggested that if they were allowed to compete they could set up the transmission system at a much lower cost.

Sponsorship and Advertising

The IBA has consistently prohibited sponsorship except under certain narrowly defined circumstances, thus limiting a potentially significant source of finance.

Advertising time is also limited to nine minutes per hour. Since audiences tend to be put off by excessive advertising it would appear that radio stations have their own incentive to limit the amount of advertising. The nine-minute limit therefore seems unnecessary.

Ownership

The IBA has a great deal of discretionary power over the ownership of stations, both through the initial franchising process and through the monitoring of subsequent mergers and take-overs. They tend to use these powers to limit the flow of funds into the industry by prohibiting certain investors, such as local newspaper owners and non-EEC companies. In addition, they effectively protect franchise holders from take-overs, especially hostile ones, which in turn reduces incentives for cost efficiency amongst the existing management.

The Continuing Role of the BBC

The BBC has been allowed to define its own role as a public service broadcaster, and since its radio monopoly was ended in 1973 it has

---

[4] This monopoly position has been referred to the Monopolies and Mergers Commission.

continued to dominate radio broadcasting. Its role as the only legitimate national broadcaster gave it an obligation to provide a variety of targeted services catering for most sections of the population. The BBC's presence in the more commercial markets of chart music and chat shows has, however, restricted the revenue potential and growth of commercial radio.

Conclusions on Current Regulation

The overall effect of the current regulatory framework seems to be to limit consumers' choice and impose high costs, especially on the commercial radio stations. Until recently, however, the limited availability of frequencies may have justified some direct regulatory control of commercial radio – due to the conflict of interest between advertisers and consumers because of the franchising process which had created a one-station local commercial radio market.

AN ASSESSMENT OF THE PROPOSED CHANGES

New Spectrum Usage

Moving the police and emergency services to another part of the spectrum will permit the use of two more nationally available FM channels and will substantially increase choice. However, dropping the universality principle could increase the average number of stations still further.

The choice of national channels, rather than more local ones, seems to run counter to experience in the ILR system (as shown in Table 2), which suggests that small stations generate higher revenue per potential listener than larger ones. In addition, the lighter regulatory touch promised by the Green and White Papers should make it easier for small stations to survive by reducing their costs.

Variety and Choice

The Government's insistence that all the new national franchises should have a variety of programming would seem to restrict any opportunity for advertising-financed radio to match consumer value. Targeted channels will enable advertisers to target audiences. And as the number of channels increases it will be in the interests of a commercial broadcaster to go for a minority audience rather than a share of the mass market.

The increase in channels is likely to be sizeable enough to justify minority programming, given the BBC's planned two new services and the opportunity for ILR stations to provide a totally new service by abandoning simulcasting.

Although a system with a number of targeted channels may not provide a perfect match with consumer preferences, it will provide a free service to listeners and facilitate the dissemination of market information and the competitive processes in the economy through the communication of product price and quality. In addition, by raising the total value of radio to advertisers it could produce enough revenue to justify the entry of still more commercial stations in the future.

In terms of the overall framework described in the first section of this chapter it could represent a significant improvement on the current system and the Government's proposals.

The Role of The BBC

The Green Paper proposals seem to support the BBC's own view that no matter what reforms occur in the commercial sector the BBC must continue to provide a full range of programme services. However, as some commercial channels would, if left to their own devices, establish channels with content similar to Radios 1 and 2, the Government should review the allocation of frequencies when the new stations have had time to establish themselves.

In addition, the allocation of more channels to the commercial sector at some future time would encourage the provision of minority-taste channels still further, and probably provide commercial news and sports channels to compete with the BBC's services.

Community Radio

The Government's proposals for community radio seem to be the most free-market orientated and appear to put consumer preferences above those of government, except in matters of political bias and obscenity.

RECOMMENDATIONS

The Government should allow applicants for the three new nationally available frequencies to decide for themselves the degree of national coverage and content of the new channels. Indeed, it should not restrict itself to three new services but instead allow applicants to bid for regions of coverage if they so wish. This will allow the market to decide the benefits of national services versus local services.

To create a competitive and free radio broadcasting industry the Government should:

o   Allow for the possibility of services becoming subscription-based.

o   Review the allocation of BBC frequencies as the new services establish themselves.

o   Significantly decrease the regulatory burden on the ILR stations.

o   End the monopoly position of PPL.

o   Establish community radio as soon as possible.

10

AMERICAN TELEVISION: FACT AND FANTASY

Raymond B. Gallagher

Director of Telecommunications Policy,
Sky Television,
London

INTRODUCTION

AMERICAN TELEVISION is getting adverse publicity in Europe. Implicitly and explicitly, both the content (seen as 'wall-to-wall Dallas') and the structure of American television (representing a market-driven, rather than public service, broadcasting philosophy) are maligned.

At the extreme, one gets the impression of American television as the 'Great Satan' of world media, representing the worst, most base, lowest-common-denominator programming. Its relatively free market is seen as a free-for-all, a crass search for profit at the expense of diversity, quality and an informed, culturally enriched society. Americans, despite having a quantity of television no one can deny (indeed, to some, *because* of this), are thus considered 'impoverished' compared to their European counterparts.

In Britain, such views are being expressed with unexpected force as policy decisions which will shape television's future draw closer, and as the stakes for vested interests grow higher. Indicative of this are the comments of a leading columnist, Simon Jenkins, in the *Sunday Times* (18 September 1988) that 'running a free market television company [in Britain] will be a grim, remorseless business, as it is in America', and accusing government policy-makers of

> 'dismantling a system that produces reasonably good television in favour of one which, *on every scrap of available evidence*, will produce incomparably worse television' (emphasis added).

In the very same newspaper, a full-page advertisement (placed by one of

178

the independent television franchise-holders) warned of the many threats posed by deregulated television and competition. Its message was explicit: 'The best way to make sure it doesn't happen here is to preserve the environment in which British television operates'. This echoes the columnist's judgement that British television 'has not been bettered under any regulatory régime abroad', and that 'We should leave well alone'.

With the 'wisdom' of media commentators and industry 'insiders' given such visibility, it is no wonder that this outlook has spread to form the general public perception of American (and deregulated) television. Consequently, there is a widespread belief – at least implicitly – that television must be controlled in many ways in order to serve the public interest – that is, to secure television's benefits, as well as to 'protect' the public from such 'dangers' as advertising and 'profit-seeking' companies.

Television Fantasy

Unfortunately, most popular opinion – and, less forgivably, much of that heard in the supposedly informed policy debate – is flawed by a distorted picture of both American television and the functioning of the medium in a deregulated market-place.

This chapter argues that many of the negative depictions of American and deregulated television (such as those listed in Table 1) are sheer fallacy, or at best half-truths, while others rely on vague or extremely subjective notions to establish the supposed inferiority or evils of the US system. Simultaneously, the strengths and benefits of America's relatively free television structure are usually ignored or obscured, as are the contradictions and deficiencies of public service broadcasting (PSB) in Britain.

The most damaging effect of the *mythos* of public service television, however, is not that it distorts the picture of American television. Rather, it is that the public is misled into accepting the 'virtues' of PSB and governmental intervention without public awareness of (a) the full range of costs imposed; (b) the additional television choice and alternatives foregone; and (c) the knowledge that many of the virtues of PSB are present even in a relatively unregulated environment. The pervasiveness of this *mythos* is due in part to ignorance, but also to calculated misrepresentation by vested interests.

It is essential to separate fact from fantasy, to debunk a number of prevalent assumptions about American television, and to question the standards and premises on which judgements are made, in order to promote more informed decision-making on the future of television in Britain. For virtually 'every scrap of available evidence' not only refutes the largely unsupported claims of the sort quoted earlier, but instead supports three contrary propositions – specifically, that:

1. American television features a greater variety of programme choice than anywhere else in the world. Not only does this include an

TABLE 1

COMMON FALLACIES ABOUT
AMERICAN/DEREGULATED TELEVISION

Programming

o American television is 'all the same' – a homogeneous output of bland, predictable sitcoms, police shows and 'wall-to-wall Dallas'.

o There is less 'serious' or 'high brow' programming than in Britain, e.g. documentaries, informational, educational, current affairs, cultural, and minority television.

o The greater the amount of commercial television, the more homogeneous and less serious the programme output.

o There is less diversity or genuine choice in American television.

News and local service

o Commercial television offers fewer news and informational programmes than public service television.

o Regulation is required to ensure adequate amounts of these types of programmes.

o American television is all network or national with little service to local communities.

o Commercial incentives and lack of regulation reduce localism.

o Strong commercial networks do not allow room for individual local or regional stations, which cannot compete.

Advertising

o There is too much advertising on American television.

o Commercial television is not free: viewers pay for the advertising in more expensive products.

o Without restrictions, stations feature non-stop advertising.

o Advertising revenue is insufficient to finance new channels or networks.

o There is inadequate finance to support local or independent stations.

New media

o Cable television is all 'second-hand' programmes and re-runs.

o Only a portion of the US has access to cable television.

o Except for new urban cable systems, most subscribers receive only a few additional channels.

o Fee-based services reduce the amount of free television.

Market forces and regulation

o Any benefits of the American system have come from government regulation.

o Regulation is needed to protect or further 'the public interest'.

o The profit motive reduces risk-taking; companies 'play it safe' rather than try anything new.

o Multiple ownership of television stations by the same company affects programme bias and restricts diversity.

o Regulation is essential to promote balance and fairness on television.

o Deregulation results in a reduction of public service programming.

o Regulatory authorities are benevolent and act in the public interest.

Other

o Americans view British television as the 'crème de la crème' and envy the PSB structure.

o American experience is irrelevant to Britain and Europe.

astonishing quantity and variety of entertainment programming, with more channels and longer programming hours, but also that claimed as the special province of PSB – that is, news, public affairs and minority interest television.

2.   Virtually all the benefits of American television – for instance, programme offerings, new technology and economic development – are due to market forces, i.e., competition and the profit motive. The corollary, supported by several decades of experience, is that regulatory efforts have generally inhibited television's growth, service to the public and economic benefits.

3.   America's relatively free-market structure serves the needs of a free society more appropriately than that of a highly regulated PSB system. It provides scope for more outlets, independent and controversial viewpoints, and local grass-roots service, with less opportunity for government abuse – in contrast to the paternalism, entry barriers and greater government role in PSB.

The 'mental map' of American television pictured by most people today resembles the first maps of North America created by the earliest explorers: so much is incorrect or missing that the picture requires almost total re-drafting. While it is possible here to re-draw only some of the most general distortions and blind spots, it is nonetheless hoped that even a brief glance at the American television landscape will dispel much of today's 'common wisdom' with common sense and self-evident realities.

TELEVISION CHOICE

Perhaps the simplest way to illustrate America's vast programme choice is a glance at Table 2, listing the 20 largest cable programme networks in the USA. It is difficult, if not impossible, to take seriously any claims of American television homogeneity or 'lack of genuine choice' with the presence of so many, and such diverse, television programme services.

Furthermore, these represent less than *one-third* of merely the *national* programme services available to cable television. There are, in fact, close to 70 national cable programme networks currently operating – *plus* more than two dozen nation-wide audio ('cable radio') and text-on-screen services – all delivered from a dozen private commercial satellites. Those carried on individual cable systems are usually supplemented by locally originated, and sometimes regional, programme services as well.

How can such choice be ignored by critics of American television? Apparently quite easily, in the first place, since viewers outside America have no exposure to these market realities. But even if evidence as to the actual quantity and variety of American television is discussed, criticism often reverts to a number of secondary or fall-back fallacies. For

TABLE 2

TOP 20 CABLE NETWORKS, 1988

(Ranked by Number of Subscribers)

	Video service	Programming	Date satellite service began	Category(a)	Systems	Subscribers (million)
1	ESPN, Bristol, CT	Sports events/programming; business news	9/79	B/A	17,000(b)	46.1(b)
2	CNN (Cable News Network), Atlanta, GA	24-hour news and special interest reports	6/80	B/A	11,000(b)	44.0(b)
3	Superstation TBS (WTBS), Atlanta, GA	Independent station: movies, sports, original and syndicated shows	12/76	B/A	12,635(b)	43.4(b)
4	USA Cable Network, New York, NY	Family entertainment and sports programming	4/80	B/A	10,100	42.0
5	MTV (Music Television), New York, NY	24-hour, all-stereo video music programming	8/81	B/A	4,590	39.4(c)
6	The Nashville Network, New York, NY	Country music and sports programming	3/83	B/A	6,100	38.0
7	Nickelodeon, New York, NY	Entertainment for kids	4/79	B/A	5,670	37.9(c)
8	CBN Cable Network, Virginia Beach, VA	Entertainment, family programming	4/77	NC/A	7,905	37.2
9	Lifetime, New York, NY	Information and entertainment especially for women	2/84	B/A	3,700	36.0
10	The Weather Channel, Atlanta, GA	Local, national, regional and international weather	5/82	B/A	3,200	33.0
11	C-SPAN, Washington, DC	House of Representatives and public affairs programming	3/79	B	2,700	33.0
12	NICK at Nite, New York, NY	Entertainment for young adults	7/85	B/A	3,860	31.5(c)
13	Headline News, Atlanta, GA	Round-the-clock half-hour newscasts	1/82	B/A	4,000(b)	30.0(b)
14	A & E Cable Network (Arts and Entertainment), New York, NY	Entertainment: series, theatre, film music, dance	2/84	B/A	2,500	30.0
15	The Discovery Channel, Landover, MD	Nature, science, technology, history, exploration	6/85	B/A	2,700	29.4
16	VH-1, New York, NY	24-hour video music programming	1/85	B/A	1,715	24.7(c)
17	WGN, Chicago, IL	Independent station: movies, sports, series	11/78	B/A	10,810(b)	24.2(b)
18	FNN (Financial News Network), Santa Monica, CA	Live financial and business news	11/81	B/A	1,850	22.75
19	FNN/SCORE, Santa Monica, CA	Live sports news and financial data	4/85	B/A	1,150	19.2
20	Cable Value Network, Plymouth, MN	Home video shopping	5/86	NC	1,730	18.5

(a) B = basic service; small fee/per subscriber paid by operator; usually no additional fee paid by subscriber. A = service accepts national advertising. NC = no charge to subscriber or operator.
(b) Includes SMATV affiliates as well.
(c) Based on A. C. Nielsen data.

Source: NCTA (National Cable Network Directory). March/April 1988. Data received from services; audio and text services not included; system figures have been rounded off.

instance, it may be claimed that, while these programme services do indeed exist:

o   only a small proportion of cable systems carry them; or

o   they are available only to the few Americans who have cable television in their area; or

o   the programming is in any case all 'second-hand' or 're-runs'; or

o   they are all expensive subscription services, unaffordable to most.

Or the 'last-ditch' fall-back may be used: that it is free broadcast television to which critics really refer when discussing the American market, since (they say) this is how most viewers receive their television, and it is this 'traditional' television service which remains an undisputed wasteland. I shall consider these claims briefly.

Cable Television

First of all, cable television is not just a peripheral part of the American television landscape. It is, in fact, the dominant form of television distribution in the USA.

Market size: Less than half of America's television homes now receive their television via broadcast aerials – as of August 1988, some 52 per cent were cable subscribers. Furthermore, cable television is available not to a minority but to more than four out of five American homes, and of those offered cable service, about two out of three homes subscribe – a total of 45 million homes.

While it is true that no individual cable system offers every available programme network, even the smallest of those listed in Table 2 is in no less than 40 per cent of cable homes. Furthermore, most of the 'Top 20' are in more than 70 per cent of cable homes and the largest are in almost every cable household. Network growth means that these figures quickly become outdated: the Arts & Entertainment network, for example, had gained another six million homes by September 1988, bringing it into some eight out of 10 cable homes.

Also, some programme networks, by their specialist nature, do not seek or expect to be carried on every cable system. Black Entertainment Television (BET), for instance, is less likely to be found outside areas where its minority audience is located. As at March 1988, the channel was, however, available on cable systems with more than 17 million subscribers (close to 40 per cent of cable homes), many of which are located in and around urban areas with a large minority population.

First-run programming: Claims that cable programming is all 're-runs' are clearly false. Most of the programming of news and information channels – e.g. Cable News Network, Financial News Network, Cable-

Satellite Public Affairs Network, Headline News – is not only original but live. These total tens of thousands of programme hours per year. Sports and premium film channels are also major contributors to new programming, the latter essential to the financing of new production for the cinema as well.

The more cable networks grow, generating a larger revenue base, the more they increase the amount of original and exclusive programming carried. The general entertainment USA Cable Network, for instance, has commissioned 24 original 'made-for-cable' movies which are to be premiered starting in April 1989; this is above and beyond the channel's current $250 million commitment to produce and acquire programmes never before seen on American television.

The Arts & Entertainment cable network, which offers 24-hours-a-day of distinctive drama, documentaries, performing arts and comedy from around the world, will co-produce more than 104 hours of special presentations and series in 1989 – an increase of over 60 per cent from its current level.

The Discovery Channel, which shows 18 hours a day of documentary programming in five categories – nature, science, technology, history and exploration – is also increasing its level of original and exclusive television output in America. Among its innovative programming in 1987, 70 per cent of which had never before been seen on American television, was the transmission of more than 60 hours of Soviet television in one week. During the Moscow Summit, the channel also carried the main Soviet nightly newscast with same-day translation for five days.

Fees: Cable television is indeed a fee-based service: in 1987 the average rate was $13.27 per month. In considering the value of this fee, however, critics and viewers would do well to take into account the number and type of channels Americans receive at an average yearly subscription of approximately £94 – less than the annual cost of a quality newspaper in Britain – on an optional basis, compared with those supplied for a compulsory licence fee of over £60 in Britain. As is evident, cable subscribers will find ample news, arts, documentary and cultural programmes considered an intrinsic part of PSB – plus much more.

It should also be noted that a number of programme networks do not charge cable operators a fee and can be received without a subscription fee via a home satellite dish. Approximately two million homes receive additional television this way, many of whom also pay for the 'scrambled' fee-based channels. Furthermore, some of these satellite programme services are beginning to expand on a free over-the-air basis via new low-power television stations.

Broadcast Television

If claims about cable television are so clearly fallacious, what of 'free' broadcast television? With more than 50 per cent of American homes on cable, some critics suggest that traditional television must be all the more impoverished. In fact, while cable and other new distribution methods have expanded the television choice of Americans vastly beyond that of traditional broadcasting, there is still a significant – and growing – selection of free over-the-air television, including local, informative, and minority-interest programming.

First, there are more channels. Whereas British viewers have a choice of four broadcast channels, more than 70 per cent of American homes can receive nine or more over-the-air channels. Viewers in large cities can choose from around a dozen. And lest it be claimed that this is the result of depriving other homes of any broadcast service, 97 per cent of American homes still receive at least five channels (*excluding* cable and satellite services) – more channels than Britain.

Besides more channels, American viewers can also find more hours of output on broadcast television than their foreign counterparts, and a greater variety of programmes at different times of the day – or the night. In New York, for instance, seven of the area's dozen broadcast stations operate 24 hours a day: the three network stations ABC, CBS and NBC; three independent television stations; and the non-commercial public broadcasting affiliate. Each night these offer a total of 28 hours of broadcast programming between 2 and 6 a.m., compared with four hours on ITV – the only 24-hour broadcast channel in Britain (and only since 1987) – and perhaps an hour on Channel 4.

To underscore the programme choice available on broadcast television, let us focus on the above stations solely between the hours of 2 and 6 a.m. on a typical week-day night (3 August 1988).

Among the 28 hours broadcast one could find a total of nine hours of purely 'informative' programmes: *Nightwatch*, four hours of news and current affairs on CBS; 30 minutes of local news on the ABC station; *Independent Network News*, 30 minutes, on independent Channel 11; and four hours of news, science, nature and other documentary programmes on the non-commercial public station WNET. To this 'serious' menu another 19 hours of entertainment programmes could be added, including three different films, several chat shows, a number of comedy and adventure series, and even a home shopping service.

Can there be any doubt as to which market offered the greatest viewer choice – and this in the middle of the night, and *excluding* the 35 channels of cable television available to New Yorkers?

It should be emphasised that the American television viewer is offered choice within as well as between programme types. In breakfast television, for example, New Yorkers could tune into three broadcast network programmes (as in most American communities), offering further viewer choice as to the presenters, guests, news and 'style' of the programme preferred – or any of the following non-network broadcast programmes at 7 a.m. on the same day as above:

o   *Good Morning New York* (local two-hour breakfast programme)

o   *Ohayo! America* (two-hour Spanish-language breakfast programme)

o   *Beverley Hills Teens* (cartoon)

o   *Sesame Street* (children's educational)

o   *Yoga* (health/fitness)

o   *El Tesoro* (Spanish-language cartoon)

o   *Success-N-Life* (religion)

o   *Cisco Kid* (western).

In terms of total programme output, the American television market adds up to a mind-boggling sum. Whereas the combined output of BBC1, BBC2, ITV (including TV-am) and Channel 4 totalled less than 24,000 hours during 1987, this was exceeded in New York by either the three commercial network stations *or* by the three 24-hour independent stations alone. Taking all New York broadcast stations into account, including another five which transmit approximately 18 hours a day, the total broadcast output in New York is around 95,000 hours per year – *almost four times* the amount of broadcast television available in London.

If cable television is taken into account, the total is several times larger. Subscribers to Manhattan Cable, for example, receive up to 35 channels, most operating 24 hours a day. Excluding the channels offering Pay-TV, the output of programming available in cable homes exceeds 250,000 hours per year.

Other Programme Comparisons

Innumerable additional programme comparisons can be made between the American and British markets, all supporting the vast choice that exists in the former, both within and between programme types.

The total amount of current affairs and general factual programmes broadcast on ITV, for example (14 hours 22 minutes per week on average in 1987), is exceeded by CBS television's *Nightwatch* alone (20 hours per week). To this can be added CBS's other current affairs and general factual programmes (including three hours per week in prime time), the output of all other broadcast channels, and such dedicated cable networks as The Discovery Channel and Cable-Satellite Public Affairs Network.

With regard to religion, one can find more than six hours of programmes – over 300 hours per year – on New York's broadcast stations alone on Sunday mornings. This compares with a total annual output of less than 200 hours on BBC1 and BBC2 (combined), and a total British PSB output of less than 400 hours annually. To the American figures can be added a variety of religious programming on broadcast channels at other times, several dozen full-time religious broadcast stations, and seven satellite-distributed religious cable networks.

Ethnic and racial minority tastes are served by a variety of outlets. For instance, more than 80 per cent of Hispanic Americans can receive at least one Spanish-language broadcast television station; some receive two. In addition, Spanish programming is carried part-time on other broadcast channels and full-time on two satellite-distributed cable networks. Cable's Black Entertainment Television network features news, films, musical specials, black college sports and music video shows 24 hours a day. National Jewish Television is another cable service offering cultural, religious and public affairs programmes for the Jewish community on Sundays.

Where there are sizeable ethnic communities one can find a variety of other specialist programming. During a typical week in August 1988, for example, New York television featured at least 10 hours each of Korean, Chinese and Japanese television programmes.

Educational and instructional programming on broadcast television is offered principally through America's 322 non-commercial public stations. On weekday mornings, for instance, approximately three hours of pre-school programmes alone (780 weekday hours per year) can be found – compared with ITV's combined total of about 314 hours of pre-school, school, children's informative and adult education programmes for the whole of 1987. As for cable/satellite services, there are two nationwide dedicated educational networks: the Learning Channel (20 hours per day), and Mind Extension University, offering college-level 'telecourses' for credit. Many individual cable systems also have local educational channels: in New York, for example, there is CUNY-TV, a 16-hour per day City University cable television channel.

News and Local Programmes

Table 3 provides one last important example of the contrast between American and British television choice, specifically in locally produced news. This has been chosen precisely because of the oft-heard warnings that local service and informational television will be threatened by a deregulated, commercial market-place.

How impoverished are Americans compared with the viewers of highly regulated and subsidised public broadcasters?

First, whereas London viewers can obtain locally produced news on two public service channels (ITV (Thames) and BBC1), New Yorkers can choose from five metropolitan-wide commercial broadcast stations alone (plus news on Spanish-language stations, public television, and cable systems not included here).

Secondly, the locally produced news available to Londoners on weekdays totals 90 minutes. On New York's commercial channels there is close to seven times this amount – some 10 hours of locally produced

TABLE 3

LOCALLY PRODUCED TELEVISION NEWS PROGRAMMES, LONDON AND NEW YORK

(Tuesday, 16 August 1988)

London[1]	BBC1 (minutes)	ITV (Thames) (minutes)
8.55 a.m.	5	
9.25		5
10.25		5
12.55 p.m.	5	
1.20		10
3.25		5
6.00		25
6.35	25	
10.30 p.m.		5
Totals	35	55

New York[2],[3]	WCBS 2 (minutes)	WNBC 4 (minutes)	WNYW 5 (minutes)	WABC 7 (minutes)	WWOR 9 (minutes)
Pre-noon[4]	10	10	[4]	10	
12.00 p.m.	30				60
5.00	60	60		60	
6.00	60	60		30	
7.00			30		
10.00			60		60
11.00 p.m.	30	30		30	
Post-midnight	30		30		
Totals[3]	220	160	120	130	120

Total Local News – London:	90 minutes (1.5 hours) on two channels
Total – New York:	750 minutes (12.5 hours) on five channels
(Less non-news material)[3]	600 minutes (10 hours)

[1] No local news is transmitted on BBC2 or Channel 4.

[2] Local television news is also broadcast in New York by additional Spanish-language and public broadcasting channels, by stations reaching only a portion of the market (e.g. Long Island), and by cable systems.

[3] New York totals include non-news material (e.g. commercials, schedule previews, public service announcements) before, during and immediately following news broadcasts. Actual news totals are estimated in parenthesis by deducting a conservative 20 per cent of programme time.

[4] Probably underestimated, e.g. because network breakfast and morning news programmes offer several 'cutaways' for local news bulletins; in addition, WNYW 5 offers a two-hour local breakfast programme, *Good Day New York*, which is not included in totals.

Source: Raymond B. Gallagher, from local television listings.

television news – after adjusting for commercials, previews and other non-news material in and around news programmes.

Thirdly, whereas most local news in London is in five or 10-minute bulletins, except for a 25-minute early evening segment, New Yorkers can view newscasts scheduled in segments of between 30 minutes and two hours. Furthermore, New Yorkers commonly have a choice of up to three competitive newscasts during the same viewing period; in London, no choice between locally produced news programmes is available at the same time.

Fourthly, as a percentage of total daily programme output, locally produced news on the commercial New York stations (after adjusting for commercials, etc.) ranged from 5 per cent to 12 per cent, with three of the five stations at more than 10 per cent of output. In comparison, locally produced news in London comprised less than 4 per cent of BBC1 or ITV's daily programme output.

And even more astonishingly, the amount of locally produced news on each of the New York stations exceeds the total amount of national news on the BBC, ITV or Channel 4 (in percentage or absolute terms), as well as the total production for all local interests (news and non-news) of virtually any BBC or ITV region.

If all locally produced New York programmes were included, as well as national news and public affairs, the American output advantage would be even more striking. To illustrate this: the Independent Broadcasting Authority (IBA) *Annual Report 1987-88* indicates that the proportion of 'informative' programmes on ITV (e.g. news, current affairs, Arts, religion and education) averages 32.9 per cent of output, excluding breakfast television (TV-am). Yet in America, several studies of television output during the late 1970s and early 1980s found that the proportion of commercial broadcasters' similar 'informative' programmes (classified as 'non-entertainment' programming) averaged between 29 and 32.5 per cent – only slightly less than ITV's present average, but still higher in absolute terms because of the larger number of American channels.

To give a more current example, my analysis of WCBS-TV (Channel 2) in New York, on a typical weekday (Thursday, 4 August 1988), indicated that approximately 43 per cent of the station's schedule (excluding breakfast television, to keep the figures comparable with ITV) was devoted to similar 'informative' programming. Furthermore, analysis of a typical Sunday schedule, when a larger amount of public affairs programming is usually offered, found some 13 hours or close to 58 per cent of the output (again excluding breakfast television) dedicated to 'informative' programmes. Both figures indicate a far greater proportion of public service-type programmes on the commercial American channel than on the highly regulated public service but commercial ITV.

MARKET FORCES AND REGULATION

The foregoing section strongly supports the proposition that American television, contrary to popular opinion, features more overall programme choice than anywhere else in the world. Furthermore, this includes both entertainment and non-entertainment programming – the latter often considered the *raison d'être* of PSB.

In absolute terms, the amount of news, current affairs, documentaries, local and minority interest television is staggering – totalling tens of thousands of hours per year. Lest it be claimed that this programming is the result of regulatory requirements, however, the purpose of this section is to state unequivocally that virtually all are provided by market-place forces, that is, consumer demand, competition and the profit motive.

Television Deregulation and the Public Interest Myth

By and large, American television is no longer looked at in a pre-ordained fashion, whereby its role, function and content are determined by government or a distanced élite who decide what is good for the public or what is the best use of the medium. While traditional broadcasters are in fact still licensed to serve 'the public interest, convenience or necessity' (deflating the other myth that American television is a totally unregulated free-for-all), it is increasingly recognised that the public interest standard is meaningless outside the normal mechanisms of the market-place, where the *actual* interests and needs of viewers are usually best perceived and served by competitive entrepreneurial venturing.

Several decades of experience confirm that regulatory efforts have generally inhibited television's growth, service to the public and economic benefits – whereas freeing market forces has encouraged innovation, the expansion of services, and consumer choice. Furthermore, this experience is highly relevant to Britain, where many of the myths heard today about market forces and deregulation are exactly the same as were heard – and subsequently exploded – in the USA.

The Cable Fable

Cable television is perhaps the best example of inhibitory regulatory intervention. For many years the growth of this service was restricted by the Federal Communications Commission (FCC). First, the FCC imposed a protectionist policy in response to broadcasters who claimed that competition would hurt their finances, and thereby their ability to provide public interest services such as news, public affairs and local programming. Similar claims were made by public service broadcasters in Britain.

Secondly, when the authorities did allow cable to expand they imposed more of a development policy, imbuing the medium with a variety of technological and service requirements to serve their now-expanded vision of the public interest in a 'wired nation' and a 'television of abundance'. But virtually every regulatory requirement, where it was unrelated to what the market-place would have provided without intervention, slowed cable's progress. In America this became known as the 'cable fable'. Similar results are seen today in Britain, where cable's failure to take off is wrongly blamed on industry or lack of demand, rather than on government's still-restrictive requirements.

Only in the 1970s did it become widely recognised in America that no one, and particularly policy-makers, could forecast the rate of development of new communications technology or viewers' evolving interests, and that regulation usually hindered the far more efficient operation of the market-place in offering innovation and choice. For example, it was the unanticipated synergy of developments like deregulated cable, satellites and Pay-TV that brought forth a greater (and swifter) diversity of services than was ever thought possible, or could have been planned and implemented by regulators defining the public interest.

From the mid-1970s to the present, detailed and systematic examination of the market-place has shown that many key regulatory assumptions in American television have in fact been false, based (in the FCC's words) on 'prognostication, not empirical proof'.[1] On the basis of a 'full and persuasive record', the FCC subsequently began to open up new distribution technologies and deregulate traditional broadcasting.

Programming Requirements

In 1984, for example, the FCC eliminated guidelines for local, informational and non-entertainment programming on broadcast television. Its detailed studies of broadcasting stations' performance showed not only that broadcasters had exceeded regulatory guidelines by a wide margin, but also indicated that these regulations had no impact on the levels of news and public affairs programming in the first place.

Similarly, before loosening controls on the number of broadcast stations a single entity could control, the FCC examined the long-held premise that this would reduce local service and a 'diversity of viewpoints' in the market. It found that:

> '[there is] no evidence that stations which are not group-owned better respond to community needs, or expend proportionately more of their revenues on local programming, or editorialize more frequently on subjects of local interest, or procure more news, investigative journalism, or issue-oriented programming'.[2]

Indeed, the FCC noted that:

---

[1] 100 FCC 2d, Report and Order in Gen. Docket No. 83-1009, Adopted 26 July 1984, Released 3 August 1984, p. 24, paras. 20 and 21.

[2] *Ibid.*, p. 35, para. 53.

'the uncontroverted evidence contained in the record indicates that group-owned stations do not impose monolithic viewpoints on their various holdings. To the contrary, we noted that the economics of each local market require autonomous decisions by each station with respect to its editorial judgement'.[3]

Furthermore, it was shown that multiple television station owners have larger news staffs, do more news programming, and are perceived by community leaders as providing greater validity and depth of news coverage, and better-quality programmes. Rather than the profit motive favouring short-term gain, it indicated that broadcasters' reputation for service is essential to their long-term economic stability.

After Deregulation

These conclusions are supported by research after deregulation. About 90 per cent of America's commercial broadcasters have local news operations, including small markets with far fewer homes than any BBC or ITV region. Of those stations without local news, many are independents operating in markets where there is already a plethora of news.

In summarising the results of a survey on the effects of news and public affairs deregulation, for instance, the Radio Television News Directors Association (RTNDA) stated unequivocally that:

'The majority of ... stations in markets of all sizes are going ahead with news and public affairs largely as they did before deregulation gave them the opportunity to cut back. They were making creditable efforts then and are doing so now, not because of regulation's presence or absence, but because high-quality news and public affairs usually pays off in goodwill and allegiance by the public and by the advertisers. It's good business.'[4]

The 'good business' of news is underscored by another RTNDA survey in 1986 which found that only 10 per cent of commercial television stations were losing money on their news operations. Even in the smallest markets, only 15 per cent were losing money, while in the largest markets none were. More significantly it found that:

'the larger the news staff, the more likely was a television station to be making money on news ... Saving money by getting by with a minimal television news staff does not appear the way to [profitability] in the majority of cases ... One way to lose money on news may be to try to hold down overheads with a staff that's disproportionately small for the market'.[5]

Service continues to grow: in 1987, for instance, the number of

---

[3] 100 FCC 2d, Memorandum Opinion and Order in Gen. Docket No. 83-1009, Adopted 19 December 1984, Released 1 February 1985, p. 83, para. 21.

[4] *RTNDA Communicator*, April 1987, p. 11.

[5] *RTNDA Communicator*, March 1987, p. 9.

television stations featuring one hour or more of locally produced news between 4 and 7 p.m. grew to a total of 249 – up from 236 stations the previous year.

In short, American experience has shown that much of what is considered public service programming does *not* depend on regulation for its existence at all. A great deal of this programming is offered even in a relatively unregulated market because there is an actual (and, usually, profitable) demand for such programmes, and because even where there is no immediate pay-off it is still in the long-term interests of a broadcaster to establish a good reputation for service and seek the goodwill and allegiance of its community.

Competition and Innovation

American communications policy today is directed towards opening up as many television distribution outlets as the market can support, with minimum governmental interference. Among these outlets are traditional broadcasting, cable television, low-power television, single and multi-channel microwave distribution systems, satellite master antenna systems and direct-to-home satellite services. The aim of policy-makers is not to force development of television technologies or services in a preconceived fashion, or to guarantee their success, but simply to free the workings of the market-place.

In this market-place, where barriers to competition and market entry have been removed, each new television entrant must offer viewers something of increased value in order to prosper. For example, new services must offer alternative programme choice, or a larger quantity or quality of already-favoured programmes, or television service at a lower cost, with better value-for-money, or with greater convenience than existing services.

Essentially, the profit motive induces each service provider to assess the actual and evolving demands and interests of the public, and to judge how efficiently these requirements are being met by others. Consequently, competition drives companies to identify and serve previously unrecognised or under-served needs, or to do a better job of satisfying existing ones.

A substantial record supports the technological, economic and consumer choice benefits of the American television market structure, as well as the considerable vision and risk-taking of entrepreneurs in introducing new and competitive services. It is because of these factors that cable television is no longer a peripheral part of the market and has grown from revenues of around $970 million in 1976 to an estimated $12 billion in 1988 – despite the fact that many people initially judged the idea of satellite programme distribution as insane. These factors also explain why cable advertising has grown from only $58 million in 1980 to around $1.5 billion in 1988. And services such as home shopping channels, non-existent anywhere at the time Channel 4 was launched in Britain, accounted for more than $1 billion in 1987 (some 10 per cent of all cable revenues), and are still growing rapidly.

The list goes on and on, and the benefits of the market can be seen not just in the 'new' television media but in the 'old' as well. Much of the expansion and improvement of American broadcast services (e.g. 24-hour schedules and increased news) is due to increased competition from cable and from new broadcast channels. These have spurred long-established and otherwise complacent participants to ensure that their service continues to offer value to viewers – knowing that if they do not, the competition will.

The productive effects of competition on viewer choice have also been seen in Britain, but only to the very limited – and largely artificial – extent that competition has been allowed – e.g. changes in the BBC after the introduction of ITV, and the development of breakfast television and Channel 4. However, there are many improvements and choices which have not developed in such a protected market. For instance, it does not occur to the average British viewer that breakfast television, 24-hour broadcasting, additional channels, more local television and so on would probably have been offered for many years now in a more open market. They are the unwitting victims of protectionist policies and the public service myth.

In contrast, American viewers are today less fooled – and broadcasters less protected – by public interest myths, or by claims that there is no demand or inadequate financial support for new services. Assertions that 'the market cannot support' such and such a development, when made either by those who face competition from it, or by those who wish to impose their own public service vision on the industry, are – when accompanied by a call for restrictions or service requirements – seen as the self-serving and irrelevant remarks they usually are. American experience has shown how entrepreneurs can create markets and tap unknown demand.

Independent Television

A prime example of this is the growth of independent commercial television stations, unaffiliated to the three major broadcast networks. The 1980s have seen a dramatic growth in these broadcast outlets, even with or despite the American cable and satellite boom. Some 320 independent stations are now in operation, around double the number at the beginning of the decade. In fact, between 1981 and 1986 at least 20 – and up to 34 – new stations were launched each year.

Independent television stations operate in more than 130 US markets, with as few as the 29,000 television homes of Ottumwa, Iowa. Many cities have several competing independents – including three markets (Los Angeles, San Francisco and Boston) which feature 11 each, in addition to their other channels. Revenue from America's independent stations – now more than $2.5 billion a year – is expected to grow to more than $6 billion by 1996. Furthermore, around 50 per cent of this comes from purely local advertising, such as restaurants, food and furniture shops, car dealers, builders and estate agents.

In Britain the prospect for even remotely similar economic growth in television is unlikely in the foreseeable future. Current proposals for just a fifth broadcast channel face an atmosphere of scepticism (there are, for instance, questions about whether there is 'sufficient' advertising finance), public service and development requirements, and political compromise (rather than demand-based criteria) as to the role and function of the service. Furthermore, rapid growth and innovation are less likely to occur in Britain to the extent that services, new or old, are unable to evolve freely within the market-place, or allowed to face the risk that goes with innovation and competition: the possibility of failure.

As previously noted, there is no guarantee of success in the American television market. A few independent television stations have indeed failed, and there has been some consolidation in the industry; similarly, a number of cable services have been unsuccessful. Yet even the failures have offered important lessons for successors, and the end-result is still a relatively expanded choice of television services.

Successes and failures in the market-place have also offered, and continue to offer, the best opportunity to discover which services individual consumers objectively value, based on the viewing time and/or finances they devote to the alternatives – in an environment where there are few barriers to the introduction of new and competitive services. Service thus reflects what the public clearly desires, instead of what is specified (or prohibited) by regulators or public appointees. In the words of Mark Fowler, a former Chairman of the FCC: 'The public's interest, then, defines the public interest'.[6]

TELEVISION IN A FREE SOCIETY

Far from impoverishing its citizens, America's relatively free-market television structure serves the needs of a free society far more appropriately than that of a highly regulated PSB system like Britain's. The former provides scope for more television outlets, local grass-roots service, independent programming decisions, few barriers to entry, alternative news sources and press rights to express controversial viewpoints, with far less opportunity for governmental manipulation of the medium – in contrast to the paternalism, entry barriers and greater governmental role in PSB.

Television Outlets

Britain's television allocation policies have created both an artificial scarcity of television outlets and (except for ITV to some extent) an

---

[6] *Texas Law Review*, Vol. 60: 207, 1982, p. 210.

unnecessarily powerful centralised structure. This has given individual television channels more social influence than is desirable – especially compared with other media – and reduced the number of media 'voices' otherwise available in a free society.

The American public, in contrast, has access to far more television outlets than daily newspapers, not just within an individual community (as previously described) but in terms of the nation's collective 'media voices' as well. Close to 1,400 individual broadcast stations are licensed on a local market basis, with more than 250 others approved. Furthermore, there are an almost equal number of new low-power television stations licensed – some 1,700 – with around 400 already on air. The latter, broadcasting to a smaller market radius, could eventually total 4,000 individual outlets.

More than 8,000 individual cable systems serve over 23,000 American communities, with hundreds more approved. In addition, there are single- and multi-channel microwave television systems being licensed on a local market basis, and nine firms have been authorised to provide direct broadcast services for small dish reception by the mid-1990s, each of them planning between eight and 32 channels of television service.

Market Entry

There are few barriers to entry in the American television market compared with Britain's. Religious organisations, racial and ethnic minorities, and other groups may – and do – own and operate their own television services, and these opportunities are increasing with the growth of such outlets as low-power television.

Britain's artificially scarce television outlets, on the other hand, make it difficult for, say, the nation's West Indian or Asian minorities to control their own broadcast service (unlike Hispanic Americans, for instance). These groups must, therefore, generally rely on programmes offered and controlled by public service broadcasters, to serve their interests. From an American perspective, it is also antithetical to a free society that religious entities are actually prohibited from owning a television station or cable system in Britain.

Local Grass-roots Service

The transmission of all but direct satellite services on a local market basis allows far greater potential for grass-roots service and local responsiveness in American communities than is allowed in Britain. As previously discussed (above, pp. 187-189), this capability is used extensively for such programming as locally produced news.

Responsiveness to local interests, however, does not have to mean the provision of locally produced programming. Local demand may be even greater for bought-in programmes, broadcast network or satellite trans-missions, or even subscription television service. The American market structure, however, focusses the assessment of local needs at far more of a grass-roots level than in Britain, with service providers aware that competitors will continually seek to identify unserved or under-served local needs.

American broadcast stations are located in more than 200 separate geographic markets, many of which are far smaller than the 12 to 14 regions the BBC and ITV each serve. In fact, close to 60 of America's broadcast television markets serve fewer than 100,000 homes – excluding even smaller low-power television communities. Cable operators must also assess which services are of interest to the public at a far smaller community level; around half (over 4,000) of the nation's cable systems actually serve fewer than 1,000 subscribers, while not even 15 per cent serve more than 10,000 subscribers.

With only two channels (BBC1 and ITV) offering limited local (in fact regional) programming in Britain, and neither having to compete for finance (each having a respective monopoly of the licence fee and advertising), it is questionable how developed service to British communities really is. Indicative of this is the relatively small difference in local output between the commercial television regions in Britain. The smallest region – the Channel Islands – featured over five hours per week for its 120,000 viewers in 1987, whilst the largest – London – offered just over 7.5 hours per week for the same period, but for almost 10.5 million (87 times as many) viewers.

Independent Programming Decisions

American television stations, contrary to much myth, are not controlled by the commercial broadcast networks (ABC, CBS and NBC). These companies are in fact limited to a maximum of 12 individual stations with no more than 25 per cent of the nation's television homes. The majority of the stations which carry their programmes (around 200 for each network) do so on a voluntary commercial basis. Furthermore, they are free to supplement (or pre-empt) the network schedule for locally produced or bought-in programmes, to switch affiliations, or to act as free independents (as more than 300 other broadcast stations do).

The programming decisions of American broadcasters are therefore independently derived and made on the basis of local needs and market forces. In contrast, Britain's public service broadcasters are required to serve the government's (or its appointees') vision of the public interest in television, with requirements for programming categories, approval of schedules and so on, and little competition. It is virtually impossible for a BBC or ITV region to opt out in order to serve its public on a similarly independent basis.

Alternative News Sources

Local news has been well documented above. At the national level, the provision of television news in Britain has been a government-created duopoly of the BBC, for its two channels, and Independent Television News (ITN), for ITV and Channel 4. In America there are far more alternative sources of news, as befits a free society: the news divisions of ABC, CBS and NBC; Independent Network News (INN), available on more than 100 independent stations; news on the Public Broadcasting Service; plus such 24-hour cable and satellite services as Ted Turner's Cable News Network (CNN) and Headline News, the Financial News Network (FNN), the Cable-Satellite Public Affairs Network (C-SPAN), and NBC's forthcoming Consumer News and Business Channel (CNBC).

C-SPAN offers two entire channels providing live coverage of the US House of Representatives and the US Senate, as well as other public affairs programmes and election coverage without parallel in Britain. In contrast to British audiences' limited exposure to their nation's political process, particularly at grass-roots level, Americans have this year been able to follow the full spectrum of developments, from local events (like the Iowa Democratic Steak Fry) to round-the-clock convention and election day coverage.

The Electronic Press

In America, television is increasingly considered as part of the electronic press, whose function is identical with that of the printed press. Its relatively free-market structure makes it but one of many outlets in a vast 'information market-place' which includes not only the aforementioned television distribution systems, but also other electronic media such as radio, home video and cinema, as well as the vast spectrum of print publishing. Together, these thousands of information sources compete for the attention of the public and contribute to the 'intellectual market-place'.

While each of these information sources has different technological and economic characteristics, there is agreement that the public does patronise a variety of outlets and, if dissatisfied with one, can always turn to – or, in America, even initiate – another. Commercial broadcasters are not considered unaccountable since they must provide a reputable service to their audiences, compete with other media and receive constant public criticism.

'Fairness Doctrine'

For these reasons, American broadcasters today have almost the same leeway as the printed press in making their own editorial judgements as to the mix of information, entertainment and advertising provided. This was even extended to the coverage of controversial issues on television in 1987 when the FCC eliminated the 'fairness doctrine', which had required coverage of controversial issues of interest in communities and obligated broadcasters to air contrasting viewpoints on any such issue already covered.

After more than 30 years of experience with this regulation the FCC found that it had the opposite effect: it inhibited the discussion of controversial issues on television, and the 'fear of governmental sanction resulting from the doctrine' created 'a climate of timidity and fear', which deterred the coverage of controversial programming.[7]

This 'chilling effect' was underscored by cases of governmental abuse, whereby officials in several presidential administrations attempted to quell the dissemination of what they viewed as 'extreme' commentary on television, and where many broadcasters – especially small ones – chose not to cover tough local issues for fear of not satisfying the government's judgement of 'balance'.

In responding to those who voiced concern about protecting the public interest from the 'private interests of broadcasters', the FCC noted that critics

'simply fail to understand ... that the public's interest in a diversity of information and viewpoints is promoted *most* when broadcasters are free to cover controversial issues of public importance without fear of subsequent governmental intervention'.[8]

As a US Supreme Court Justice noted, the concept of fairness is 'too fragile to be left to government bureaucrats to accomplish'.[9] The FCC also noted that partisan debate is essential in a democracy, and that it is vehement and robust debate which best serves the search for truth.

In the same vein, Supreme Court Justice Byron White stated that, while the press is not always accurate or responsible, and may not present full and fair debate on public issues:

'society must take the risk that occasionally debate on vital matters will not be comprehensive and that all viewpoints may not be expressed ... Any other accommodation – any other system that would supplant private control of the press with the heavy hand of government intrusion – would make the government the censor of what the people may read and know'.[10]

It is in this, perhaps more than any other, context that America's television market structure serves the needs of a free society more appropriately than that of a highly regulated PSB system. Indeed, it is questionable to what extent the latter can present controversial issues which challenge those who grant broadcasters' licence fees and monopoly franchises in the first place.

It is difficult to envision, say, a Watergate (or Irangate) being pursued with such vigour by the television media in Britain, where public service broadcasters have constantly been subjected to inhibiting criticism and

---

[7] *Syracuse Peace Council v. Television Station WTVH Syracuse*, 2 FCC Rcd at 5052.

[8] Memorandum Opinion and Order in Docket No. 83-131, Adopted 24 March 1988, Released 7 April 1988, footnote 57.

[9] *CBS v. DNC*, 412 US at 145-46 (Stewart, J., concurring).

[10] *Miami Herald Publishing Co. v. Tornillo*, 418 US 241, 260 (1974) (White, J., concurring).

reporting restrictions – and, in the case of the BBC, even had staff 'vetted' by the government security services. Similar governmental intervention would be extremely difficult in the American television market today, with broadcasters' increased independence and multiplicity of outlets.

Furthermore, local investigative television reporting and local issue coverage is a growing feature in America, serving its citizens' democratic needs. There is no equivalent in Britain, where the television structure and programme balance requirements weigh heavily against similar vigorous coverage of such issues as local government corruption.

WHAT THE CRITICS MEAN

As this chapter has shown, the realities of American television contravene both popular conceptions and the assertions of many industry observers and insiders. Most of the criticisms commonly heard about the 'inferiority' or 'evils' of American television, and the 'dangers' of deregulation and competition, are in fact sheer fantasy, taken out of context, or based on vague or extremely subjective criteria. More significantly, the strengths and benefits of American television have generally been ignored or obscured, as have the contradictions and deficiencies of PSB in Britain.

Contrary to critics' claims, there is no evidence that running free-market television companies is a 'grim, remorseless business': witness the 'profit-seeking' companies which are in fact the source of unparalleled news, public affairs, Arts and documentary services in America. Nor can it seriously be claimed that British television 'has not been bettered under any regulatory régime abroad', when the American market structure has created economic and consumer benefits only dreamed of elsewhere; compare the meteoric rise of cable television in the United States with the almost stillborn industry under Britain's regulatory structure.

Not least, there are strong arguments (and concrete examples) that the American television structure has served – and continues to serve – the needs of a free society far more appropriately than highly regulated PSB: witness the aggressive and unencumbered search for truth by the many alternative American news organisations in the Iran-Contras débâcle, versus the muzzling of the British broadcasting duopoly on Zircon, *Spycatcher* and other controversial issues of public importance.

Yet, in spite of all the evidence to the contrary (of which only a small portion could be presented here), many critics still continue to malign American television and claim that deregulation and competition will impoverish the British public. I shall therefore briefly examine some common criticisms and contradictions, and consider what critics really mean when they malign American television and maintain that the medium must be controlled in order to serve the public interest.

Quality and Diversity

Undoubtedly the most common criticism levelled at American television, regardless of the facts and figures presented, is that it somehow offers less real choice or genuine diversity than British PSB, and that deregulation heralds a lowering of television standards or quality. What is usually obscured, however, is the totally subjective nature of such criticisms.

Programme diversity, for instance, applies not simply between programme types (e.g. sport and news offer two different types of television choice for the viewer), but also within programme types (e.g. local versus national news, or different types of sport). Furthermore, real choice is not merely the existence of more or different types of programmes for their own sake, but the availability of the particular programmes an individual prefers and the overall value they offer the viewer. Therefore, such factors as the convenience (i.e. availability of preferred programmes at different times of day and night) and cost of television (in terms of the alternative use of one's time and/or licence or subscription fees) must be considered as well. Critics, however, usually obscure this proper context for evaluating television.

The same argument applies to the subjective notion of quality. For example, the expenditure, talent and production standards used in an individual programme (or across a full television schedule) mean little apart from the overall value offered to the viewer. A so-called 'quality' drama programme (e.g. with higher expenditure, more noted writers or actors, and more sophisticated production techniques) is of little value to a viewer who would actually prefer a less acclaimed non-drama programme not requiring such resources. In fact, the former can even be seen as detrimental to consumer choice if resources could have been redirected to the creation of *more* alternative programmes which offer viewers equal or greater relative value.

In reality, there are few barriers to providing what critics commonly refer to as higher-quality or more diverse television in a relatively free market – if indeed there is a demand for such programmes and viewers find adequate value in them (enough to devote their viewing time and/or finances to them). Should viewers find existing programme choice bland and boring, or not satisfying their full range of taste, there is every incentive and opportunity in the open market-place for competitors to offer more quality or diversity (i.e. a higher-value service). Thus we have seen the development of such services as Arts, documentary and news channels in the American market.

By their choices – the ultimate being to switch off completely – the public constantly sends (and programmers are constantly on the look out for) messages about television's relative value, and services demonstrate their worth among many possible alternatives. This process, however, is distorted in a highly regulated PSB environment, where the number of channels is artificially restricted, and where many programmes are required by regulation, as well as being subsidised by compulsory licence fees or television advertising monopolies.

Who Decides?

What critics usually mean when they condemn the lack of quality, diversity or genuine choice on television is that there is not enough of the programming which they (the critics) think people ought to be watching, or what suits their personal tastes.

The implication of this attitude was best expressed almost 30 years ago by Sir Robert Fraser, the first Director-General of Britain's Independent Television Authority (ITA):

> 'If you decide to have a system of people's television, then people's television you must expect it to be. It will reflect their likes and dislikes, their tastes and aversions, what they can comprehend and what is beyond them. Every person of common sense knows that people of superior mental constitution are bound to find much of television intellectually beneath them. If such innately fortunate people cannot realise this gently and considerately and with good manners, if in their hearts they despise popular pleasures and interests, then of course they will be angrily dissatisfied with television. But it is not really television with which they are dissatisfied. It is with people.'[11]

There never has been a true system of 'people's television' in Britain, however, which would reflect the full scope and proportions of public likes and dislikes, tastes and aversions, and so on. Instead there has been a highly controlled television system which gives people some of what they want, but also what paternalistic policy-makers and broadcasters think people ought to have. Furthermore, this structure serves to prevent people from choosing too much of what the controlling élite considers either poor-quality programmes or television which is unsuitable for British tastes.

Even today, attempts to create a system of 'people's television' are being restrained by what appears to be a fundamental distrust of the public. This particularly applies to concerns about the possible Americanisation of British television, and the loss or dilution of cultural values. Yet if PSB truly serves the public's real needs and interests, the new choices will have limited appeal. And if the British public does choose to view foreign programmes (American or otherwise), or what critics consider lower-quality television, or to patronise channels which feature a larger number of advertising messages, the basic truth is that this reflects their freely chosen values, rather than those accepted only through manipulation by an élite which defines and freezes the culture at its particular standards.

---

[11] Speech delivered to the Manchester Luncheon Club, 17 May 1960, cited in Denis Thomas, 'Commercial TV – and After', in *TV: From Monopoly to Competition – and Back?*, Hobart Paper 15 (revised edition), London: Institute of Economic Affairs, 1962.

Generally, critics' claims – like the principles of PSB – are full of contradictions and arbitrary distinctions. For instance, American television is 'unwatchable' (yet it is essential to limit American imports). British television is the 'envy of the world' (yet Super Channel, the much-heralded 'Best of British' satellite programme service, has been a near total loss). The expansion of channels in America has meant 'worse' television (yet these new services are among the leading buyers and co-producers of British television). Broadcasting is a 'national asset' requiring extraordinary controls (but newspapers do not require such controls). And the BBC, with its guaranteed income, uses its resources to purchase such programmes as *Dallas* and *Neighbours* (the latter repeated twice a day), when these are among those programmes most certain to be provided free to viewers in an open commercial market, and certainly not reflective of critics' cultural aspirations.

In addition to much ignorance regarding American television, many critics and (to the public's detriment) policy-makers also display an astonishing degree of arrogance. This is captured brilliantly in the remarks of one member of a parliamentary committee, during 1988 hearings on an issue no less significant than 'The Future of Broadcasting':

> 'It is possible, is it not, to watch television in your hotel bedroom in the United States and switch to about 30 channels and find them all equally mediocre, apart from the odd one which comes in from Britain.'[12]

Only to be followed by the chairman's comment that:

> 'I can recall watching the proceedings of a legislative authority on a television programme in the States and I cannot think of anything more boring! Presumably the public would exercise its taste by not watching . . .'[13]

Behind the first remark is the frequently unvoiced attitude that American television is mediocre not on grounds of quality or diversity *per se*, but because it is simply 'too American'. One gets the impression that these critics would be satisfied only by turning on American hotel television to find peculiarly British subject matter, with Americans sporting (less 'mediocre') British speaking mannerisms and British styles of programme presentation. Yet American-style television is quite naturally what will be found in the largest proportion, from the commonest chat shows (featuring American hosts and largely American topics) to some religious programmes which reflect (only) some Americans' stronger fundamentalist beliefs.

It is also possible that many foreign viewers of American television have not identified the programmes which meet their interests, due to the initial difficulty in following the programme scheduling and channel

---

12 *The Future of Broadcasting*, Vol. II, Home Affairs Committee Third Report, Session 1987-88: HC 262-II, comments of Miss Janet Fookes, p. 67, para. 208.

13 *Ibid.*, para. 211, comments of Mr John Wheeler, Chairman.

structure; some even resent the overwhelming number of channels from which to choose and the necessity to consult more complicated programme listings. Yet (on a smaller scale) it is no less perplexing for the American visitor in London to discern the nature of Britain's PSB channels when one finds *Dallas* on the BBC, *Dynasty* on ITV and *Hill Street Blues* on Channel 4.

With regard to the second comment, the American public presumably demonstrates its poor taste *en masse*, for there are more than 10.8 million regular viewers of C-SPAN, the channel featuring live coverage of the House of Representatives and public policy programmes. This taste for the 'boring' – first-hand monitoring of one's government representatives and public policy-making, with frequent viewer participation programmes – is exercised for an average of 9.5 hours per month, by viewers who vote at twice the national rate, with a hard-core audience viewing 20 or more hours per month. Presumably such arrogance and ignorance in critical public policy decision-making would be more exposed in Britain, to the benefit of citizens and the chagrin of politicians, if similar American-style television choice was available. For, among its programmes, C-SPAN televises hearings like the one above from the Congressional committees which make communication policy in America.

Envy of the World?

Both of the above quotes also reflect one of the most sacred claims in broadcasting mythology: that British television is the 'crème de la crème' and the 'envy of the world' – including America. Such arrogance could be put into perspective quite easily, however, if anyone were to consider that few Americans, given a choice, would actually be willing to have the British television structure and content substituted for their own.

It is sheer fantasy to think that the average American would be willing to trade nine or more free broadcast and 30-plus optional cable channels for less than a handful of PSB channels, and agree to a compulsory licence fee equivalent to more than $100 a year – funds which could be spent on a variety of alternative information and entertainment services, or indeed anything of greater relative value. It would be equally impossible to convince the average viewer of his or her 'impoverishment' in television service compared to the British public, and to demonstrate that the switch would bring Americans more genuine diversity or real choice.

For most Americans, there would be a diminution of choice under the British model: for example, little overnight broadcasting; the replacement of extensive local newscasts by shorter bulletins; locally based programming on fewer channels in fewer communities; less dedicated programming for significant ethnic and minority groups within a community (e.g. Hispanics, Koreans, Japanese, etc. in New York); and less opportunity to tune in to channels dedicated to a specific programme type (such as sport, music, Arts, documentaries, children's) whenever the viewer desires. Furthermore, few Americans would be likely to welcome a duopoly of national news services; less scope for covering controversial issues; the extensive barriers to market entry, competition and innovation of the British system; or indeed the fundamentally greater influence of government and its appointees in determining what is 'best' for the television public.

Exactly who would be the beneficiaries of the British television model in America? Essentially, the same special interests who benefit from the television structure in Britain: (a) the few broadcasters on whom viewers would become dependent, now wielding increased influence and monopoly sources of finance; (b) ambitious regulators, with greater centralised control over the structure and content of television; and (c) certain individuals and groups who wish to impose their personal standards of quality and diversity on all television viewers.

It is no accident that these few special interests are those to whom critics and policy-makers usually refer, when indeed they can identify Americans who find British television an unqualified object of envy and admiration – for instance, the non-commercial Public Broadcasting Service (PBS), which has long sought funding as guaranteed as the BBC's licence fee. For this claim clearly does not hold true for the vast majority of Americans, and it is doubtful that many supporters of even particular aspects of British television (e.g. 'quality' drama productions) would adopt the latter at the cost of the wider American choice.

Undoubtedly one of the critics' greatest fears is that PSB channels like the BBC will follow the path of PBS as increasingly minority channels – that is, services patronised only by a specific audience segment (e.g. 'high-brow' audiences) or by many viewers only a small portion of the time – because of the success of a freer commercial market in satisfying public preferences. During 1987, public broadcasting stations in America received only 5 per cent of television viewing in homes that did not subscribe to cable, and only 2 per cent of viewing in homes which subscribed to both pay (principally movie channels) and basic cable (e.g. news, Arts and documentary channels).

The traditional dominance of commercial broadcasters, public service or otherwise, is not exempt either. In America, viewership of the mass audience commercial networks has fallen from around 90 per cent in the early 1970s, when there was little alternative choice, to only 75 per cent in non-cable homes in 1987 – due largely to the growth of alternative independent broadcasting stations. More threateningly, however, network viewing in pay-cable homes dropped to only 47 per cent in 1987, with the new pay- and basic-cable channels accounting for 18 and 24 per cent of audiences respectively.

Ghetto or Oasis?

The American television market demonstrates that viewers, when offered alternative choice, indeed exercise that choice where additional value is presented, thus weakening the hold of traditional commercial and public service broadcasters. This loss of long-established and previously unchallenged power and privilege is one of the central concerns of those cautioning against television deregulation in Britain. Much of this self-interest is, however, cloaked in terms of 'the public interest'. Commercial broadcasters, for instance, are more than willing to promote and accept public service obligations in a protected regulatory environment: this is a relative 'bargain' for not having to prove their value against others in an open market.

Perhaps the most absurd criticism heard in this context regards the future of the BBC as a possible 'cultural ghetto'. This contradiction in terms clearly gives the game away, for it suggests that rather than offer a television 'oasis' – providing (and financing) only quality or diversity programming otherwise unavailable in the market-place – the only way the public can be led to what is 'good' (and institutional power can be retained) is by pandering to, and charging for, 'popular' tastes as well.

The Myth of Public Service Broadcasting

In sum, the realities of America's (relatively) free television market challenge not only critics' claims, but many of the fundamental premises of PSB as well. It is the author's view that the British public, long subject to the *mythos* of the latter, has been – and largely continues to be – misled about the role and function of television, and the 'benefits' of a public service regulatory structure.

Most British viewers, for instance, pay their compulsory licence fee in the belief that their television would not exist, or would be extremely restricted, without PSB. They are therefore grateful when there is an expansion of choice by public service broadcasters, e.g. breakfast television, a fourth channel, 24-hour service, an additional regional news bulletin, and so on. Few are aware that such services – and many more – would not only still be offered in a freer market, but probably would already have been available for many years.

Nor does the average viewer generally recognise that when a new service like Channel 4 is given a 'mission' (by policy-makers) to offer 'complementary' and 'minority interest' television on a national basis, this forecloses the possibility of the market-place providing more local service or more of the type of programmes already enjoyed.

Even fewer realise that the premises of spectrum scarcity and universal service are among the most fundamental broadcasting myths perpetuated, and that many viewers could have had a fifth, sixth or even seventh channel for some time now. To American eyes it is astonishing that European ministries, ostensibly serving free societies, were actually able to withhold information on spectrum allocation for so many years.

It is as if the public were convinced that there could be only four newspapers in a nation, with a host of similar restrictions in the 'public interest': for example, two financed by a mandatory fee on all newspaper-reading homes and two financed solely by advertising; news articles provided only by two organisations; regional news in only two of the newspapers; the fourth allowed to cater to 'minority' tastes only; and each required to be impartial, with no specific editorial opinion allowed.

Indeed, such an idea is equivalent to policy-makers looking at the printing press and seeing only their conception of 'public service publishing' – say, a 'quality' newspaper – while missing the prospect, and subsequent economic and consumer benefits, of books, magazines, circulars, weekly, local and free-circulation newspapers, specialised high-quality subscription publications, and so on.

Unfortunately, unlike publishing, policy-makers, public service broadcasters and other special interests in Britain *have* been able to impose *their* vision regarding the role, function and content of broadcasting on the rest of society. Consequently, much of the public is, and will remain, convinced it is being regulated (and in the case of licence fees, virtually robbed) for its own good – until fact replaces fantasy regarding both American and British television.

11

CABLING AMERICA:

Economic Forces in a Political World

Thomas W. Hazlett

University of California, Davis

'Over the last thirty years, the American cable television industry has gone from a relatively minor commercial adjunct to the over-the-air television broadcasting business to the dominant video distribution medium in the country, with over 80 per cent of all US television households passed by cable and projected 1988 revenues of about $12 billion derived from serving about 52 per cent of 90 million homes.'[1]

US CABLE TELEVISION TODAY

AMERICA'S TELEVISION MARKET-PLACE has been remarkably transformed by cable. As recently as 1979 the typical US viewer had a choice of just four broadcast television stations, and only the luckiest 20 per cent could select from as many as eight.[2] Today over 90 per cent of the USA's 45 million cable households enjoy more than 20 channels.

As the service has evolved, cable has been sold as a 'basic' package of 12 to 45 channels transmitting off-air programming and selected satellite fare (such as sports channels, news channels and distant city stations). These basic channels can be augmented by buying one or more 'premium' channels showing mostly late-run (i.e. recently released) movies and high-quality special features. The average cost for the basic system in 1987 was about $13

---

[1] National Telecommunications and Information Administration (NTIA), 'Video Program Distribution and Cable Television: Current Policy Issues and Recommendations', *NTIA Report*, US Department of Commerce, June 1988, p. 1.

[2] T. L. Schuessler, 'Structural Barriers to the Entry of Additional Television Networks: The Federal Communications Commission's Spectrum Management Policies', *Southern California Law Review*, Vol. 54, 1981, p. 983.

per month, and about $11 per month for the premium channels. The average cable viewer subscribed to basic plus one premium channel. The standard state-of-the-art 450 megahertz cable system now supplied 64 channels which can be used to send all locally available off-air signals and some combination of 52 basic, nine premium and four pay-per-view channels available via satellite.[3]

Network television (American Broadcasting Company (ABC), Columbia Broadcasting System (CBS), National Broadcasting Company (NBC)) audiences have been dropping sharply in response to this competitive pressure, and the operating profits of the largest single cable operator, Telecommunications, Inc. (which serves about one in five US cable subscribers), are now higher than the combined revenue of the three networks.

A Benefit or a Cost?

Television is a very large component of contemporary American life, and it is changing dramatically as a result of the cable revolution. Specialised programming is increasingly turned to by viewers no longer held hostage by the 'scarcity' of broadcast television.[4]

While television critics have often castigated the new programming fare as going from the sublime to the ridiculous, the enhanced choice available on cable is clearly an improvement from the consumer's point of view. For instance, the emergence of rock videos as an art form owes much to MTV, a 24-hour rock'n'roll channel, and subsequent imitators. While the critical eye may see little merit in this genre, it is clearly a choice many viewers would like to make.

Programmes have expanded in virtually all dimensions: more sport, movies, old television series, rock videos, comedy specials, children's programming, news and public affairs shows, health and science, concerts and 'high' culture. The presence of more 'bad' programming is a reality from any particular perspective, but is irrelevant to all but the professional critic: the dial allows the viewer to benefit from more diverse television while flipping past the 'costs'.

Hence, such programming amounts to virtually no cost at all. Indeed, the mere availability of greater choice can be seen as a benefit, particularly as sampling the unknown is so cheap. This is a very important consideration wherever tastes are not rigidly defined which, one suspects, is generally true for television viewers. It is nonetheless observable that

3 NTIA, *op. cit.*, p. 11.

4 The 'physical scarcity' of the electromagnetic broadcast spectrum has been the legal premise for regulating off-air radio and television since 1943. It has been criticised by economists and lawyers as theoretically inconsistent, and a new public choice analysis of the origins of broadcast regulation finds that the regulatory framework then established had nothing substantially to do with 'physical scarcity'. (See Thomas Hazlett, 'The Rationality of US Regulation of the Broadcast Spectrum' (working paper), University of California, Davis, 1989.)

television critics frequently prefer to focus on what they perceive as offensive cable programming – a witty put-down is likely to be more interesting than a thoughtful endorsement. The conclusion that the presence of such programming on cable lowers consumer satisfaction is therefore refuted by the simple fact that people generally prefer to have more choice rather than less.

Several sectors have reaped rewards from this explosion of choice, in addition to the viewing public. New demand for programming has been a boon to Hollywood – a vast new source of revenue for producers, leading to a leap in demand for directors, actors, writers, technical personnel and distributors.

The marketing industry has also been quick to cash in, as direct television selling has secured a very large toehold in cable. Indeed, the Home Shopping Network allows buyers to make automated telephone credit card purchases of televised merchandise around the clock.

Even political discussion has experienced a growth period with whole networks such as C-SPAN devoted to the broadcasting of Congressional deliberations, unedited ('gavel-to-gavel') political convention coverage, speeches, policy debates and other forums of note.

But these changes, while adding up to no less than a social bonanza, were held in check for years by a regulatory climate that froze cable's development. Public policy towards the medium has experienced an on-again, off-again cycle that has confused the market-place and withheld social gains which technology made possible long ago. And while the emergence of cable television is often associated with dramatic break-throughs in space-age science, the more formidable advances in cable development involve the classical machinations of interest-group politics.

THE RISE OF CABLE TELEVISION

The Early Days

The cable television industry began just after commercial television itself. In 1948, an entrepreneur from Mahoney City, Pennsylvania, connected some local household television sets to a common antenna, which had been raised to high ground to improve reception. Thus, a business was born: community antenna television (CATV) – later to become 'cable'.

The first systems were modest retransmitters of off-air broadcast or microwaved signals to hilly and/or distant localities. They delivered between one and three channels for $3 to $5 monthly. But they quietly spread out around the country. By the mid-1960s over 1,500 systems were in place, and the average system served about 1,000 households (Table 1).

Cable's economic impact was just beginning to be felt. Through the 1950s the Federal Communications Commission (FCC), which regulated radio and television broadcasters, tried to figure out what to do with CATV. By definition, cable did not beam 'physically scarce' airwaves (the

TABLE 1

GROWTH OF THE CABLE TELEVISION INDUSTRY, 1955-88

Year	Subscribers million	Number of Systems	Penetration %
1955	0.15	400	0.5
1960	0.65	640	1.4
1965	1.2	1,325	2.3
1970	3.9	2,500	6.6
1975	8.5	3,681	12.4
1977	11.3	3,832	15.8
1980	15.2	4,225	19.8
1982	23.7	4,825	25.3
1985	38.0	6,600	44.6
1988	45.0	8,000	51.1

Source: *NTIA*, 1988, p. 10.

domain the Commission was charged with regulating); it simply took existing signals and ran them more strongly and clearly to a cluster of local television sets. The FCC saw this function as essentially benign; it was as if the cable operator were simply providing individual users with improved 'antenna power'. The FCC decided to leave cable free to develop without governmental regulation.

Economic pressure was to influence the politics of the situation, however. As cable grew, over-the-air broadcasters came to see it as a threat to their audiences. In fact, the expansion of cable benefitted broadcasters, by spreading their signals to hitherto untapped regions, and also competed with them, as new channels were introduced into established markets. The broadcasters concluded that, on the whole, cable did more harm than good. They lobbied the FCC to disarm the encroaching rival, and by the early 1960s the agency took strong measures to do so.

Stanley Besen, an economist with the Rand Corporation, describes the episode thus:

'Cable development did not concern the Commission during the early 1950s since it occurred largely in places which did not have over-the-air television . . .'[5]

By the end of the decade, however, cable had begun to move into markets which had television service by bringing programmes from other cities to its subscribers. As a result, broadcasters petitioned the FCC to

[5] Stanley Besen, 'The Economics of the Cable Television "Consensus"', *Journal of Law and Economics*, Vol. XVII, April 1974, p. 39.

prevent cable systems from being established in their markets. Under increasing pressure from broadcasters, the FCC began to regulate the industry.

Regulation

By 1966 a freeze, in effect, was placed on all cable development in the top 100 US television viewing markets. This was accomplished by FCC rules requiring that any cable system in such areas should carry all local off-air television channels, while barring them from 'importing' any competitive signals unless they could obtain special permission from the FCC, issued only upon 'a finding that such importation was in the public interest'.[6] In order to protect the financial position of the over-the-air broadcasters, permission was seldom granted. Competition had, in effect, been rendered illegal in the interests of established television stations.

Curiously, the FCC was rather forthright in its anti-consumer stance. In 1971, its Chairman, Dean Burch, told a congressional panel that, while they (the FCC) hoped cable would develop:

> 'We also feel that it would be in the public interest for over-the-air broadcasting not to be adversely affected. You can translate that into short-term protectionism for over-the-air broadcasting, but we feel there is a public interest consideration as well.'[7]

The regulations shackling cable became progressively more Byzantine, growing and contracting in different directions at once. In 1969, for example, the FCC prevented cable systems from featuring pay channels which showed movies more than two years after they had been released in cinemas, sporting events which had been televised less than two years previously, and regular series of any kind.

The Launch of Satcom I

The possibilities of cable's expanding technology literally skyrocketed in December 1975, when the Satcom I satellite was launched. This gave local cable systems the distribution technology they needed to receive distant programming easily, cheaply, quickly and *en masse*. By this time, the protectionist stance of the FCC had sparked a deregulatory backlash; regulators were moving to let viewers be the arbiters of whether they should receive their channels from the airwaves or by cable.

In 1972 a long, gradual shift away from Federal government controls began, with the government at first relaxing the most arcane prohibitions, and then scrapping regulation altogether. The Federal courts hurried the process along, ruling a series of FCC anti-cable regulations illegal.

When Home Box Office became the first pay service to use Satcom I in 1975, beamed simultaneously to thousands of communities via satellite, it

---

[6] Besen, *ibid.*, p. 40. [7] Cited in Besen, *loc. cit.*, p. 41.

immediately found itself involved in litigation. In the Federal court, it won the right to compete freely with broadcast television, thus paving the way for cable to establish itself: at last it had product to sell. Hence,

'it was only after the Home Box Office decision in 1977, that large city cable systems became attractive investments'.[8]

Deregulation Gains Momentum

Deregulation was just beginning. Pay channels had price controls removed in 1979; city franchise fees were limited to a 5 per-cent-of-gross maximum in 1984; the 1984 Cable Communications Policy Act removed all local control over basic cable pricing as of 29 December 1986; and a number of court decisions[9] declared regulation of cable programming unconstitutional. Spurred on by the elimination of Federal controls and the availability of an unwired continent, cable investors built systems fast and furiously, increasing the number of subscribers from six million to 45 million households in the decade and a half following 1972.

Today, cable passes eight in 10 American homes, and is purchased by almost 60 per cent of those. And business is good – very good. As the *Wall Street Journal* notes:

'. . . prices for cable systems are soaring. They have topped the $2,000-per-subscriber mark, five times the purchase price for a system a decade ago'.[10]

One obvious reason for this is that investors are willing to pay a premium to buy into a steady business that faces no direct competitors and is seen as recession-proof (cable system prices scarcely budged following the October 1987 stock market crash).

In a long and strenuous twist of public policy, cable television has been transformed from a medium restrained from competing by Federal regulation, to the lofty status of a locally licensed monopoly protected from competitors. Indeed, even as cable operators have enjoyed unprecedented freedom to set their own rates, package their own products and run their own businesses, they have clung to one relic of their regulation-fraught past – the franchise monopoly. Increasingly, the tension between the consumer's interest in free competition and the franchise-holder's interest in protectionism has fuelled controversy as to the economics of the cable market-place.

DIRECT COMPETITION IN CABLE

While cable operators are most comfortable with a franchise monopoly, particularly given deregulated rates and services, direct competition has

---

[8] Stanley Besen and Robert Crandall, 'The Deregulation of Cable Television', *Law and Contemporary Problems*, Vol. 44, Winter 1981, p. 111.

[9] For example, *Quincy Cable TV Inc. v. FCC* (1985).

[10] Laura Landro, 'As Cable-TV Industry Keeps Growing, Rivals Demand Deregulation', *Wall Street Journal*, 17 September 1987, pp. 1, 23.

come to play an increasingly important role in the market-place. This is entirely to be expected. As the withdrawal of regulation has eliminated the (arguable) rationale for protecting firms from competition, why should public policy protect unrestricted monopoly?

'Overbuilding'

If the Federal deregulation of cable has allowed consumers to enjoy inter-media competition, the economics of the market-place have made direct 'head-to-head' rivalry between cable firms increasingly likely. As recently as 1982, a consulting report for the City of Monroe, Georgia, could see a new trend developing in direct cable competition – called 'overbuilding', i.e. the increasing tendency of newcomers to build new systems in areas already served by established cable operators:

'In the pre-1978 years, most cable multiple system operations (MSOs) did not seek to enter or sustain an overbuilt franchise ... [which would entail] accepting lower returns ... when more attractive alternatives are available. Now such alternatives are increasingly scarce. In recent years, the growth in the availability and acceptance of Pay-TV has increased internal cash flow and enhanced operators' ability to secure the external financing necessary to support the development of overbuilt franchises. The diversity of programming available has strained the capacity of some older systems to deliver all the services that their subscribers would like to receive. For all these reasons, and, in some cases, because of deteriorating service quality from existing franchises, more and more well-financed operators are responding.'[11]

In 1986 and 1987, overbuilding activity achieved new heights, as new companies entered to compete with established operators in Easton, Pennsylvania; Colorado Springs, Colorado; Huntsville, Alabama; Sacramento, California; and Orange County, Florida. Scores of other markets await competition, as soon as legal impediments to competitive entry are cleared away.

The reason for this boom in overbuilding is straightforward. There are two ways to enter any particular cable market: one is by purchasing the system already in place, and the other is by building a competitive system to go head-to-head. At current market prices, it is often much more expensive to purchase an existing system than to build a competing one. Whereas it typically costs between $1,800 and $2,500 per subscriber to purchase an existing monopoly firm (i.e. an average system with 20,000 subscribers would sell for between $36 million and $50 million), that average market can be overbuilt for between $500 and $1,000 per subscriber.

---

[11] Alan Pearce, Roger Paterson and Mary Frederickson, 'Competitive Cable Franchising: An Analysis of Economic Theory and Empirical Data' (unpublished study for the City of Monroe, Georgia), 1982, p. 14.

TABLE 2

CABLE SYSTEM VALUES, 1985-88

Period	No. of System Sales	No. of Basic Subscribers Involved	Price/ Subscriber $	Price/HP* $
Jan.-June 1985	138	2,607,543	1,074	487
Jan.-June 1986	211	4,608,724	1,343	681
Jan.-June 1987	176	5,856,004	1,506	814
Jan.-June 1988	202	7,635,198	1,997	1,153

* HP = Number of homes passed.

Source: Cable TV Investor. Data Extra, 31 July 1988, p. 4.

Profitability of Cable

The disparity between market value and capital cost indicates that a monopoly in the typical cable franchise is very valuable. Table 2 shows that the average US cable subscriber was worth some $1,997 to the franchise-holder in 1988 – almost double the 1985 figure. Using capital cost data supplied by Albert Smiley in 1986,[12] and employing industry averages for homes per mile of 92 and basic penetration ratio of 0.58 (58 per cent),[13] the average investment in a 50,000 home market is about $600 per subscriber. This indicates a q ratio of approximately 3.37 – well above the value of unity likely to be seen in a competitive market.[14]

A recent report by a Washington telecommunications consulting firm found that the average US cable system (in December 1986) was valued by the market at 2.81 times its capital cost as compared with a US non-financial firm mean of 0.805. By any current measure, the implication is that cable systems enjoy far higher returns than those required to attract capital.[15]

---

[12] Albert Smiley, 'Direct Competition Among Cable Television Systems', Washington DC: US Department of Justice, Antitrust Division, EAE Paper No. 86-9, June 1986.

[13] Homes/mile means the density of a cable system – how many potential subscribers there are along one mile of cable. Penetration ratio is the rate at which these potential customers actually subscribe.

[14] On the logic of using ratios to deduce market power, see Eric Lindenberg and Stephen Ross, 'Tobin's q Ratio and Industrial Organization', *Journal of Business*, Vol. 54, 1981, pp. 1-32.

The q ratio = $\frac{\text{capital value}}{\text{capital cost}}$. In a competitive market (abstracting from depreciation and disequilibrium issues), q = 1 for an average firm. Ratios significantly above one are evidence of monopoly profits. (This is sometimes called a 'Tobin q', after Professor James Tobin, Nobel prize winner at Yale University.)

[15] The basic point is that it costs about $600 to create a cable subscriber, but once you own such a system (serving a number of subscribers) you can sell it for about $2,000 per subscriber. The difference between capital cost ($600) and capital value ($2,000) is *monopoly* rent (or the right to an above-competitive return). The market data cited above are very compelling evidence on this point and should give the sophisticated lay reader a good idea of how monopolistic local cable franchises

[*Contd. on p. 216*]

215

The increasing profitability of cable stems from both the supply and demand sides of the market. For suppliers, capital costs have declined significantly in recent years, as real interest rates have moderated and as newer and better technologies have emerged in a dynamic industry. The effect of such innovation, in economic terms, is that state-of-the-art 64-channel cable systems can be constructed today for roughly what it cost to build much smaller (20- or 35-channel) systems only five or 10 years ago.

One 1984 study of the economics of cable television found that the expense of laying a second cable in a region covered by an established monopolist incurred relatively low cost penalties compared with the advantages gained by the new competitor through the use of superior technology. Columbia University economist, Eli Noam, in a statistical analysis using data for 4,800 cable systems, concluded that while

'the effect of economies of scale is relatively small, by far the largest contribution [to efficiency] is made by the "external" development of technology, as expressed by the contribution of new vintages to cost reduction'.[16]

Interestingly, Noam's findings were so convincing he concluded that cable was not a natural monopoly but that 'existing operators are not contested by competitive entry and are instead protected by legal barriers such as *de facto* franchise monopolies'.

Increasing Competition

These legal barriers appear to be falling. Some local authorities see little reason to protect unregulated monopolies, and are quick to issue competing franchises. Even more important, however, are the Federal courts which have declared franchise monopolies to be unconstitutional restrictions on the free speech/free press rights of those cable competitors which have been excluded.[17] The clear trend is for increasing market rivalry within the industry, which can take any of three forms:

o   Direct competition, as in an overbuild.

o   Potential competition, as when new or neighbouring firms can credibly threaten to overbuild an existing monopolist.

o   Contract competition, when new firms enter markets by contracting with a developer, landlord or homeowners' or tenants' association. This form of 'private cable' provides vigorous competition with CATV,

---

are in the USA. (See H. Shooshan & C. Jackson, 'Opening the Broadband Gateway: The Need for Telephone Company Entry Into the Video Services Marketplace', (unpublished) Report prepared for the United States Telephone Association, Washington DC, October 1987, p. 14.)

16 E. M. Noam, 'Private Sector Monopolies: The Case of Cable Television Franchises', in M. Holzer and S. Nagel (eds.), *Productivity and Public Policy*, Beverley Hills, California: SAGE Publications, 1984, p. 211.

17 *Pacific West v. Sacramento* (1987), *Century Federal v. Palo Alto* (1987), and *Group W Cable Inc. v. Santa Cruz* (1987).

particularly in 'wholesale' markets where service is often negotiated at a group or bulk rate.[18]

Overbuilds have occurred in more than 100 US cable markets at one time or another, and current estimates find over 40 instances of such rivalry today. This competition has recently been intensified by the factors already mentioned: deregulation of cable prices and services, vanishing virgin cable territory, lucrative cable investment opportunities, the superiority of newer video technology, and the ending of exclusive monopoly franchises by the courts. Industry insiders now claim that direct competition between cable systems in the same geographical area is the new reality. At the December 1987 Western Cable Show in Anaheim, California, Dr Samuel Book, of the cable consulting firm Malarkey-Taylor & Associates, noted:

'Overbuilds are here to stay. They are not an ephemeral one-in-a-thousand fluke as they have been in the cable industry during its history up to now. They are likely to become a permanent and growing feature on the cable landscape.'

Similarly, in a frank article, a senior editor of *Cable Television Business* wrote in the 1 December 1987 issue:

'By now everyone in the cable business recognizes that it's often cheaper to build a new system than to buy an existing one. But the overbuild threat has been brushed aside with such arguments as "You'll never be able to get the financing", or "No cable operator would ever intrude on another operator's territory". There's nothing wrong with those arguments. But what happens when you already have the financing or when you aren't among the top 50 MSOs?'

The heated condemnation of competition in cable television has mainly come from municipalities and established monopolists. Logically enough, the majority of existing franchise-holders would like to retain exclusive rights to cable consumers. As additional firms are permitted to compete in the market, incumbent monopolists must react in one of two ways. They either (a) upgrade their product and/or lower their price due to competitive pressure (i.e. a new entrant significantly increases both market demand and firm elasticity of demand); or (b) petition the local government to deny a franchise to a potentially competitive cable firm. Petitioning the local government is generally preferred, because it is usually cheaper (and if it fails, prices may then be lowered and product

---

[18] Thomas Hazlett, 'Private Contracting versus Public Regulation as a Solution to the Natural Monopoly Problem', in R. Poole (ed.), *Unnatural Monopolies*, Lexington, Mass.: Lexington Books, 1985, pp. 71-114; and Thomas Hazlett, 'Competition *v.* Franchise Monopoly in Cable Television', *Contemporary Policy Issues*, Vol. IV, April 1986, pp. 80-97.

upgraded). Expanding a menu of programme offerings can be expensive, particularly if it implies completely rebuilding a system to carry more channels. Moreover, should the new firm enter directly, price competition is often vicious.

Two econometric studies of prices in overbuilt markets[19] found a statistically significant lowering of rates under overbuilt competition, holding other factors constant; several consulting reports have noted a similar phenomenon. A study by Touche Ross[20] found that basic cable rates for overbuilt systems averaged about $9 monthly in 1986, as against a national average of $11.10.

The most recent overbuild numbers, compiled in mid-1987, are listed in Table 3. Importantly, these monopoly and competitive systems are compared during the period of rate deregulation. Prices, and prices-per-channel, are substantially lower for the duopoly (or overbuilt) systems. The combined monthly rate for a package consisting of basic plus one pay channel (the typical subscription) is nearly 24 per cent less under competition, a difference statistically significant at the 95 per cent confidence level.

This information does not take into account other differences (apart from the existence of competition) between markets. However, in a survey of seven cable television markets (in different geographical areas) experiencing competitive entry over the past two years, pre-competition prices were, on average, above the August 1987 Multichannel News Survey mean used as a control in Table 3 ($13.82 *v.* $13.35), while offering a lower mean number of basic channels (30.4 *v.* 35.5). These markets included Colorado Springs, Colorado; Rigeland/Madison, Mississippi; Easton, Pennsylvania; Citrus, Dade, and Orange County, Florida; and Huntsville, Alabama. With competition, the price of basic cable in these markets dropped to an average of $8.09 monthly – a reduction of 41.5 per cent.

This is to be expected: we anticipate entry against less efficient, relatively over-priced systems first. But it also suggests that the low prices from competitive systems are not the result of peculiar features of their geographical location, but a clear consequence of pro-consumer economic rivalry.

WHAT'S LEFT OF CABLE POLICY?

With the Federal deregulation of cable, and, importantly, the pre-emption of local government regulation, a public interest analysis would predict the

---

[19] Douglas Webbink, 'The Impact of Regulation and Competition on Cable TV Service Prices, Channels and Pay Tiers' (unpublished), Bureau of Economics, US Federal Trade Commission, May 1985; and Thomas Hazlett, *op. cit.*, April 1986.

[20] Touche, Ross, 'Report on Overlapping Cable Franchise Study' (Consulting Report for Dade County (Florida) Cable Commission), October 1987, p. 40.

TABLE 3

DUOPOLY v. MONOPOLY CABLE PRICES, 1987

Duopoly System	Entry Status	Year Overbuild Began	No. of Basic Channels	Basic Price $	1st Pay Price $	$P_B + P_P$ $
S. W.-Allentown, PA	se[1]	1964	32	10.25	7.95	18.20
T. C.-Allentown, PA	se	1964	35	10.00	8.95	18.95
Sammons-Easton, PA	i[3]	1986	38	7.25	9.95	17.20
Consolidated-Frankfurt, KT	i	1962	24	6.50	9.00	15.50
Suburban-Delaware, Co., PA	se	1981	30	9.50	7.95	17.45
American-Delaware, Co., PA	se	1981	31	9.50	8.95	18.45
Telesat-Orange Co., FL	fs[2]	1987	40	9.95	9.95	19.90
Cablevision C.F.- Orange Co., FL	i	1987	27	6.50	6.50	13.00
Cablevision C.F.- Orange Co., FL	i	1987	33	6.50	6.50	13.00
Telesat-Dade Co., FL	fs	1987	42	9.95	9.95	19.90
Dynamic-Dade Co., FL	i	1987	40	9.95	9.95	19.90
Citizens-Colo. Sps., CO	fs	1986	40	15.00	7.45	22.45
Century-Colo. Sps., CO	i	1986	30	12.50	11.95	24.45
Comcast-Huntsville, AL	i	1986	29	8.50	9.95	18.45
Cable America- Huntsville, AL	fs	1986	43	7.95	10.00	17.95
Alsea-Waldport, OR	fs	1979	23	9.00	8.15	17.15
TCI-Waldport, OR	i	1979	26	9.27	8.19	17.46
Televents-Citrus Co., FL	fs	1987	41	9.95	9.95	19.90
Telesat-Citrus Co., FL	fs	1987	n.a.	9.95	9.95	19.90
(1) 19-system unweighted means			33.6	9.37	9.01	18.38
(2) 24 monopoly-system means			35.5	13.35	10.67	24.02
(3) Difference [(2) - (1)]/(2)			5.4%	29.8%	15.6%	23.5%

[1] se = simultaneous entrant (or reasonable approximation).

[2] fs = fully sequential entrant (i.e., overbuilder).

[3] i = incumbent supplier (i.e., overbuilds).

Sources: T. W. Hazlett, for duopoly statistics; 'Cable System Retail Pricing Comparison', *Multi-channel News*, 10 August 1987, p. 34, for 24 monopoly systems' figures. (These were from a 25-system sample, Comcast-Huntsville being omitted because of its status as an overbuild.)

falling away of exclusive cable franchise. As the rationale for regulation has evaporated, and with municipalities prohibited from constraining prices to quasi-competitive levels, the public interest approach to regulation would point towards use of a new policy tool to control monopoly pricing – potential entry.

Yet this solution has been employed infrequently; the overwhelming majority of US municipalities cling to monopoly franchise barriers even at the cost of monopoly pricing. Indeed, the trade association for city governments – the National League of Cities – has vigorously fought open-entry claims in the courts, and has consistently advised its members against allowing competition in cable.[21]

The aim of the local franchise authorities is to claim available economic rents. The opportunity to collect such rents has arisen as a result of the withdrawal of Federal regulation, combined with municipal monopoly power over local streets and rights-of-way. A cable operator must obtain permission from the local municipal government to construct the necessary aerials and underground cable plant, which enables franchising to operate. This sets in motion a process wherein potential cable franchise-holders will bid for the right to wire a city for cable television.

The demand curve for monopoly franchises will reflect the profits available from obtaining such a licence. Assuming, for the moment, selfless and omniscient public franchising agents, the franchising authority could organise the bidding for entry rights so as to maximise consumer surplus, or to maximise the present value of payments to the agency. The former method would require output-price bids by rival firms, with the franchise being awarded to the applicant offering the lowest price schedule (or schedules).[22]

In the end, this would produce the competitive welfare outcome with a monopoly market structure. This sort of 'Demsetzian' auction, however, would obviously require just the sort of price controls which are now ruled out for the US cable market by Federal law.

The second sort of auction – direct dollar bids for franchise rights – leads to the predictable monopoly outcome of a lower level of output than that which maximises consumer welfare, as industry profits are maximised by a régime of monopoly pricing. A potential monopolist, in other words, will be able to outbid any collection of competitive firms because its derived demand is higher. (At the extremes perfect market competitors would bid nothing for the franchise while a monopolist would bid up to the entire present value of monopoly rents.)

Yet again, Federal law constrains such bids, as municipalities have been prevented (since the late 1970s) from obtaining cable payments in excess of 5 per cent of total receipts. This, it turns out, is a binding price control in the sense that at 5 per cent of gross, there is excess demand for franchises. Just as in any similar price-controlled situation, buyers (would-be franchise cable monopolists) and sellers (local governments) tend to think of new margins on which to deal.

---

21 Thomas Hazlett, 'The Demand to Regulate Franchise Monopoly: Evidence from CATV Rate Deregulation in California' (working paper), University of California, Davis, 1989; and 'Cities Awaiting Word from Cable on First Amendment Immunity', *Communications Daily*, 22 September 1988, p. 1.

22 Harold Demsetz, 'Why Regulate Utilities?', *Journal of Law and Economics*, Vol. XI, April 1968, pp. 55-66; Oliver Williamson, 'Bidding for Natural Monopolies – In General and With Respect to CATV', *Bell Journal of Economics and Management Science*, Vol. 7, Spring 1976, pp. 73-104; Richard Schmalansee, *The Control of Natural Monopolies*, Lexington, Mass.: Lexington Books, 1979; and Thomas Hazlett, in R. W. Poole (ed.), *op. cit.*

The Cable Franchising Process

In this market, the trading is a highly structured affair, revolving around a formal cable franchising process. This typically begins with a municipality's 'Request for Proposals', which is followed by the submission of several (usually two to eight) 'bids' by rival cable firms to obtain a *de facto* monopoly franchise for the jurisdiction in question (although the franchise will be nominally 'non-exclusive', only one will usually be issued).

Such bids are evaluated by City Hall staff or outside consultants, and then put to the city council (or other public body assigned this statutory responsibility) for a formal vote on which applicant is to be awarded the franchise. The process, which has been known to take as long as 20 years in some cities, was devised to allow the excess demand to be dissipated, to the benefit of those who effectively assign the franchises. Such an auction process differs from classic excess demand rationing under rent controls, for instance, in that the 'landlords' are public officials. Hence, their property rights to the rent streams they assign are limited not simply by a Federal price control law, but also by a complex web of political considerations and anti-bribery statutes.

Such circumstances often present a fascinating public choice experiment, which answers the question: How do public officials behave towards a 'regulated' industry when they lose their ability to force Pareto-efficient improvements? The observable data demonstrate that officials will only rarely jettison their remaining control in an attempt to enhance consumer welfare through a greater reliance on competitive forces. Instead, they shift to a different rationale for regulation, claiming a cross-subsidy purpose as a substitute for efficiency. They will argue that monopoly franchises are necessary so as to promote various 'public interest' considerations, such as subsidisation of public access and local origination channels (televising community activities or activists), government channels (broadcasting city council meetings or a talk show with the mayor), education channels, and universal service. Of course, political agencies will always gain from owning the right to use their discretion to engage in unconstrained cross-subsidy schemes so as to maximise their political support. This premise for regulation therefore becomes a non-economic brief for incumbent office-holder expediency.

In short, these franchise auctions assign monopoly rights to private cable companies in exchange for (a) the compensation of incumbent politicians with cash and in-kind gifts (legal or illegal); (b) the endowment (through subsidies) of local origination and public access cable services with channel capacity and programming resources far beyond those that consumers would be willing to pay for; and (c) the granting of corporate stock to well-connected 'pillars of the community' who have influence with the relevant office-holders (routinely called 'rent-a-citizen'). Scientific selection of the 'best' cable system – from the vantage point of rate-paying customers – is not what the franchise process looks like in the flesh.

Franchise Assignment in Practice

An illustration may be helpful. In a lengthy and interesting 1985 study of the Minneapolis (Minnesota) cable franchise, Peter Edwards found a city with high hopes for its selection process. Beginning in 1972, Minneapolis convened a committee (composed of seven city council members) to plan rationally for an optimal municipal policy towards cable. A combination of local, state and federal regulation conspired to delay a final award, however, until November 1982.

The decade-long process, which had begun so promisingly with the employment of citizens' commissions, special boards, consulting cable experts and a state regulatory body (not to mention the FCC), broke down into a jungle war of raw political might. As Edwards concludes: 'That the Minneapolis process became famous for going wildly out of control is, therefore, more than a little unexpected . . .'.[23] What went wrong was that, in shifting the focus of competition from consumers to a monopoly-granting agency, public policy created a rent-seeking process which would predictably exact large social costs.

What made the process so sensational, however, was the juxtaposition of supposedly high-minded public purpose with this starkly self-interested rivalry. Though claiming a governmental interest in regulating a 'natural monopoly', bringing about a diversity of news and entertainment sources and controlling the almost inevitable disruption to the public entailed in constructing a cable system (digging up roads, for instance), none of these 'technical' matters concerned the actual decision-makers in the heat of a very real franchising process. Indeed, Edwards found:

'. . . the crucial factor in the Minneapolis cable franchise decision was politics. The cable companies followed the pattern which was to become commonplace in cable franchise contests. Each company went to considerable effort to align themselves favorably within the local political dynamic. Lawyers, lobbyists, local investors, public relations firms and community groups were all involved . . .'

'Local politicians, motivated almost exclusively by political concerns, were typically uninformed about cable television and lacked any sense of broader, national developments in telecommunications, yet they selected cable operators. Concern for the welfare of their local communities was frequently absent; concern for more national issues almost never existed.'[24]

---

23 Peter Edwards, *Cable Television Franchising: A Case Study of Minneapolis, Minnesota*, New York: Communications Media Center, New York Law School, 1985, p. 87.

24 Edwards, *ibid.*, pp. 90 and 95.

THE MORAL OF THE CABLE REGULATION STORY

After three decades of cable television regulation in America, it is safe to say that cable consumers receive essentially no benefit from the specialised political institutions nominally pledged to protect their interests. Cable is now an unregulated monopoly in upwards of 90 per cent of all US cities, and the great majority of those cities employ legal entry barriers to ensure that 'natural' monopoly is never threatened by 'unnatural' competition. But these are the golden days of consumer welfare maximisation compared with the sorry episode of broadcast television protectionism in the 1960s and 1970s. Even at monopoly price levels, some output is preferred to none.

What the American experience seems to suggest is that ambitious regulatory policies towards a complex communications product such as cable television make very easy prey for rent-seekers. Challenged incumbents will be quickest to react to the protectionist possibilities of regulation, and are likely to lobby for the suppression of dynamic change. An existing industry with large, well-defined rents will tend to out-perform an emerging technology with uncertain potential and ill-defined ownership. (In other words, it is difficult to internalise the gains from lobbying for new entry when it is not clear who the entrants will be nor how large the gains.) The bias of regulation in technically dynamic areas will therefore be reactionary, and this may add years or even decades to the economic hurdles faced by newcomers in an emerging market-place.

But the dramatic expansion of the television 'dial' afforded by cable has eventually proved a vital enough economic force to surmount federal hostility, and to establish cable firmly as the primary form of home video entertainment in America. Local regulators have done little to facilitate this revolution. Rather, they have acted as self-interested auctioneers, attempting to ransom off entry rights to top political bidders, and often preventing all entry for several years.

This type of auction without a (public) purpose may one day be ended at the hands of the US Constitution. But in the meantime it serves as an important lesson in the ubiquity of competitive market forces, which divert energies to all activities where entrepreneurs – and political agents – believe that gains outweigh costs.

12

MODELS OF BROADCAST REGULATION:
The UK and North American Experience

Martin Cave

Brunel University

and

William H. Melody

University of Oxford;
Simon Fraser University, Vancouver

THE TERM 'REGULATION' is generally used to indicate any intervention by government to constrain or direct the activities of industry. 'Deregulation' is the removal of such constraints. The simplistic model of regulation assumes that regulation is a direct substitute for market forces and that government can achieve its objectives through regulation. In fact, although regulation can restrict and direct certain market forces, it can only constrain them to a limited extent, and cannot prevent them from having significant effects.

In some circumstances competition can be harnessed within a framework of regulation to facilitate the achievement of non-market public policy objectives. However, in the broadcast industries in particular, certain regulatory functions cannot be totally eliminated. Given the special features of broadcast markets, regulation in some form is likely to persist – if necessary, by the industry itself.

Thus, 'deregulation' really involves changes in the structure of regulation and in the role of market forces. The effects of these changes will depend very much on the particular framework and structure of regulation, as well as on the specific market forces that are brought into greater play. It cannot be presumed in advance that any particular change in regulatory structure will automatically achieve any particular public policy objective.

CYCLES OF REGULATION

The claim that the form and structure of regulatory institutions make a difference may not seem an especially bold one. But it is implicitly or explicitly denied by those writers in the field who focus entirely on the formulation of policy either by a benevolent government or through the interplay of interest groups and those exercising political power.

When policy is formulated by a benevolent government, the aim of regulation is simply to identify and correct market failure; the institutions through which it is implemented make little difference. Equally, when regulation is treated as a good like any other for which there is a demand by those who are regulated, and which is supplied by political leaders, the institutional arrangements through which regulation is exercised are assumed to have little effect. It is more realistic, however, to recognise that institutional factors are important and change over time. In many countries industrial regulation was established only after market failure so severe as to require it,[1] and most deregulation movements are driven primarily by a perception that regulation is failing to live up to its objectives. The process of regulation and deregulation is thus a cyclical one.

Saying that the structure of regulatory institutions matters does not mean that they are autonomous. The decision-making process will inevitably be influenced by the distribution of economic power and by the political system. But once the structure of regulatory decision-making is established, it acquires a more independent role; and if the structure is changed the effect may be considerable.

This chapter examines the structure of the regulatory system for broadcasting in North America and in Britain. It starts from the proposition that the framework through which regulation is exercised does make a difference, particularly in determining the pace of change but also sometimes its direction. We suggest that the growing involvement of the European Community in broadcasting regulation in Britain is going to have an effect not only through the interaction of a new set of players with different preferences and interests, but also through the emergence of a new set of procedures for the making and implementation of policy. The effects may be very different from those which have been generally anticipated.

WHO REGULATES?

Taking a wide definition, regulation can include anything from the 'background' legal system (e.g. the prevention of theft) to direct control through public ownership. For our purposes it is useful to concentrate on

---

[1] British broadcasting is an exception here, as a draconian form of regulation took effect from the outset. The outcome was partly influenced, however, by observation of unregulated interference of one signal by another in the United States.

measures specific to broadcasting, though we recognise that more comprehensive regulations (such as those enshrined in property law, competition policy and industrial policy) are becoming increasingly important to the broadcasting industry.

Regulatory authority for broadcasting is divided in most countries among several institutions, including the legislature, government departments, independent regulatory agencies and the courts. In any particular case, immediate regulatory authority will be shared among them, in ways that may have a significant effect upon the functioning of the system.

The Legislature and the Executive

The role of the legislature is to establish the broad objectives and limitations of regulation through legislation establishing the regulatory system – and in some cases to supervise the regulatory agencies created by that legislation. In constitution-based political systems like the USA, where separation of powers gives the legislature a role that is substantially independent of the executive, Congress plays a major role not only in passing legislation, but also in accepting or rejecting executive nominations to the regulatory agency, setting the agency's budget and providing overall control of its activities.

In executive-led systems like the UK, the role of Parliament is to pass, or more rarely reject, legislation proposed by the government. The decisive voice often belongs to the department or departments concerned with broadcasting. Policy is formed by seeking to reconcile divergent aims – for example, objectives of industrial policy, public finance and regulation of broadcast content – or to satisfy divergent interest groups.

Independent Regulatory Agencies

The next level of regulatory player is the quasi-independent regulatory agency, exercising powers that are typically delegated to it by legislation and often shadowed by a government department. In some cases the legislation specifies what the agency may do only in broad terms – as in the statutory requirement placed on many US regulatory bodies to act in 'the public interest, necessity and convenience'. In other cases, such as the UK Broadcasting Act 1980, the powers and obligations of the regulatory bodies are set down in considerable detail.

The Courts

Finally, the courts play a role in many regulatory proceedings. This will vary from country to country. In the UK the courts have shown reluctance to intervene in regulatory proceedings, except in cases where proper procedures have not been observed. In the US, by contrast, the Federal courts – especially the Court of Appeals of the District of Columbia and the Supreme Court – have been active in reviewing the substance of regulatory decisions, as well as ensuring that proper procedures are adhered to. They have thus had a significant impact on many of the major issues of broadcasting policy.

VARIETIES OF REGULATORY EXPERIENCE

There are many reasons for the various ways in which regulatory power and responsibility are divided in different countries. This has led to considerable diversity in each country's approach to the regulation of broadcasting. The UK government-led system has tended to promote periods of stability interrupted by occasional major shake-ups. The US agency- and court-led model tends to promote incremental change arising from the successive interactions of interest groups. The Canadian model represents a mixture of the two, but with its own unique set of objectives.

Historically, the three crucial stages in broadcast regulation have been (a) the initial regulation of radio; (b) the introduction and diffusion of terrestrial television broadcasting; and (c) the incorporation of the newer technologies of cable, satellite and integrated telecommunication systems.

United Kingdom

In the UK[2] the first stage (regulation of radio) led to the creation of a monopoly public broadcasting organisation with major emphasis on public service broadcasting (PSB) – encapsulated by Reith's famous remark in 1922 that 'few [listeners] know what they want, and very few want what they need'.[3]

As elsewhere, radio broadcasting in Britain began after the First World War, largely as a commercial service promoted by radio manufacturers and operating within a highly regulated environment. But a decision was taken to place radio (from the beginning of 1927) in the hands of a newly created British Broadcasting Corporation (BBC) controlled directly neither by government nor industry but by a regulatory body – the Board of Governors.

Over the following years the BBC fought to maintain its monopoly against encroachments from continental broadcasters and even some fledgeling radio cable systems. Lord Reith later noted – in evidence to the Beveridge Committee – that 'it was the brute force of monopoly that enabled the BBC to become what it did; that made it possible for a policy

---

[2] Detailed references are not provided for this section. For the United Kingdom, see Asa Briggs, *History of Broadcasting in the United Kingdom*, Vol. I: *The Birth of Broadcasting*, Oxford University Press, 1961, Vol. II: *The Golden Age of Wireless*, Oxford University Press, 1965; A. Smith (ed.), *British Broadcasting*, Newton Abbot: David and Charles, 1974; B. Sendall, *Independent Television in Britain*, Vol. I: *Origin and Foundation 1946-62*, London: Macmillan, 1982, Vol. II: *Expansion and Changes 1958-68*, Macmillan, 1983; R. Coase, *British Broadcasting: A Study in Monopoly*, London: Longmans, Green, 1950; B. Paulu, *Television and Radio in the UK*, Macmillan, 1981.

[3] Quoted in Coase, *op. cit.*, p. 47.

of moral responsibility to be followed'.[4] In 1926, the monopoly principle was accepted by the Conservative Government with few misgivings.

The Birth of Commercial Television

When television broadcasting began in 1936, it too was assigned to the BBC, despite a proposal from the General Electric Company (GEC), a major electrical company, that a consortium of 'responsible' private companies should provide the service. But after the Second World War, as television ownership became widespread, there occurred one of those sudden government-driven changes in policy that have occasionally disturbed the serenity of broadcasting regulation in Britain.

The background to this major decision illustrates the importance of control of the legislature in British regulatory policy. The BBC's Charter was renewed in 1946 until the end of 1952. A Committee chaired by Lord Beveridge was appointed in 1946 to consider broadcasting policy, and its majority reported in 1951 in favour of maintaining the BBC's monopoly. The Labour Government was not, however, able to realise its intention of re-chartering the BBC as a monopoly before it fell in October 1951. The issue thus passed to a Conservative Government which had misgivings about the BBC's monopoly and was subject to pressure to allow commercial (i.e. advertiser-supported) programmes.

Among the various groups which combined in lobbying for commercial television were: advertising agencies seeking new outlets for promotional material; a number (initially small) of Conservative Members of Parliament opposed to the BBC's monopoly; and some former BBC employees. Opposition was bipartisan and intense (Lord Reith, for example, likened the introduction of commercial television to that of dog-racing or smallpox),[5] but the Conservative Party was finally won over. An Act establishing commercial broadcasting was passed in 1954.

The provisions of that Act failed to satisfy the most fervent proponents of free enterprise. An Independent Television Authority (ITA) was created which would own and operate transmitting stations, and would supervise (but not provide) the programmes. The programmes would be made by contracting companies appointed by the Authority. The Authority was required to ensure competition in the supply of programmes and 'a proper balance in their subject matter'.

In relation to advertising, the Act required the Authority to limit the duration of commercial messages and to produce and publish an advertising code. It specifically forbade sponsorship of programmes (the form of advertising then prevalent in the United States).

The 1954 Act imposed numerous obligations on the ITA but at the same time gave it wide discretion over how to satisfy them. The requirement to ensure competition was particularly onerous, as the

---

[4] Quoted in Paulu, *op. cit.*, p. 17.   [5] Quoted in Smith, *op. cit.*, p. 103.

spectrum allocation policy adopted by the Government restricted each area of the country to a single channel. The plan the ITA chose involved making different contractors responsible for programmes on different days of the week. But it also intended to introduce further competition by allowing companies to sell programmes to one another on a competitive basis.

The ITV Cartel

This latter aim was not realised. Commercial television was initially unprofitable, and the companies responded by developing 'networking' arrangements with one another for the exchange of programmes. The ITA had initially envisaged programme exchanges on a competitive basis, but what emerged was a monopolistic 'network carve-up' in which the major companies divided the production of network programmes among themselves. This co-ordinated programme planning obviously had a strong commercial logic, as each major company could save on production facilities, but the arrangement thwarted the Authority's aim of achieving competition between programmes.

The ITA sought advice on the legality of the companies' arrangements, and was told that it could be argued that the companies were putting themselves outside their contractual obligations. But in the event the ITA acquiesced in the arrangement, its tolerance surviving even into the age of enormous profits. Although television in Britain ceased to be a monopoly in 1955, commercial television itself effectively became a cartel.

The existence of the cartel, and of the excess profits it permitted, enabled the regulatory agency to impose public service obligations on the commercial broadcasters. Specific requirements were imposed in respect of news, current affairs, religious, children's and other programmes. And compliance was made more likely by a contract renewal process in which holders of the monopoly franchises competed every 10 years or so against potential entrants on the basis of their past record. However, the rules of the game were not explicit, and the decision-making process was anything but transparent.

The regulatory framework created in 1926 and in the early 1950s has, until recently, remained virtually unchanged. Over the past 25 years, new radio and television channels (independent local radio (ILR), BBC2 and Channel 4) have been integrated within it. Significant authority has rested with the regulators – the BBC Board of Governors and the Independent Broadcasting Authority (IBA), which took over from the ITA in 1972. They have exercised that power to achieve the goals of PSB within a framework largely devoid of competition for revenue.

United States

Not surprisingly, the pattern of regulation differs markedly between the UK and the USA.[6] Whereas in the UK the government enjoyed draconian powers under the 1904 Wireless Telegraphy Act to prohibit radio broadcasting in its early days, in 1923 a US court ruled that the Commerce Department had no power to refuse anyone a licence to broadcast, and a subsequent ruling denied the Department the power to assign radio frequencies. The resulting confusion provoked Congress to pass the Radio Act of 1927, which entrusted the allocation of radio licences to the Interstate Commerce Commission (ICC) which was to act 'as public interest, convenience or necessity requires'.

Apart from prohibitions on limiting freedom of expression, and certain other provisions, the Act gave little guidance as to how the ICC's brief should be interpreted. It did, however, provide for court review of Commission decisions. The broadcasting provisions of the Radio Act were repeated in the Federal Communications Act of 1934, which established the Federal Communications Commission (FCC); they have not been superseded.

The Federal Communications Commission

Although quasi-independent from other branches of government, in practice the FCC has been anything but free from political or other interference. Legally it has a great deal of discretion, but in fact it is subject to competing pressures of many kinds.

In the first place, the President nominates candidates for the Commission and can thereby gradually change its composition. Secondly, because of the political importance of broadcasting, Congress supervises the FCC closely. The Senate has to confirm nominees; and Congressional committees of both Houses control its budget and monitor its performance with annual reviews. The Committees also hold hearings on major broadcasting policy issues. As well as exercising pressure on its own account, Congress also provides a channel through which other interests can use Congressional influence to exert pressure on the Commission. Thus, lobbyists can work through Congress, as well as seeking to communicate directly with the FCC.

Thirdly, FCC decisions are subject to judicial review on grounds of both procedure adopted and the substance of decisions made. In practice, all major decisions are likely to go first to the Court of Appeals of the District of Columbia, and many (such as the cable jurisdiction issue and restrictions on pay-cable) are finally resolved by the Supreme Court. In this way, changing legal interpretations influence broadcasting policy.

---

[6] See Erik Barnouw, *A History of Broadcasting in the United States*, Vol. I: *A Tower in Babel*, New York: Oxford University Press, 1966, Vol. II: *The Golden Web*, Oxford University Press, 1968; Erwin G. Krasnow *et al.*, *The Politics of Broadcast Regulation* (3rd edition), New York: St Martin's Press, 1982.

Finally, the broadcasting industry has a powerful influence over the FCC. This is exercised unofficially at the stage of appointment, through the industry's contacts with the Executive and with Congress. Commissioners and senior staff members are subject to blandishments and pressures of various kinds during their period of office, and often return to work for the industry, typically as members of the Communications Bar. Some restrictions are placed on this so-called 'revolving door' at the FCC. Nevertheless, the close relationship between FCC members and the industry is highly likely to influence regulatory decisions.

The FCC and Cable Television

This interplay of forces can be seen in many instances. The best documented is the Commission's approach to new broadcasting technologies – and to cable, in particular. At first the FCC declined to take regulatory authority over cable. In 1965, however, in response to pressures from broadcasters who feared that cable would take away their audiences, the FCC asserted that it had regulatory authority over cable and imposed a range of restrictions on the signals that cable could carry. These prevented a cable company from making available to its subscribers both certain pay-TV channels and signals imported from commercial stations outside the region.

The FCC justified the measures as an attempt to protect local stations, especially weaker ones, which ran the risk of losing audiences to the imported programmes. The evidence was doubtful, however, and the restrictions were first relaxed and then in 1980 finally eliminated, with significant help from the courts. Since then, under successive chairmen of the FCC now committed to a market-place approach to regulation, a whole range of other regulatory restrictions have been discarded. In the intervening period, the broadcast industry has established substantial ownership interest in cable, and *vice versa*; and the cable industry's power and influence have gradually expanded.

Canada

During the 1920s, radio stations were established in most major cities in the USA, and the relatively few major cities in Canada.[7] With most of Canada's substantially smaller, geographically scattered population within reach of US radio signals, and many Canadian stations acting primarily as relays for US network programmes, it became clear that unless the Canadian Government intervened, Canada would remain simply an extension of the US commercial radio networks.

---

[7] Caplan-Sauvageau Task Force, *Canada, Report of the Task Force on Broadcasting Policy*, Ottawa, 1966; W. H. Melody, 'The Canadian Broadcasting Corporation's Contribution to Canadian Culture', *Royal Society of Arts Journal*, Vol. CXXXV, No. 5368, March 1987, pp. 286-297; W. H. Melody, 'The Communications Regulatory Process in the United States and Canada', in M. Gerace (ed.), *Accountability and Responsibility in North American Communication Systems: Future Perspectives*, Windsor, Ontario: University of Windsor, 1979.

In 1932, Conservative Prime Minister R. B. Bennett told Parliament:

'. . . this country must be assured of complete control of broadcasting from Canadian sources, free from foreign interference or influence . . . without such control it can never be the agency by which national consciousness may be fostered and sustained and national unity still further strengthened . . .'[8]

During the late 1920s and 1930s, there was an active political battle between public and private broadcasting interests. The 'public' interests were Canadian, the 'private' interests primarily American. (Or, as Graham Spry proclaimed, 'The question is, the state or the United States?'.)[9]

The Canadian Broadcasting Corporation (CBC) was created in 1936, modelled in part on the BBC, but differing in several fundamental respects. The CBC mandate was:

o   to provide a national radio programming service that was primarily Canadian, but that also included quality programmes from other sources;

o   to programme in both major languages, English and French;

o   to promote national unity;

o   to extend the service to all Canadians, a task that entailed substantial investment in transmission facilities;

o   to license and regulate the private radio stations, many of which would distribute the CBC service. (CBC financing was partly by government grant, and partly by advertising.)

Broadcasting policy in Canada has been under investigation almost continuously by a succession of Royal Commissions, special committees and task forces. There have been at least six major government policy statements. Legislation has been proposed on many occasions and two Broadcasting Acts passed.

Throughout its existence there have been significant changes in the structure of Canadian broadcasting: the licence fee was abolished and advertising on CBC radio was dropped when television was introduced; and the regulatory functions were transferred in 1968 to a special regulatory commission (the Canadian Radio-Television and Telecommunication Commission, or CRTC), which regulates the CBC as well as the commercial broadcasters. This regulatory commission was modelled in significant part on the US FCC.

Canadian communications policy (although not necessarily the CRTC) has promoted, and often subsidised, the development of new

---

[8] Prime Minister R. B. Bennett, introducing Bill 94 on Broadcasting, *Debates of House of Commons*, 18 May 1932, p. 3,035.

[9] G. Spry, 'The Canadian Broadcasting Issue', *Canadian Forum*, April 1931, p. 247.

communication technologies that have been used to import US television programmes. Canada pioneered the introduction of cable television, becoming the first nation to achieve substantial penetration, at least a decade ahead of the USA. Yet the Canadian cable industry does little more than import US programmes to those areas of the country already well served by over-the-air broadcasting.

Canada was also the first nation to have a commercial domestic satellite system and has pioneered the development of direct broadcast satellites to small roof-top receiving dishes. Canada now leads the world in satellite television viewing, almost all of which is received from US television distributors' satellites.

Regulation as a Barrier to Entry

The history of Canadian broadcast regulation has been primarily that of attempting to resist market forces and to protect a favoured broadcaster. Commercial broadcasting was initially seen as complementary to the CBC, simply permitting an extension of service. Regulation attempted to restrict competition between commercial broadcasting and the CBC. But from its inception, the CRTC almost immediately became a captive of the established commercial broadcast industry. The major thrust of its regulation was to protect established commercial broadcasters from competition from cable television. However, the CRTC was frequently over-ridden by policy decisions taken at administrative level and generally proved ineffective. In recent years, the Commission has been attempting to protect the cable industry from competition from direct broadcast satellites to small roof-top receiving dishes. And this too is proving ineffective.

The CRTC differs from the FCC, but parallels UK regulation in attempting to establish and implement specific content requirements to ensure that broadcasting operates in the public interest. Yet these regulations have been consistently eroded over time.

DIFFERENCES BETWEEN REGULATORY SYSTEMS

Procedural Issues

Both the USA and Canada have had substantial experience with broadcast regulatory authorities that have had broader remits than regulatory agencies in the UK. They have already had occasion to address the regulatory and policy implications of the new cable and satellite technologies. And they have also had to attempt to find a balance between market forces and public service obligations. Although the broad regulatory objectives of the FCC and the CRTC have much in common, and both authorities are supposedly independent, there are substantial differences in the way they function, partly because of the role of the courts in each country.

The courts in Canada have been extremely passive. There are few appeals to them over broadcasting issues and the common practice is for them to examine only procedural and not substantive matters. In going out of their way to avoid issues of substance, the Canadian courts are much closer to those of the UK than of the USA.

Although the CRTC is not under any real pressure to justify its decisions, the Commission is subject to immediate overturn by Cabinet on political grounds. In the USA, the system is more complex and indirect, with a more decentralised exercise of power. The active role of the US courts contributes to delay and increases legal costs. But the requirements for thorough justification of decisions tend to increase the role of evidence and analysis and make those decisions less vulnerable to sudden political reversal.

In terms of openness, the Canadian regulatory process is much closer to the US than the UK. It encourages wide participation by the public as well as by parties with major commercial interests at stake. Frequent regional hearings are held for the purpose of receiving public evidence and opinion – hearings which are informal and not bound by rigid legal procedure. This process of openly seeking public information to inform the policy formulation process stands in stark contrast to policy-making procedures in the UK, where public consultation is confined to the details of policy.

The differences between the UK, Canada and the USA reflect historical, political, economic and cultural differences, and their effects upon the policy-making process. Nevertheless, a common characteristic of regulation in all three countries has been that the regulatory authorities have almost universally identified their interests with those of the established segment of the industries they regulate.

The result is that they have often been advocates for the preservation of the monopoly power of the established industry when it is in competition with new technologies such as cable and satellite. They may be able to achieve certain public policy objectives under conditions of a stable industry and institutional structure. But they have not been capable of fashioning policy to accommodate the changing technologies, even when they nominally have the power to do so.

Ownership and Control

Rules concerning the ownership and control of media are a regulatory device affecting entry. All these countries have had complex rules on the extent of ownership within a single medium (for instance, how many television stations a single company can own or have an interest in) and cross-ownership (for instance, the extent to which a company owning a newspaper can also own or have an interest in television and radio stations in the same locality).

When new delivery technologies become available, the question arises as to how to adapt the cross-ownership rules. A permissive policy which allows incumbents to invest in new services is likely to reduce their resistance to them, while a restrictive policy may promote greater competition. Ownership rules thus become another dimension of regulatory strategy, and their importance grows as the number of delivery systems increases and as alternative sources of finance – especially Pay-TV – become feasible.

Regulatory Capture

Regulatory agencies have been subject to a substantial amount of criticism, not confined to their role in broadcasting. Governments often set up agencies as independent and expert bodies capable of making decisions in complex areas, and give them substantial discretion.[10] For whatever reasons they are established, however, they often end up 'captured' by the very industry they are created to control. The industry is able to concentrate its efforts on influencing the regulators, whereas consumers – normally the losers in this process – have diffuse interests which do not serve as an effective counterweight.

The notion of regulatory capture has been deployed at different levels of sophistication.[11] The simplest level sees the process as akin to corruption. More elaborate economic theories of regulation, which spring from path-breaking work by Stigler,[12] emphasise that regulatory authority is a commodity of which there is a supply – determined through the political process – and a demand which comes from the interest groups involved. The extent and nature of regulation emerges from a bidding process in which producers' interests dominate consumers' interests. The interaction of supply and demand for regulation determines who are the gainers and losers in the regulatory game.

The history of restricted entry in broadcasting has increased the potential gains to the industry from successful capture. And the discretionary power of regulators in the UK has been enhanced by the process of franchising, whereby the licence or franchise to provide television programming and sell advertising time in a particular area is periodically open to a form of competition. In this competition, applicants seek to persuade the regulator to give them the franchise on the basis of their programming and other plans. In the past, such franchises have not been sold to the highest bidder, but possession of them has sometimes imposed obligations, such as a requirement to make programmes available to the network.

---

[10] See R. Baldwin and C. McCrudden (eds.), *Regulation and Public Law*, London: Weidenfeld and Nicolson, 1987.

[11] R. Posner, 'Theories of Economic Regulation', *Bell Journal of Economics*, Vol. 5, No. 2, 1974, pp. 335-358.

[12] G. J. Stigler, 'The Theory of Economic Regulation', *Bell Journal of Economics*, Vol. 2, No. 1, 1971, pp. 3-21.

Franchising

Franchising has been subject to a battery of criticism, both for its secrecy and arbitrariness and because it allows the television contractors to make excessive profits from their monopoly of the air waves.[13] But in the UK it became the linchpin of the regulatory structure for commercial television, locking the IBA and the franchise-holders into an embrace of mutual dependence. Recognising this dependence, the government has in the past been tempted to assign potential broadcasting entrants to a new regulatory body, unencumbered by ties to existing broadcasters. Thus, the task of regulating cable television in the UK was initially entrusted in 1984 to a new Cable Authority, charged with regulating the industry with a light touch and promoting its development.[14]

Similarities and Differences

The experience of broadcasting regulation in Canada, the UK and the USA is thus broadly consistent with more general theories about regulatory behaviour. In all three countries there are powerful vested interests in broadcasting. These comprise on the one hand existing commercial broadcasters with a desire to exclude further entry, and on the other public broadcasters, who are often supported by a domestic programme production industry. Though competing for audiences, the two often agree on the desirability of restricting competition.

New technologies challenge the incumbents. They create opportunities both for broadcasters and for equipment manufacturers. The strength of the new forces is such that the regulatory process seeks a way of accommodating them. In the USA the structure of the regulatory system makes the process incremental – based on a succession of separate decisions often taken through a judicial process. As already mentioned, the Canadian process is more open to public participation, but not notably successful in adapting to new technologies. In the UK regulation is characterised by periods of stability punctuated by major upheavals when critical regulatory authority is taken from the agencies and reclaimed by government.

Recent events have shown that the onset of a period of upheaval has a galvanising effect on regulatory agencies as well. It is noticeable that the IBA has responded to outside attack, and the suggestion that it has out-lived its usefulness, with a radical self-reappraisal. Thus, its 1988 policy document, *Independent Television in the 1990s*,[15] adopts a more favourable view of new entrants than its previous statements, and contemplates a

---

13 R. Baldwin, M. Cave and T. Jones, 'The Regulation of Independent Local Radio and its Reform', *International Review of Law and Economics*, Vol. 7, 1977, pp. 177-191.

14 See C. G. Veljanovski, 'Cable Television-Agency Franchising and Economics', in R. Baldwin and C. McCrudden (eds.), *op. cit.*, pp. 267-297.

15 Independent Broadcasting Authority, *Independent Television in the 1990s: A Policy Statement by the IBA*, April 1988.

number of innovations in the ITV system, including franchise au and abandoning the requirement that franchise-holders should production facilities. This response demonstrates – like other sin deregulatory proposals emanating from equivalent US agencies – that traditional patterns of regulatory behaviour can be overturned through decisive action by governments and legislatures.

CURRENT CHANGES IN THE UK

The broadcasting industry in the UK is undergoing a major transition which is likely to amount to a complete reorganisation and reform of regulation in the industry. Because of the growing internationalisation of broadcasting and the increasing regulatory involvement of supra-national bodies such as the European Commission and the Council of Europe, the issues go beyond national policy.

The decisions that have been implemented to date have changed only the margins of television broadcasting. Cable has so far attracted a relatively small audience and the three-channel high-powered Direct Broadcasting by Satellite (DBS) service authorised by the IBA does not begin operating until late 1989. In addition, early in 1989 a medium-powered satellite will start to transmit as many as 16 channels across Europe, many of them in English.

The White Paper's Fundamental Changes

More fundamental changes, however, are proposed in the Government's White Paper, *Broadcasting in the '90s*,[16] and these include:

o   The creation of a fifth and possibly a sixth UHF terrestrial channel.

o   The allocation to broadcasting of additional microwave frequencies capable of transmitting up to about 12 channels by line of sight.[17]

o   The transfer of the night hours of one BBC television channel to commercial use.

o   The use of auctions – subject to quality safeguards – to allocate both existing television franchises and any new terrestrial services in the next contract round in 1992.

o   Encouragement to the BBC to develop subscription services.

o   The possible reorganisation or privatisation of the transmission of terrestrial television channels, currently undertaken by the BBC and the IBA.

---

[16] *Broadcasting in the '90s: Competition, Choice and Quality*, Cm. 517, London: HMSO, 1988.

[17] Microwave transmission, known as MMDS or MVDS, uses parts of the spectrum not previously used in the UK for broadcasting purposes. It has, however, been used successfully for this purpose in the USA and elsewhere.

o   The further expansion of 'independent production' of broadcast programmes by specialist companies rather than by the broadcasters themselves.

o   The creation of a new Independent Television Commission (ITC) replacing both the IBA and the Cable Authority and operating a lighter form of regulation than the IBA.

This section does not aim to examine the merits and demerits of these possible policy changes, but to describe the process by which they occur and examine their likely impact upon the regulatory system. The first and most obvious point to note is that the changes will come about through decisions taken by government, and that the role of the legislature is limited to the approval or introduction of minor amendments.

The principal actors are therefore the major government departments involved in broadcasting, which are the Home Office and the Department of Trade and Industry (DTI). Whereas the former is often credited with a conservative approach to broadcasting, based upon an appreciation of the merits of the existing broadcasting system, the responsibilities of the DTI for industrial and technological policy have sometimes led it to support chosen new technologies – initially cable and more recently satellite broadcasting. There is scope for conflict here. Such is the importance of broadcasting, however, that other politicians and departments are drawn into the debate and play a role in the determination of policy – for instance, through membership of the appropriate inter-departmental committees of ministers or civil servants.

Switching the critical regulatory decisions from regulatory agencies to the government alters the range of interest groups affected by and seeking to intervene in the policy-making process. Existing or potential broadcasters, advertisers and equipment manufacturers lobby civil servants and ministers over a wider range of possible policy options. And considerable expense and ingenuity are devoted to commissioning independent studies by outside experts. A by-product of this process is a useful extension of knowledge in such areas as the economic feasibility of subscription broadcasting and the revenue potential of television advertising markets. Once the decisions are made, however, the regulatory system is likely to revert to more routine operation of a newly established system.

Effects of Reforms on Broadcasters and Regulators

The UK system of broadcasting was characterised above as a highly regulated one in which – in the long periods between major policy changes – control is exercised on a discretionary basis by the regulatory agencies of the BBC Board of Governors and the IBA. If the potential changes outlined above – or some approximation of them – are implemented, what are the major implications likely to be?

First, the introduction of competitive pressures will place a much greater strain on relations between commercial broadcasters and regulators. With economic rents eliminated through such mechanisms as franchise auctions, broadcasters will have much less room to manoeuvre over such issues as the maintenance of quality standards. In such circumstances they are likely to seek judicial review of regulatory decisions which go against them. It can be expected that the government (and possibly the courts too) will seek to prevent major issues being resolved through the legal system, but a greater involvement by the courts seems likely.

Secondly, a new set of regulatory bodies will come into being: an Independent Television Commission (ITC) responsible for all commercial television, a Radio Authority, and a Broadcasting Standards Council (BSC) responsible for content regulation. The relationship between the ITC and the BSC may involve conflict if the BSC seeks to impose content restrictions which the ITC views as excessive.

A more radical scheme of reorganisation would amalgamate broadcasting regulation with that of telecommunications, which is now undertaken by the Office of Telecommunications (OFTEL). The resulting body, analogous to the FCC or CRTC, would in principle be able to deal in a unified way with the increasingly inter-linked issues of broadcasting and telecommunications. Some proponents of this change also hope that the outcome would be a more competitive and deregulated system.

In an age when new technology is constantly eroding the technical distinctions between communication technologies and services, a proliferation of specialist regulatory agencies is unlikely to generate effective regulation. Co-ordinated public policy across the broadcast-related sectors of the economy, if not all of telecommunications, would seem to be necessary. An abundance of regulatory agencies, each with a narrow remit and limited power, is likely to make co-ordinated policy development within the UK more difficult, if not impossible. The specialist regulators will be tempted to view their 'clients' as allies on major issues, while at the same time adopting a public posture of toughness on minor ones. Moreover, it is likely to leave the UK in a weaker position to influence developments relating to Pan-European regulation by the European Commission.

PAN-EUROPEAN REGULATION

The development of a truly international or global television market is affecting virtually all countries. It opens up opportunities, but the pursuit of these opportunities will have significant implications for all television programming. There has been very little serious examination of how global television markets are likely to develop, what the characteristics of international or global television are likely to be, and what the economic, social, political and cultural implications might be.

This is an important issue because it is possible that programming for global markets will displace many traditional forms of programming for domestic markets, including both commercial and public service programming. The BBC, for example, has a potentially lucrative opportunity to enter global television markets, substituting programmes that have been produced for the global commercial market for a major portion of its traditional domestic public service programming developed historically for its UK audience.

In Canada, the CBC is being forced into international programming. For many years the CBC has imported the great majority of its prime-time entertainment television programmes from the USA because of the high cost of original programme production, the relatively low cost of purchasing US programmes and ever-tightening budget constraints. But the CBC has now been instructed by the Canadian Government to direct what programming it does produce to global markets, as a means of increasing revenue and thereby reducing its subsidy from the public treasury.

Even in the USA, despite its enormous domestic market, producers aiming at foreign markets are no longer simply trying to sell television programmes that were produced for US domestic consumption. 'High-volume programme producers in many countries – including most major public service institutions – are now developing their strategies to exploit the 'export' potential of television programmes as part of national industrial policies.

A Common Market in Broadcasting?

In 1984 the European Commission (EC) published a Green Paper on the establishment of a common market in broadcasting, especially by satellite and cable, entitled *Television without Frontiers*.[18] It aims to illustrate the relevance of the EC Treaty to broadcasting, and invites discussion as a basis for possible future proposals for legislation that would attempt to unify the present diversity among national laws and regulations of the member countries concerning broadcasting, copyright and related matters.

The Green Paper seizes on the satellite and cable technologies as a way to create a European focus – a European common market in television broadcasting. The new technologies will support new television services that will be made Pan-European by the nature of the distribution technologies. As a new European-wide television service, it need not raise the difficult issues associated with entrenched national institutions and established national television services. Rather it will require only 'liberalisation of controls in order that national restrictions should not obstruct the operation of the common market'.

The major obstruction that concerns the EC is national control over

---

[18] Commission of the European Communities, *Television without Frontiers*, Brussels: CEC, 1984.

broadcasting signals that can be received within the country. Nations could retain the power to place restrictions on programme production within their respective countries, but the EC would like to establish harmonised (i.e. uniform) reception regulations. In essence, these EC regulations would be the same or less restrictive than those of the EC country with the least restrictive regulations, in order to provide access to Pan-European television for the maximum amount of programming from all potential sources. Put simply, the EC compromise is that the individual nations will determine what television programmes are produced in and sent from the respective countries, while the EC will determine what can be received across all the EC countries.

Restricting one's own domestic producers in respect of the nature or source of programmes would simply place them at a competitive disadvantage in European and global television markets. Within this global market structure, a powerful incentive is thus created to eliminate all regulations in order to maximise a nation's competitive advantage in programme production.

Nevertheless, the EC has proposed a series of regulations that attempts to balance commercial and cultural interests, as well as reflecting the general public interest. These include an initial quota for European programming of 30 per cent, rising to 60 per cent after three years; restrictions on advertising to 15 per cent of airtime; and a ban on tobacco and paid political advertising. It also includes regulations relating to children's television, taste and decency, as well as copyright.

Controversy over Quotas and Advertising Controls
The greatest controversy surrounds the use of quotas and restrictions on advertising. Experience in Canada clearly demonstrates that quotas are unlikely to be an effective long-term solution. Quotas will not get European programmes produced, and might amount to little more than protectionism. Cultural programming can best be promoted directly by examining alternative ways of financing – perhaps subsidising – programming that is not driven by commercial imperatives, within an overall broadcasting system that ensures access to a diversity of programme sources.

The advertising debate rests on the extent to which commercial considerations control the supply of broadcast material. The basic principles that have been espoused by the Council of Europe, as well as many nations, are: (a) that advertising must not affect the broadcasting organisations' autonomy in the matter of programming; and (b) that advertising must not, in either its form or content, compromise the public service function of radio and television.[19]

Application of these principles has brought strong support for the

---

19 Council of Europe, 'Advertising in Radio and Television Broadcast', Mass Media Files, No. 1, 73.460/ 06.1, Strasbourg: Council of Europe, 1982; also James Michael, 'The Regulation of Broadcasting by European Institutions: Convention or Chaos?', PICT Policy Research Paper, No. 5, London: Economic and Social Research Council, 1988.

proposition that television films and documentaries should be broken only if they are longer than 45 minutes, and news and current affairs programmes of less than 30 minutes should not be interrupted at all; these are standards approximating those used in West Germany today. But this would result in long advertising segments and provide significantly less advertising revenue than short advertising breaks throughout the programmes. Some analysts argue that these advertising restrictions could jeopardise the financial viability of satellite broadcasting in Europe, which they believe is dependent upon the establishment of a favourable European regulatory structure that applies uniform regulations across all countries with few restrictions on advertising.

It is not, of course, possible to insulate programme production from commercial considerations. The real issue is the extent to which programming decisions will be influenced by commercial considerations. Generally, the greater the commercial influence, the greater the revenue. If the objective of public policy is to promote a diversity of programming, then a uniform level of commercial influence in all programming decisions is not likely to achieve it. Rather, the policy should promote a diversity of levels of commercial influence to stimulate a heterogeneous mix of programmes.

Direct broadcast satellites in Europe will attract primarily US programmes and advertising from trans-national corporations. This should expand viewer choice, at least in the short term, while restricting advertising options for regional and national advertisers; and in some countries, restricting options for domestic programme production.

Perhaps the most significant long-term policy issue will be whether the international broadcast markets can be kept reasonably competitive, ensure access to diverse sources of programming and permit new entry at all levels. Satellite broadcasting depends upon the use of scarce orbital locations and radio frequencies. There is no alternative to the licensing of entry. In addition, the concentration of ownership in the industry is increasing steadily, including both horizontal and vertical integration. The difficulties of access and new entry could be just as severe under a new liberalised European regulatory régime as under the inherited structure.

The process of consultation, negotiation and debate is now nearing completion. We can expect a Pan-European regulatory authority to be established in the not too distant future, along the general lines described here. The form and structure of that regulatory authority, and its relation to UK regulatory authorities in the field, may be the most significant determinant of the effectiveness of UK broadcast regulation in future.[20]

---

[20] For further discussion of these developments from a variety of perspectives, W. H. Melody, 'Pan-European Television: Commercial and Cultural Implications of European Satellites', in P. Drummond and R. Paterson (eds.), *Television and its Audience: International Research Perspectives*, London: British Film Institute, 1988, pp. 267-281; W. H. Melody, 'Future Developments of New Media in the European Community: Some Implications Drawn from the North American Experience', in E. De Bans (ed.), *Future Trends in Mass Media Forecasts 1985*, Brussels: Commission of the European Communities, FAST Programme, 1986; M. Ferguson (ed.), *New Communications Technologies and the Public Interest*, London: SAGE Publications (Communications in Society Series), 1986.

CONCLUSION

We have emphasised the importance of the form and structure of regulation to the successful implementation of UK public policy in broadcasting. Our analysis has led us to the conclusion that the dominant thrust of the current debate over the appropriate role of UK broadcasting regulation or deregulation not only misses many of the key dimensions of the issue, but also sets up a framework for incomplete, and possibly misleading, analysis. The establishment of an effective UK broadcasting regulatory structure will require a much stronger focus on the inter-relations between the many converging sectors of broadcasting and telecommunications, and on the implications of potential Pan-European regulation upon the options, objectives and structure of UK regulations.

SELECT BIBLIOGRAPHY

SELECT BIBLIOGRAPHY

Abel, J. D., R. A. Hill and M. W. Spicer, 'The Political Economy of Broadcasting', *Lloyds Bank Review*, Vol. 119, 1976, pp. 23-37.

Altman, W., D. Thomas and D. Sawers, *TV: From Monopoly to Competition – and Back?*, Hobart Paper 15, London: Institute of Economic Affairs, 2nd edn., 1962.

Baldwin, R., M. Cave and T. H. Jones, 'The Regulation of Independent Local Radio and Its Reform', *International Review of Law & Economics*, Vol. 7, 1986, pp. 177-191.

Barwise, P. and A. Ehrenberg, *Television and its Audience*, London: SAGE Publications, 1988.

Baxter, W. F., 'Regulation and Diversity in Communications Media', *American Economic Review*, Vol. LXIV, 1974, pp. 392-401.

Beebe, J. H., 'Institutional Structure and Program Choices in Television Markets', *Quarterly Journal of Economics*, Vol. 91, 1977, pp. 15-37.

Besen, S. M., 'The Economics of the Cable Television Concensus', *Journal of Law and Economics*, Vol. 17, 1974, pp. 39-52.

Besen, S. M., 'The Value of Television Time', *Southern Economic Journal*, Vol. 42, 1976, pp. 435-41.

Besen, S. M. *et al.*, *Misregulating Television – Network Dominance and the FCC*, New Haven: Yale University Press, 1985.

Besen, S. M. and R. Soligo, 'The Economics of the Network-Affiliate Relationship in the Television Broadcasting Industry', *American Economic Review*, Vol. 63, 1973, pp. 259-68.

Besen, S. M. and B. Mitchell, 'Economic Analysis and Television Regulation: A Review', Santa Monica: *Rand Report*, Vol. R-1398-MF, 1973.

Besen, S. M., W. G. Manning and B. M. Mitchell, 'Copyright Liability for

Cable Television: Compulsory Licensing and the Coase Theorem', *Journal of Law and Economics*, Vol. 21, 1978, pp. 67-95.

Besen, S. M. and R. W. Crandall, 'The Deregulation of Cable Television', *Law and Contemporary Problems*, Vol. 44, 1981, pp. 77-124.

Booz, Allen & Hamilton, *Subscription Television: A Study for the Home Office, Final Report, May 1987*, London: HMSO, 1987.

Booz, Allen & Hamilton, *The Economics of Television Advertising in the UK*, London: The Economist Publications, Special Report No. 1,143, 1988.

Bowles, R., M. Cave and P. Swann, *An Economic Appraisal of Subscription Television*, Home Office: Report for the Committee on Financing the BBC, 1986.

Briggs, A. and J. Spicer, *The Franchise Affair*, London: Century, 1986.

Briggs, A., *History of Broadcasting in the United Kingdom*, Vol. I: *The Birth of Broadcasting*; Vol. II: *The Golden Age of Wireless*, Oxford: Oxford University Press, 1961 and 1965.

Brittan, S., 'The Fight for Freedom in Broadcasting', *Political Quarterly*, Vol. 58, 1987, pp. 3-20.

Broadcast Research Unit, *The Public Service Idea in British Broadcasting – Main Principles*, London: Broadcast Research Unit, 1986.

Brown, A., *Commercial Media in Australia – Economics, Ownership, Technology and Regulation*, Brisbane: University of Queensland Press, 1986.

Budd, A., *Channel Four – Post Peacock – The Financial Implications of Recommendation 14*, London: Channel Four, 1986.

Budd, A., 'The Peacock Committee and the BBC: Liberal Values and Regulation', *Public Money*, December 1986, pp. 29-33.

Budd, A., *A Fifth Television Channel*, London: London Business School, 1988.

Cabinet Office, *Cable Systems*, London: HMSO, 1982.

Caine, S., *Paying for TV?*, Hobart Paper 43, London: Institute of Economic Affairs, 1968.

Cave, M., 'Financing British Broadcasting', *Lloyds Bank Review*, No. 157, July 1985, pp. 25-35.

Cave, M., 'The Conduct of Auctions for Broadcast Franchises', *Fiscal Studies*, Vol. 10, No. 1, February 1989, pp. 17-31.

Cave, M. and P. Swann, *The Effects on Advertising Revenues of Allowing*

Advertising on BBC Television – A Report for the Committee on Financing the BBC, London: HMSO, 1985.

Coase, R. H., *British Broadcasting: A Study in Monopoly*, London: Longmans Green, 1950.

Coase, R. H., 'The Federal Communications Commission', *Journal of Law and Economics*, Vol. 2, 1959, pp. 1-40.

Coase, R. H., 'The Economics of Broadcasting', *American Economic Review*, Vol. LXI, 1966, pp. 440-57.

Collins, R., N. Garnham and G. Lockley, *The Economics of Television*, London: SAGE Publications, 1988.

Comanor, W. S. and B. N. Mitchell, 'Cable Television and the Impact of Regulation', *Bell Journal of Economics*, Vol. 2, 1971, pp. 154-212.

Comanor, W. S. and B. N. Mitchell, 'The Costs of Planning: The FCC and Cable Television', *Journal of Law and Economics*, April 1972, pp. 177-206.

Commission of the European Communities, *Television without Frontiers*, Brussels, 1984.

Council of Europe, 'Advertising in Radio and Television Broadcast', Mass Media Files, No. 1, 73.460/06.1, Strasbourg: Council of Europe, 1982.

Crandall, R. W., 'FCC Regulation, Monopsony and Network Television Program Costs', *Bell Journal of Economics and Management*, Vol. 3, 1972, pp. 483-508.

Crandall, R. W., 'Regulation of Television Broadcasting: How Costly is the Public Interest?', *Regulation*, January/February 1978.

De Vany, A. S., R. D. Eckert, C. J. Meyers, and D. J. O'Hara, 'A Property System Approach to the Electromagnetic Spectrum: A Legal-Economic-Engineering Study', *Stanford Law Review*, Vol. 21, 1969, pp. 1,499-1,561.

Demsetz, H., 'Why Regulate Utilities?', *Journal of Law and Economics*, Vol. 11, 1968, pp. 55-66.

Department of Trade & Industry, *Deregulation of the Radio Spectrum in the UK*, London: HMSO, 1987.

Department of Trade & Industry, *Evolution of the United Kingdom Communications Infrastructure Phase 1 – Discussion Paper*, London: DTI, 1987.

Department of Trade & Industry, *The Development of UK Communications Systems*, Discussion Document, London: PA Consulting Group, April 1987.

Department of Trade & Industry, *The Infrastructure for Tomorrow*, Communications Steering Group Report, London: HMSO, 1988.

Department of Trade & Industry, *Evolution of the United Kingdom Communications Infrastructure*, London: HMSO, 1988.

Department of Trade & Industry, *Report on the Potential for Microwave Video Distribution Systems in the UK*, London: HMSO, 1988.

Domberger, S. and J. Middleton, 'Franchising in Practice: The Case of Independent Television in the UK', *Fiscal Studies*, Vol. 6, 1985, pp. 17-32.

Domberger, S., 'Economic Regulation through Franchise Contracts', in J. Kay *et al.* (eds.), *Privatisation and Regulation – The UK Experience*, Oxford: Oxford University Press, 1986.

Federal Communications Commission, *New Television Networks: Entry, Jurisdiction, Ownership and Regulation*, Washington DC: FCC, 1980.

Ferguson, M. (ed.), *New Communications Technologies and the Public Interest*, London: SAGE Publications, 1985.

Fisher, F. M., J. J. McGowan and D. S. Evans, 'The Audience-Revenue Relationship for Local Television Stations', *Bell Journal of Economics*, Vol. 11, 1980, pp. 694-708.

Fisher, F. *et al.*, 'Community Antenna Television Systems and Local Television Station Audience', *Quarterly Journal of Economics*, Vol. 80, May 1966, pp. 227-51.

Fournier, G. M., 'Nonprice Competition and the Dissipation of Rents from Television Regulation', *Southern Economic Journal*, Vol. 51, 1985, pp. 754-65.

Fournier, G. M. and D. L. Martin, 'Does Government-Restricted Entry Produce Market Power?: New Evidence from the Market for Television Advertising', *Bell Journal of Economics*, Vol. 14, 1983, pp. 44-56.

Fowler, M. and D. Brenner, 'A Market-Place Approach to Broadcast Regulation', *Texas Law Review*, Vol. 60, 1982, pp. 207-57.

Goldberg, V. P., 'Marginal Cost Pricing, Investment Theory and CATV: Comment', *Journal of Law and Economics*, Vol. 14, 1971, pp. 513-16.

Green, D., 'Cable TV in France – A Non-Market Approach to Industrial Development', *National Westminster Bank Quarterly Review*, August 1984, pp. 13-24.

Greenberg, E., 'Wire Television and the FCC's Second Report and Order on CATV Systems', *Journal of Law and Economics*, Vol. 10, 1967, pp. 181-92.

Greenberg, E. and H. S. Barnett, 'TV Program Diversity – New Evidence and Old Theories', *American Economic Review*, Vol. LXI, 1971, pp. 89-93.

Hazlett, T., 'Private Contracting versus Public Regulation as a Solution to the Natural Monopoly Problem', in R. W. Poole (ed.), *Unnatural Monopolies*, Lexington, Mass.: Lexington Books, 1985, pp. 71-114.

Hazlett, T., 'Competition v. Franchise Monopoly in Cable Television', *Contemporary Policy Issues*, Vol. 4, 1986, pp. 80-97.

Hazlett, T., 'Private Monopoly and the Public Interest: An Economic Analysis of Cable Television Franchise', *University of Pennsylvania Law Review*, Vol. 134, 1986, pp. 1,335-1,409.

Hazlett, T., 'Duopolistic Competition in CATV: Implications for Public Policy,' working paper, University of California, Davis, 1988.

Hazlett, T., 'The Demand to Regulate Franchise Monopoly: Evidence from CATV Rate Deregulation in California', working paper, University of California, Davis, 1988.

Hollins, T., *New Technologies, New Policies*, London: British Film Institute, 1982.

Hollins, T., *Beyond Broadcasting: Into the Cable Age*, London: British Film Institute, 1984.

Home Office, *Report of the Committee on the Future of Broadcasting*, Cmnd. 6752, London: HMSO, 1977.

Home Office, *Direct Broadcast by Satellite*, London: HMSO, 1981.

Home Office, *The Report of the Independent Review of the Radio Spectrum (30-960 MHZ)*, Cmnd. 9000, London: HMSO, 1983.

Home Office, *Report of the Committee on Financing the BBC* (The Peacock Report), Cmnd. 9824, London: HMSO, 1986.

Home Office, *Research on the Range and Quality of Broadcasting Services*, Report of the Committee on Financing the BBC, Appendix G, Part 17, 'Programme Range and Quality', London: HMSO, 1986.

Home Office, *Radio: Choices and Opportunities – A Consultative Document*, Cm. 92, London: HMSO, 1987.

Home Office, *Subscription Television*, London: HMSO, 1987.

Home Office, *Broadcasting in the '90s: Competition, Choice and Quality – The Government's Plans for Broadcasting Legislation*, Cm. 517, London: HMSO, 1988.

Home Office/Department of Trade & Industry, *Report of the Inquiry into*

Cable Expansion and Broadcasting Policy, Cmnd. 8679, London: HMSO, 1982.

Home Office/Department of Trade & Industry, *The Development of Cable Systems and Services*, Cmnd. 8866, London: HMSO, 1985.

House of Commons, Home Affairs Committee Report, *Broadcasting in the 1990s: The Challenge of Maintaining Standards*, House of Commons, 1988.

House of Lords, *Select Committee on the European Communities: Television Without Frontiers*, Session 1985-86, 4th Report, HL 43, London: HMSO, 1985.

Huettner, D. A., 'Optimal Second Best Pricing of CATV Pole Attachments', *Southern Economic Journal*, Vol. 48, 1982, pp. 996-1,015.

Hutchison, R., *Cable, DBS and the Arts*, London: Policy Studies Institute, 1984.

Independent Broadcasting Authority, *Independent Television in the 1990s: A Policy Statement by the IBA*, London: IBA, 1988.

Johnson, L. L., *The Future of Cable Television: Some Problems of Federal Regulation*, Santa Monica: Rand Corp., Vol. RM-6199-F, January 1970.

Kuhn, R. (ed.), *The Politics of Broadcasting*, Beckenham: Croom Helm, 1985.

Lees, F. A. and C. Y. Yang, 'The Redistributional Effect of Television Advertising', *Economic Journal*, Vol. 76, 1966, pp. 328-36.

Levin, H., 'Spectrum Allocation Without Market', *American Economic Review*, Vol. LX, 1970, pp. 209-18.

Levin, H., 'Program Duplication, Diversity and Effective Viewer Choices: Some Empirical Findings', *American Economic Review*, Vol. LXI, 1971, pp. 81-96.

Levin, H., *Fact and Fancy in Television Regulation – An Economic Study of Policy Alternatives*, Baltimore: Johns Hopkins University Press, 1980.

Lewis, P., 'IBA Programme Awards', *Public Law*, 1975, pp. 317-40.

Lewis, P. M., *Community Television and Cable in Britain*, London: British Film Institute, 1979.

Liebowitz, S. J., *On the Canadian Broadcasting Corporation's Costs of Operation*, Vancouver: Fraser Institute, 1985.

Litman, B. and S. Eun, 'The Emerging Oligopoly of Pay-TV in the USA', *Telecommunications Policy*, Vol. 5, 1981, pp. 121-35.

MacAvoy, P. W. (ed.), *Deregulation of Cable Television*, Washington DC: American Enterprise Institute for Public Policy Research, 1977.

MacCabe, C. and O. Stewart (eds.), *The BBC and Public Service Broadcasting*, Manchester: Manchester University Press, 1986.

Melody, W. H., 'The Communications Regulatory Process in the United States and Canada', in M. Gerace (ed.), *Accountability and Responsibility in North American Communication Systems: Future Perspectives*, Windsor, Ontario: University of Windsor, 1979.

Melody, W. H., 'Radio Spectrum Allocation: Role of the Market', *American Economic Review*, Vol. 70, 1980, pp. 393-97.

Melody, W. H., 'Future Developments of New Media in the European Community: Some Implications Drawn from the North American Experience', in E. De Bans (ed.), *Future Trends in Mass Media Forecasts*, Brussels: Commission of the European Communities, FAST Programme, 1986.

Melody, W. H., 'The Canadian Broadcasting Corporation's Contribution to Canadian Culture', *The Royal Society of Arts Journal*, Vol. CXXXV, No. 5368, 1987, pp. 286-97.

Michael, J., *The Regulation of Broadcasting by European Institutions: Convention or Chaos?*, PICT Policy Research Paper, No. 5, London: Economic and Social Research Council, 1988.

Milne, A. *et al.*, *The Cable Debate – A BBC Briefing*, London: BBC, September 1983.

Minasian, J. R., 'Television Pricing and the Theory of Public Goods', *Journal of Law and Economics*, Vol. 7, 1964, pp. 75-76.

Mitchell, B. M., 'Cables, Cities and Copyrights', *Bell Journal of Economics and Management*, Vol. 5, 1974, pp. 235-63.

Nadel, M. S., 'Comcar: a Marketplace Cable Television Franchise Structure', *Harvard Journal of Legislation*, Vol. 20, 1983, pp. 541-73.

National Telecommunications and Information Administration, *Telecom 2000: Charting the Course for a New Century*, Washington DC: US Department of Commerce, 1988.

National Telecommunications and Information Administration, 'Video Program Distribution and Cable Television: Current Policy Issues and Recommendations', United States Department of Commerce, NTIA Report 88-233, June 1988.

NERA, *1992 and Beyond ... Options for ITV: An Assessment for the ITV Association by National Economic Research Associates*, London: NERA, 1988.

Noam, E. M., 'Private Sector Monopolies: The Case of Cable Television

Franchises', in M. Holzer and S. Nagel (eds.), *Productivity and Public Policy*, Newbury Park, Ca.: SAGE Publications, 1984, pp. 193-217.

Noam, E. M. (ed.), *Video Media Competition: Regulation, Economics, and Technology*, New York: Columbia University Press, 1985.

Noll, R. G., M. J. Peck and J. J. McGowan, *Economic Aspects of Television Regulation*, Washington DC: The Brookings Institution, 1973.

Office of Fair Trading, *Thames Television Limited*, London: OFT, 1984.

Owen, B. M., J. H. Beebe and W. G. Manning, Jr., *Television Economics*, Lexington, Mass.: D.C. Heath, 1974.

Owen, B. M., *Economics and Freedom of Expression*, Lexington: D.C. Heath, 1975.

Owen, B. M., 'The Rise and Fall of Cable Television Regulation', in L. Weiss and S. Strickland (eds.), *Regulation – A Case Approach*, New York: McGraw-Hill, 1982.

Pacey, P. L., 'Cable Television in a Less-Regulated Market', *Journal of Industrial Economics*, Vol. 34, 1985, pp. 81-92.

Park, R. E., *Cable Television and UHF Broadcasting*, Santa Monica: Rand Corp., Vol. R-689-MF, 1971.

Park, R. E., 'The Growth of Cable TV and its Probable Impact on Over-the-Air Broadcasting', *American Economic Review*, Vol. 61, 1971, pp. 69-73.

Paulu, B., *Television and Radio in the UK*, London: Macmillan, 1981.

Peacock, A. T., *Making Sense of Broadcasting Finance*, Robbins Lecture, University of Stirling, 1986.

Peacock, A. T., 'The "Politics" of Investigating Broadcasting Finance', *Royal Bank of Scotland Review*, Vol. 153, 1987, pp. 3-16.

Perrakis, S. and J. Silva-Echenique, 'The Profitability and Risk of CATV Operations in Canada', *Applied Economics*, Vol. 15, 1983, pp. 745-58.

Peterman, J., 'Concentration of Control and the Pricing of Television Time', *American Economic Review*, Vol. 61, 1971, pp. 74-80.

Posner, R. A., 'Natural Monopoly and its Regulation', *Stanford Law Review*, Vol. 21, 1969, pp. 548-643.

Posner, R. A., *Cable Television: The Problems of Local Monopoly*, Santa Monica: Rand Report, Vol. RM-6309-FF, 1970.

Posner, R. A., 'The Appropriate Scope of Regulation in the Cable Television Industry', *Bell Journal of Economics and Management Science*, Vol. 3, 1972, pp. 98-129.

Powe, L. A., Jr., *American Broadcasting and the First Amendment*, Berkeley: University of California Press, 1987.

Rothenberg, J., 'Consumer Sovereignty and the Economics of TV Programming', *Studies in Public Communications*, Vol. 4, 1962, pp. 45-54.

Saliba, M., 'Television Programming and the Public Interest: Subscription TV versus Public Ownership', *Antitrust Law and Economic Review*, Vol. 6, 1973, pp. 111-17.

Samuelson, P. A., 'Public Goods and Subscription TV: Correction of the Record', *Journal of Law and Economics*, Vol. XVII, 1974, pp. 81-96.

Schmalansee, R., *The Control of Natural Monopolies*, Lexington, Mass.: Lexington Books, 1979.

Schuessler, T. L., 'Structural Barriers to the Entry of Additional Television Networks: The Federal Communications Commission's Spectrum Management Policies', *Southern California Law Review*, Vol. 54, 1981, pp. 875-1,000.

Sendall, B., *Independent Television in Britain*, Vol.I: *Origin and Foundation 1946-62*; Vol. II: *Expansion and Change 1958-68*, London: Macmillan, 1983.

Smiley, A., 'Direct Competition Among Cable Television Systems', Washington DC: US Department of Justice, Antitrust Division, EAE Paper No. 86-9, 1986.

Smith, A. (ed.), *British Broadcasting*, Newton Abbot: David and Charles, 1974.

Spence, M. and B. Owen, 'Television Programming Competition and Welfare', *Quarterly Journal of Economics*, Vol. 91, 1977, pp. 103-26.

Spitzer, M. L., 'Controlling the Content of Print and Broadcast', *Southern California Law Review*, Vol. 58, 1985, pp. 1,349-1,405.

Steiner, P., 'Program Patterns and Preferences and the Workability of Competition in Radio Broadcasting', *Quarterly Journal of Economics*, Vol. LXVI, 1952, pp. 194-223.

Steiner, P., 'Monopoly and Competition in Television: Some Policy Issues', *Manchester School*, Vol. 24, 1967, pp. 107-31.

Thomas, D., *Competition in Radio*, Occasional Paper 5, London: Institute of Economic Affairs, 1965.

Veljanovski, C. G. and W. Bishop, *Choice by Cable – The Economics of a New Era in Television*, Hobart Paper 96, London: Institute of Economic Affairs, 1983.

Veljanovski, C. G., 'UK Cable Policy in the Eighties', *Fiscal Studies*, Vol. 4, 1983, pp. 29-45.

Veljanovski, C. G., 'Regulatory Options for Cable TV in the UK', *Telecommunications Policy*, Vol. 7, 1984, pp. 290-306.

Veljanovski, C. G., 'Cable Television – Agency Franchising and Economics', in R. Baldwin and C. McCruddin (eds.), *Regulation and Public Law*, London: Weidenfeld & Nicolson, 1987.

Veljanovski, C. G., 'British Cable and Satellite Television Policies', *National Westminster Bank Quarterly Review*, November 1987, pp. 28-40.

Veljanovski, C. G., *Commercial Broadcasting in the UK – Over Regulation or Mis-Regulation?*, London: Centre for Economic Policy Research, Working Paper No. 175, 1987.

Veljanovski, C. G., *Cable and Satellite: The Market for Programmes?*, London: Centre for Economic Policy Research, Working Paper No. 176, 1987.

Veljanovski, C. G., 'Broadcasting – Auctions, Competition and Policy', *Economic Affairs*, Vol. 8, No. 6, 1988, pp. 33-37.

Veljanovski, C. G., *Television, Advertising and the Economy*, London: Incorporated Society of British Advertisers, 1987.

Vogel, H. L., *Entertainment Industry Economics: A guide for financial analysis*, Cambridge: Cambridge University Press, 1986.

Waterson, M., 'Issues in the Regulation of Cable TV', *International Review of Law & Economics*, Vol. 4, 1984, pp. 67-82.

Webb, G. K., *The Economics of Cable Television*, Lexington, Mass.: D.C. Heath, 1983.

Webbink, D., 'The Impact of Regulation and Competition on Cable TV Service Prices, Channels and Pay Tiers', Washington DC: Federal Trade Commission, Bureau of Economics, 1985.

Wiles, P., 'Pilkington and the Theory of Value', *Economic Journal*, Vol. LXXIII, 1963, pp. 185-200.

Williamson, O., 'Franchise Bidding for Natural Monopolies in General and with Respect to CATV', *Bell Journal of Economics and Management Science*, Vol. 7, 1976, pp. 73-104.

Yarrow, G. K., C. G. Veljanovski *et al.*, *The Effects on Other Media of the Introduction of Advertising on the BBC – A Report for the Committee on Financing the BBC*, London: Home Office, 1985.

Young, Sir Brian, 'The Paternal Tradition in British Broadcasting 1922-?', Watt Club Lecture, Edinburgh: Heriot-Watt University, 1983.

THE AUTHORS

THE AUTHORS

Samuel Brittan has been principal economic commentator on the *Financial Times* since 1966 and Assistant Editor since 1978. He was with the *Financial Times* (1955-61); Economics Editor of the *Observer* (1961-64); an Adviser at the Department of Economic Affairs (1965). He was the first winner of the Senior Wincott Award for financial journalism in 1971; awarded the George Orwell prize for political journalism in 1980. He was a Research Fellow of Nuffield College, Oxford, in 1973-74 and a Visiting Fellow, 1974-82. In 1978 he was a Visiting Professor at the Chicago Law School. In May 1985 he was appointed a member of the Peacock Committee on the financing of the BBC, whose report was published in 1986. He is an honorary D.Litt. of Heriot-Watt University, Edinburgh (1985); Hon. Professor of Politics, University of Warwick (1987-); and an Hon. Fellow of Jesus College, Cambridge (1988-).

He is the author of numerous books, of which the most recent is *A Restatement of Economic Liberalism* (1988). For the IEA he has written *Government and the Market Economy* (Hobart Paperback 2, 1971), *Participation without Politics* (Hobart Paper 62, 1975, 2nd edn., 1979), *How to End the 'Monetarist' Controversy* (Hobart Paper 90, 1981, 2nd edn., 1982), and his Wincott Memorial Lecture, *Two Cheers for Self-Interest* (Occasional Paper 73, 1985).

Alan Budd is Chief Economic Adviser to Barclays Bank. He was previously Professor of Economics at the London Business School (1981-88) and is now Visiting Professor there. He was Senior Economic Adviser to the Treasury (1970-74), and taught at the University of Southampton (1966-69). He has been a Visiting Professor at Carnegie-Mellon University (1969-70) and at the University of New South Wales (1983). He is a member of the IEA's Advisory Council and has contributed to a number of its collections: *The Taming of Government* (Readings 21, 1979); *Keynes's General Theory: Fifty Years On* (Hobart Paperback 24, 1986); *Monetarism and Macro-economics* (Readings 26, 1987); he also contributed a Commentary to *The State of the Market* (Occasional Paper 80, 1988).

Martin Cave is Professor of Economics at Brunel University. He was educated at the University of Oxford and worked as a Research Fellow in the Centre for Russian and East European Studies at Birmingham, before going to Brunel. He has been a Visiting Professor at the University of Virginia and a Visiting Fellow at the Australian National University and La Trobe University. Much of his early work was in economic planning; this includes *Computers and Economic Planning: the Soviet Experience* (1980), and (with Paul Hare) *Alternative Approaches to Economic Planning* (1981). Recently he has worked primarily on issues of regulation, especially of telecommunications and broadcasting and the measurement of public sector performance. He has acted as consultant to various government departments and regulatory bodies, and was an adviser to the Peacock Committee on Financing the BBC.

John Fountain is a Senior Lecturer in Economics at the University of Canterbury, Christchurch, New Zealand. He holds a PhD in Economics from Stanford University (1976) and a BA (Honours) (1969) from the University of British Columbia. Currently his teaching and research is in the areas of micro-economics, public economics, and the economics of telecommunications.

Raymond B. Gallagher is Director of Telecommunications Policy for Sky Television in London. A US citizen, he began his communications career during the American cable TV boom in the late 1970s. Initially he served in local government cable TV regulation in Syracuse, New York, where he also obtained a Bachelors Degree in Communications and a Masters Degree in Public Administration from Syracuse University.

Subsequently, he served in staff and consulting capacities for the US Department of Commerce, National Telecommunications and Information Administration (NTIA) in Washington DC – the principal White House advisory agency for communications policy. He was co-director and a principal author of *The Emergence of Pay Cable Television* for NTIA, a landmark study of the US cable and Pay-TV market-place which concluded that cable television systems could not reasonably be built to fulfil overambitious expectations for both entertainment and advanced communications services.

From 1980 to 1982 he assisted local governments with the solicitation and evaluation of cable TV franchise proposals, with the Cable TV Information Center, and served as Telecommunications Development Specialist for the American Newspaper Publishers Association (ANPA). In mid-1982 he began providing independent consultancy services in Europe, becoming resident in the UK in 1983.

Mr Gallagher has written for US and European new media publications and has been a frequent speaker at industry conferences, as well as conducting a number of corporate seminars on European market

260

developments and opportunities in television. He joined Sky Television in 1989.

Thomas Hazlett is Assistant Professor of Agricultural Economics, University of California, Davis, and contributing editor of *Reason* magazine. He is also an economic commentator for two radio stations in the USA and a contributor to the *Economist.* He has addressed many conferences and has written numerous articles and book reviews. He specialises in law and economics, applied price theory, public choice and telecommunications policy.

William H. Melody is Senior Research Associate, St. Antony's College, University of Oxford. He has been appointed the founding Director of the Centre for International Research on Communication and Information Technologies (CIRCIT), Melbourne, and Visiting Professor, University of Melbourne. He was founding Director of the UK Programme on Information and Communication Technologies (PICT), London (1985-88). He has held a number of Professorships in American and Canadian universities. Professor Melody is the author of many books and articles about the communication industries, technologies, economics and public policies, and is a member of the editorial board of 12 publications. He has lectured all over the world.

Mark Oliver is a management consultant specialising in the media and telecommunications industries working for the Deloitte Media Group. He has worked on a number of assignments for broadcasting organisations. These have involved analysis of the media sectors in the UK, Europe and the USA.

Sir Alan Peacock, a Trustee of the IEA, divides his time between being Executive Director of The David Hume Institute, Chairman of the Scottish Arts Council, and Research Professor in Public Finance, Heriot-Watt University. He has held a wide variety of academic, business and public positions in the UK and elsewhere, including Professorships in Economics at Edinburgh, York and Buckingham Universities, Chief Economic Adviser, Department of Trade and Industry (1973-76); he was the Principal and later first Vice-Chancellor of the independent University of Buckingham (1978-84). He has written extensively on the economics of public policy and is currently writing a monograph, *Public Choice Analysis in Historical Perspective.* He chaired the Committee on Financing the BBC (1985-87) and was knighted for public services in 1987.

David Sawers is a writer and consultant who specialises in industrial economics. He spent 18 years as an economist in the government service, and has also worked as a journalist and an academic. His major publications are (with John Jewkes and Richard Stillerman) *The Sources of Invention* (1958), a classic study of industrial innovation, and (with Ronald Miller) *The Technical Development of Modern Aviation* (1968), a study of innovation in the aircraft industry. For the IEA he has written, with Wilfred Altman and Denis Thomas, *TV – From Monopoly to Competition – and Back?* (Hobart Paper 15, Revised Edition 1962), and *Competition in the Air* (Research Monograph 41, 1987).

Brian Sturgess works in the Media Team of Barclays de Zoete Wedd, has lectured at the University of Nottingham and the City University Business School, and was responsible for the development of an MBA programme aimed at the academic needs of the City. He holds degrees from the universities of Oxford and Newcastle upon Tyne. He was the consultant to the BBC in their submission to the Peacock Committee. He spoke at the Home Office's fact-finding seminar on television advertising ahead of publication of the White Paper on broadcasting. He has published widely on advertising and the media and specialises in economic analysis, statistics and econometric forecasting. He joined Barclays de Zoete Wedd in December 1987.

Cento Veljanovski is Research & Editorial Director of the Institute of Economic Affairs. He was previously in private practice, Lecturer in Law & Economics, University College, London (1984-87), and Research Fellow, Centre for Socio-Legal Studies, Oxford (1978-84). He has held visiting posts at a number of North American universities and worked for a short period after graduation with the Australian Treasury. He was educated in Australia and the UK, holding several degrees in law and economics (BEc, MEc, DPhil). He has advised government and industry on privatisation and regulation and is a Director of Putnam, Hayes & Bartlett, management and economics consultants. He was an expert adviser to the Peacock Committee and has undertaken assignments for the BBC, cable and radio companies and, recently, for the Australian Government and UK television industry. He is the author of *Selling the State – Privatisation in Britain* (1987), (with W. Bishop), *Choice by Cable* (Hobart Paper 96, 1983), and has written widely on the economics and law of cable, television and the media.

Hobart Paperback 28

PRIVATISATION & COMPETITION

A Market Prospectus

Edited by Cento Veljanovski

Privatisation of the nationalised industries has been the hallmark of the Thatcher government's efforts to rejuvenate the British economy. Yet in key industries privatisation has not been accompanied by a coherent or consistent attempt to maximise competitive pressures. There is growing concern that in the utility industries — telecommunications, gas, electricity, water and transport — monopolies have been transferred to private ownership and that regulation has replaced public ownership.

The fifteen contributors to *Privatisation & Competition* examine the interplay between privatisation, competition and regulation so far to identify the trade-offs, tensions and the probable consequences of the sacrifice of market forces and competitive pressures in Britain's privatisation programme. Many of the contributors put forward proposals for reform and blueprints for the privatisation of those industries which are still in the public sector — British Coal, the Electricity Supply Industry, British Rail and the Post Office.

Privatisation & Competition brings together an authoritative collection of original essays on one of the most radical and profound changes in industrial policy in Britain this century.

Contents

ISBN 0-255 36211-0   Royal Octavo   249 pages

THE INSTITUTE OF ECONOMIC AFFAIRS
2 Lord North Street, Westminster
London SW1P 3LB

Price £9·50